By A. J. Liebling

They All Sang *(with Edward B. Marks)*

Back Where I Came From

The Telephone Booth Indian

The Road Back to Paris

Republic of Science

The Wayward Pressman

Mink and Red Herring

The Honest Rainmaker

Normandy Revisited

The Sweet Science

The Earl of Louisiana

The Press

The Most of A. J. Liebling

Between Meals

Mollie & Other War Pieces

Chicago: Second City

A Neutral Corner

Liebling at *The New Yorker*

The Sweet Science

A. J. Liebling

THE SWEET SCIENCE

Foreword by Robert Anasi

NORTH POINT PRESS

A division of Farrar, Straus and Giroux

New York

North Point Press
A division of Farrar, Straus and Giroux
18 West 18th Street, New York 10011

Copyright © 1951, 1952, 1953, 1954, 1955, 1956 by the Estate of A. J. Liebling
Foreword copyright © 2004 by Robert Anasi
All rights reserved
Distributed in Canada by Douglas & McIntyre Ltd.
Printed in the United States of America
Originally published in 1956 by The Viking Press
First North Point Press paperback edition, 2004

The text of this book originally appeared in *The New Yorker*.

Library of Congress Cataloging-in-Publication Data
Liebling, A. J. (Abbott Joseph), 1904–1963.
The sweet science / A. J. Liebling ; foreword by Robert Anasi.
p. cm.
ISBN-13: 978-0-374-27227-2
ISBN-10: 0-374-27227-1
1. Boxing—United States—History. I. Title.

GV1125. L5 2004
796.83'0973—dc22
2004049509

Designed by Jonathan D. Lippincott

www.fsgbooks.com

9 11 13 15 16 14 12 10 8

To Whitey, Freddie, and Charlie, my Explainers

Contents

Ahab and Nemesis

Foreword
by Robert Anasi

No one wrote about boxing better than A. J. Liebling. This is saying something, as the competition is pretty fierce, running as it does through Norman Mailer all the way back to *The Aeneid*. Liebling's first boxing essays appeared in the 1930s, but his great run didn't start until 1951. Between that year and 1963, he churned out thirty-four pugilistic masterpieces for *The New Yorker*, a publication that cared little for the "sweet science of bruising" but appreciated Joe Liebling.* Liebling wasn't a boxing writer per se; a man of commodious inclination, he wrote with equal facility about the racetrack, World War II, France, the press, politicians (and other con-men), the low-life, and food. Yet boxing held a particular allure for him. He had boxed enough to enjoy the niceties of the sport, and the characters of the prize ring provided abundant material for his writing. I like to think that Liebling was foreordained to write about boxing: the first newspaper article he remembered reading, at age seven, was about an Oklahoma fighter. Tellingly, boxing analogies and anecdotes permeate his non-boxing books such as *Between Meals* and *The Telephone Booth Indian*.

On boxing Liebling is a joy to read. It would be redundant to

---

* The balance of the essays are collected in *A Neutral Corner* (1990).

list the many virtues of his prose—like handing out an instruction manual for a sunset. More useful, perhaps, is to mention what he *doesn't* do. These essays avoid the dazzled mystification of much "literary" boxing prose and the hard-boiled sentimentality of the sports journalism of Liebling's day. From time to time Liebling's erudition will send you running for the dictionary—choice mots include *pyknic* and *succedaneum*, and there are oddball references to Greek tragedy and an Arab philosopher named Ibn Khaldun. The intent, however, is not to overawe but to entertain (he calls one Southern politician "a peckerwood Caligula").

Although Liebling's observations are suffused with humor, generally at the expense of his principals—fighters and trainers, managers and fans—his drollery is never malicious. As often as he satirizes fight people, he credits them with shrewdness and insight, though often it may filter through a guttural idiom. Liebling writes with bemused tolerance, the hallmark of an artist whose work took him through every stratum of urban life to Indian reservations and the D-Day beaches of Normandy. One thing Liebling certainly is not is a racist, although no less an authority than Joyce Carol Oates makes a claim to the contrary. Liebling does refer to African-Americans as "colored" or "Negro," but that is simply the diction of his period. What Oates fails to realize is that Liebling had more empathy for fighters than he did for anyone else. Compared to how Liebling treats southern politicians and prudes, boxers get off easy.

Liebling's voice is urbane, his tastes cosmopolitan. He appreciates the crowd and is attuned to the minute interactions and exchanges of city life. Like a man out for a weekend stroll, Liebling takes his time; the typical essay meanders from gym to training camp and through the city, making stops at various centuries and continents. Liebling is the educated stand-in for the man on the street, delighted to take the time to look at what's happening around him—though he is also entirely capable of taut, dramatic writing (best demonstrated in "Charles I," the book's shortest essay).

Liebling's good fortune, and ours, rests in the fact that *The New Yorker* of his day trusted its top writers to expound upon whatever inspired them. While *The Sweet Science* focuses mostly on title fights, the outcome is less important than the route Liebling takes to get there. So he toddles over to Ireland for a modest bout simply because it's being held in the town that gave its name to every all-out brawl—Donnybrook. Such whimsy is rarely visible in today's celebrity and scandal-driven market, where every article must reduce to a one sentence "idea," and fact is king. The rare opportunities writers have to treat their subjects goes a long way toward explaining their compressed, overheated prose—they know they aren't likely to get the chance again, and only have a few thousand words to fit everything in. By contrast, the Liebling pace is leisurely. What he can't treat in one essay can be easily taken up in the next; themes evolve and intertwine throughout the eighteen pieces. Celebrities are disdained, scandals absent. By the time Sonny Liston became heavyweight champion in 1962, he had attracted notoriety equal to that of Mike Tyson today, yet Liebling barely refers to Liston's criminal past. The rough champion is humanized through his exchanges with a sympathetic Liebling. The obvious goes unmentioned.

To most contemporary Americans the customs and traditions of fighters appear as bizarre and savage as those of Kandangai headhunters. In the 1950s, however, boxing was much closer to the general public. This familiarity, and Liebling's own boxing experience, allowed him to represent the sport *as* sport. His stance toward its sometimes disturbing violence might seem blasé to us—as when he describes Ezra Charles's disfigurement at the hands of Rocky Marciano—but Liebling saw boxing as the pros do: a job, more difficult than most but also more rewarding. He doesn't make the ring over into the setting for a morality play or an alternate site for Armageddon (he had witnessed the real thing on the battlefields of Europe).

This is not to say that Liebling didn't take boxing seriously. As far as he was concerned, boxing deserved to be called "science." He understood the intellectual and physical effort necessary to master the craft. Although he recognized the brute force of a Marciano, he preferred technicians to sluggers—a suitable predilection for one of the great stylists of his generation. Hence his disapproval of Ingemar Johansson's lax training methods and his appreciation of the shrewd old artist Archie Moore, whom he called "a boxer's boxer, as Stendhal was for a long time a writer's writer." Liebling rarely covered unproven fighters, but his eye for talent was acute enough to recognize, in late 1961, the aura around a brash young heavyweight named Cassius Clay (he also enjoyed Clay's verbal prowess).

Liebling knew he was covering a sport in decline. He had watched boxing descend from a pinnacle in the 1920s, when it rivaled baseball as a national pastime and Jack Dempsey garnered more headlines than Babe Ruth. Even during the Depression-era doldrums of 1938, New York City counted more than a thousand registered professional boxers who performed weekly at seven city clubs, while amateurs fought as often as every other day for prizes that could easily be pawned (a useful quality in the twentieth century's worst economic crisis). When Liebling returned to the beat fourteen years later, New York had only 241 pros; all but one of the clubs had shut down, and the old Madison Square Garden, world capital of boxing, was a ghost kingdom with spectral tiers of empty seats.

Liebling's prose is shaded by the recognition that his time is passing. Time hangs over all of us, but it strikes no one more swiftly than boxers, who can become old men in three minutes. Even the great champions, men who have defeated every other opponent, are helpless against this threat. *The Sweet Science* opens with the last stand of Joe Louis, hero of Liebling's young manhood, and closes with a thirty-nine-year-old (at least) Archie Moore succumbing to Marciano. The succession of title-holders is the central story of prizefighting, and no reign ends without bloodshed. Liebling's sympathies rest with the old men in their futile struggle (his terse sentences on Louis's downfall are the most affecting in the book). With a self-proclaimed "insatiable nostalgia for the past," Liebling is perfectly suited to the task of eulogizing the fighters of his youth.

His nostalgia, however, encompasses more than a fading generation of fighters. A much larger world was disappearing, that blue-collar, urban America Liebling covered in the 1930s and left for the Second World War. Boxing was that era's canary in the coal mine. Like Kerouac with his railroad hobos and skid-row mantras, Liebling laments the vanishing underworld of the Depression, although in rather a different context. Liebling blamed boxing's suffocation on an invention he had little use for: "a ridiculous gadget called television . . . utilized in selling beer and razor blades." (Liebling had commensurate disdain for baseball and Chicago, Illinois, which he famously dubbed "the Second City"). Television, for Liebling, had strangled boxing by taking audiences from the boxing clubs and paydays from club fighters. As he put it: "Television gives so plausible an adumbration of a fight, for nothing, that you feel it would be extravagant to pay your way in . . . Men are becoming slaves of their shadows."

In postwar America, boxing was losing its audience for the very same reasons cities were losing their inhabitants. The new Levittown culture was killing the community that sustained Liebling. For Liebling the city was the center of American life, and New York was America's central city. Yet the New York he walked through was at the grim commencement of a forty-year decline. Postwar America was trending away from the city of pedestrians toward the isolation of the suburbs, where TV screens and passenger automobiles filtered reality. (One woman who spent the fifteen years after the war abroad told me, "When I came back, all everyone talked about was their lawn and their car.") This exodus transformed cities from communities to wastelands, and new suburbanites looked at those left behind not as fellow citizens but as criminals and murderers. Boxing has always been a primarily urban pastime (whereas the defining suburban sport is auto-racing, in which the machine and its anonymous mechanics hold far greater importance than the driver). When white Americans left the cities, they left boxing as well.

One of my great literary regrets is that Liebling didn't live to cover Cassius Clay's triumph over Liston and Clay's subsequent transfiguration into Muhammad Ali—Liebling died a few months before their first bout. The world Ali ushered in was a new one, its Day-Glo struggles more in tune with Tom Wolfe's hyperkinetic prose. Yet, like all true artists, Liebling looked forward as well as back, and would surely have kept his equipoise through the turmoil of the '60s. Literary journalism is as old as newspapers, but what Wolfe dubbed "New Journalism" can be directly traced through Liebling and his brittle colleague Joseph Mitchell. Moving beyond the clever parochialism of *The New Yorker* and the false objectivity of traditional news writing, Liebling helped to legitimize a narrator whose subjective stylings enrich reality. Early Tom Wolfe reads a lot like Liebling on speed.

I can only surmise about what Liebling would make of today's pugilistic dark ages. In his era, fighters fought rematches of close fights, even title fights, almost automatically. Ray Robinson and Jake LaMotta met *six* times, inconceivable for champions today. In the 1950s a quality pro thought himself underemployed if he had only eight or ten bouts a year, and the amateur scene was thriving. Nowadays pros who make a living from boxing are about as common as Yetis, and amateurs can't get enough fights to learn the rudiments of the craft. It has been several generations since the tinsel meccas of Las Vegas and Atlantic City displaced the Garden as showcases of the sweet science. My own experiences as an amateur boxer looking for fights, and as a writer writ-

ing about them, took me back and forth across the five boroughs
on an often-futile quest. Today's boxer is an endangered species;
at times I felt like a zoologist searching for a rare snail in the
Amazon basin.

Over a century intervened between Liebling's efforts and
those of his beloved Pierce Egan; evidently, great boxing and
great journalism come together only at rare intervals. Yet although the sport has become a part-time avocation for most,
there is no danger that boxing will go extinct, or that writers will
lose their fascination with it. Liebling took the long view: ". . . the
desire to punch other boys in the nose will survive in our culture . . . [Boxing] is an art of the people, like making love."

The Sweet Science

Introduction

"Sweet Science of Bruising!"
—*Boxiana*, 1824

"I had heard that Ketchel's dynamic onslaught was such it could not readily be withstood, but I figured I could jab his puss off. . . . I should have put the bum away early, but my timing was a fraction of an iota off." —Philadelphia Jack O'Brien, talking, in 1938, about something that had happened long ago

It is through Jack O'Brien, the *Arbiter Elegantiarum Philadelphiae*, that I trace my rapport with the historic past through the laying-on of hands. He hit me, for pedagogical example, and he had been hit by the great Bob Fitzsimmons, from whom he won the light-heavyweight title in 1906. Jack had a scar to show for it. Fitzsimmons had been hit by Corbett, Corbett by John L. Sullivan, he by Paddy Ryan, with the bare knuckles, and Ryan by Joe Goss, his predecessor, who as a young man had felt the fist of the great Jem Mace. It is a great thrill to feel that all that separates you from the early Victorians is a series of punches on the nose. I wonder if Professor Toynbee is as intimately attuned to his sources. The Sweet Science is joined onto the past like a man's arm to his shoulder.

I find it impossible to think that such a continuum can perish, but I will concede that we are entering a period of minor talents. The Sweet Science has suffered such doldrums before, like the long stretch, noted by Pierce Egan, the great historian of *Boxiana*, between the defeat of John Broughton in 1750 and the rise of Daniel Mendoza in 1789, or the more recent Dark Age between the retirement of Tunney in 1928 and the ascension of Joe Louis in the middle thirties. In both periods champions of little worth succeeded each other with the rapidity of the emperors who followed Nero, leaving the public scarce time to learn their names. When Louis came along he knocked out *five* of these world champions—Schmeling, Sharkey, Carnera, Baer, and Braddock, the last of whom happened to be holding the title when Louis hit him. A decade later he knocked out Jersey Joe Walcott, who nevertheless won the title four years afterward. His light extended in both directions historically, exposing the insignificance of what preceded and followed.

It is true there exist certain generalized conditions today, like full employment and a late school-leaving age, that militate against the development of first-rate professional boxers. (They militate also against the development of first-rate acrobats, fiddlers, and *chefs de cuisine*.) "Drummers and boxers, to acquire excellence, must begin young," the great Egan wrote in 1820. "There is a peculiar *nimbleness* of the *wrist* and exercise of the shoulder required, that is only obtained from growth and practice." Protracted exposure to education conflicts with this acquisition, but if a boy has a true vocation he can do much in his spare time. Tony Canzoneri, a very fine featherweight and lightweight of the thirties, told me once, for example, that he never had on a boxing glove until he was eight years old. "But of course I had done some street fighting," he said to explain how he had overcome his late start. Besides, there are a lot of unblighted areas like Cuba and North Africa and Siam that are beginning to turn out a lot of fighters now.

The immediate crisis in the United States, forestalling the

one high living standards might bring on, has been caused by the popularization of a ridiculous gadget called television. This is utilized in the sale of beer and razor blades. The clients of the television companies, by putting on a free boxing show almost every night of the week, have knocked out of business the hundreds of small-city and neighborhood boxing clubs where youngsters had a chance to learn their trade and journeymen to mature their skills. Consequently the number of good new prospects diminishes with every year, and the peddlers' public is already being asked to believe that a boy with perhaps ten or fifteen fights behind him is a topnotch performer. Neither advertising agencies nor brewers, and least of all the networks, give a hoot if they push the Sweet Science back into a period of genre painting. When it is in a coma they will find some other way to peddle their peanuts.

In truth the kind of people who run advertising agencies and razor-blade mills have little affinity with the Heroes of *Boxiana*. A boxer, like a writer, must stand alone. If he loses he cannot call an executive conference and throw off on a vice president or the assistant sales manager. He is consequently resented by fractional characters who cannot live outside an organization. A fighter's hostilities are not turned inward, like a Sunday tennis player's or a lady M.P.'s. They come out naturally with his sweat, and when his job is done he feels good because he has expressed himself. Chain-of-command types, to whom this is intolerable, try to rationalize their envy by proclaiming solicitude for the fighter's health. If a boxer, for example, ever went as batty as Nijinsky, all the wowsers in the world would be screaming "Punch-drunk." Well, who hit Nijinsky? And why isn't there a campaign against ballet? It gives girls thick legs. If a novelist who lived exclusively on applecores won the Nobel Prize, vegetarians would chorus that the repulsive nutriment had invigorated his brain. But when the prize goes to Ernest Hemingway, who has been a not particularly evasive boxer for years, no one rises to point out that the percussion has apparently stimulated his intellection. Albert Camus, the French probable for the Nobel, is an ex-boxer, too.

I was in the Neutral Corner saloon in New York a year or so ago when a resonant old gentleman, wiry, straight, and whitehaired, walked in and invited the proprietors to his ninetieth birthday party, in another saloon. The shortly-to-be nonagenarian wore no glasses, his hands were shapely, his forearms hard, and every hair looked as if, in the old water-front phrase, it had been drove in with a nail. On the card of invitation he laid on the bar was printed:

Billy Ray
Last surviving Bare Knuckle Fighter

The last bare-knuckle fight in which the world heavyweight championship changed hands was in 1882. Mr. Ray would not let anybody else in the Neutral buy a drink.

As I shared his bounty I thought of all his contemporary lawn-tennis players, laid away with their thromboses, and the golfers hoisted out of sand pits after suffering coronary occlusions. If they had turned in time to a more wholesome sport, I reflected, they might still be hanging on as board chairmen and senior editors instead of having their names on memorial pews. I asked Mr. Ray how many fights he had had and he said, "A hundert forty. The last one was with gloves. I thought the game was getting soft, so I retired."

When I was last in Hanover, New Hampshire, faculty members were dropping on the tennis courts so fast that people making up a doubles party always brought along a spare assistant professor.

This discussion of the relative salubrity of the Sweet Science and its milksop succedanea is what my friend Colonel John R. Stingo would call a labyrinthian digression.

It is because of the anticipated lean aesthetic period induced by television that I have decided to publish this volume now. The transactions narrated in it happen to comprise what may be the last heroic cycle for a long time. The Second World War, which began to affect American boxing when the draft came along in 1940, stopped the development of new talent. This permitted aging prewar boxers like Joe Louis and Joe Walcott to maintain their dominance longer than was to be expected under normal conditions. By the late forties, when the first few postwar fighters were beginning to shine, television got its thumb on the Old Sweetie's windpipe, and now there are no clubs to fight in. But in between these catastrophes Rocky Marciano appeared out of the shoe-manufacturing town of Brockton, Massachusetts, and Sandy Saddler, the pikelike featherweight, out of Harlem. Randy Turpin looked, briefly, like the first Heroic British fighter since Jimmy Wilde. Marcel Cerdan made an unforgettable impression before his premature death in an airplane accident. (He is not in this book, because he died too soon.) Archie Moore, a late-maturing artist, like Laurence Sterne and Stendhal, illuminated the skies with the light of his descending sun, and Sugar Ray Robinson proved as long-lasting as he had been precocious—a tribute to burning the candle at both ends.

It was in June of 1951 that it occurred to me to resume writing boxing pieces, and that was only four months before Marciano, then an impecunious, or "broken," fighter, arrived, as narrated early in this volume. There was no particular reason that I came back to boxing—"Suddenly it came to me," like the idea to the man in the song who was drinking gin-and-water. It was the way you take a notion that you would like to see an old sweetheart, which is not always the kind of notion to act on.

I had written a number of long boxing pieces for *The New Yorker* before 1939, but I dropped them then, along with the rest of what Harold Ross used to call "low-life," in order to become a war correspondent. Low-life was Ross's word for the kind of subject I did best.

When I came back from the war in 1945 I wasn't ready to write about the Sweet Science, although I continued to see fights and to talk with friends in Scientific circles. I became a critic of the American press, and had quite a lot of fun out of it, but it is a pastime less intellectually rewarding than the study of "milling," because the press is less competitive than the ring. Faced with a rival, an American newspaper will usually offer to buy it. This is sometimes done in Scientific circles, but is not considered ethical. Besides, the longer I criticized the press, the more it disimproved, as Arthur MacWeeney of the *Irish Indepen -dent* would put it.

My personal interest in La Dolce Scienza began when I was initiated into it by a then bachelor uncle who came east from California when I was thirteen years old, which was in 1917. He was a sound teacher and a good storyteller, so I got the rudiments and the legend at the same time. California, in the nineties and the early 1900s, had been headquarters: Corbett, Choynski, Jeffries, Tom Sharkey, Abe Attell, and Jimmy Britt were Californians all, and San Francisco had been the port of entry from Australia, which exported the Fitzsimmonses and Griffos. Uncle Mike could talk about them all. After my indoctrination I boxed for fun whenever I had a chance until I was twenty-six and earning sixty-three dollars a week as a reporter on the Providence *Journal and Evening Bulletin*. I continued to box occasionally for many years more, generally just enough to show I knew what was all about it, as the boys say. I went shorter rounds every time. The last was in about 1946, and the fellow I was working with said he could not knock me out unless I consented to rounds longer than nine seconds.

When I returned to the realms of higher intellection in 1951 Joe Louis was entering his eighteenth year as the most conspicuous ornament of the "fancy"—the highest feather in its hat. Within a few months Marciano appeared. This began a new cycle: Marciano and the Old Men, like Louis and the Old Men in 1934–38. During the immediately subsequent episodia, to borrow a word from Colonel Stingo, Marciano knocked out three world's heavyweight champions, Louis, Walcott, and Ezzard Charles, and wound up beating Moore, the heavyweight-light-heavyweight, who challenged for the title at thirty-nine. Marciano was then himself thirty-one, which was a fairly advanced age for a boxer, but all his big fights have been against men still older, because nobody was coming up behind him. With the Moore fight on September 16, 1955, the cycle was complete. It is certain that neither Hero will ever be better than on that night, and highly improbable that either will be again that good.

All the Heroic transactions recorded within this book thus occurred within the four-and-a-fraction years, June, 1951–September, 1955, and they have a kind of porous unity, like the bound volumes of *Boxiana* Egan used to get out whenever he figured he had enough magazine pieces about the ring of his day to fill a book. There is as main theme the rise of Marciano, and the falls of everybody who fought him, and there are subplots, like the comeback of Sugar Ray after his downfall before Turpin, and his re-downfall before Maxim, but not his current re-comeback. There is some discussion of the television matter, and there are exploits of minor Heroes like Sandy Saddler, the featherweight champion, and a lot of boys you never heard of. The characters who hold the book, and the whole fabric of the Sweet Science together, are the trainer-seconds, as in Egan's day.

Egan, to whom I refer so often in this volume, was the greatest writer about the ring who ever lived. Hazlitt was a dilettante who wrote one fight story. Egan was born probably in 1772, and died, certainly, in 1849. He belonged to London, and no man has ever presented a more enthusiastic picture of all aspects of its life except the genteel. He was a hack journalist, a song writer, a conductor of puff-sheets and, I am inclined to suspect, a shakedown man. His work affords internal evidence that he was self-educated; if he wasn't he had certainly found a funny schoolmaster. In 1812 he got out the first paperbound installment of *Boxiana; or Sketches of Ancient and Modern Pugilism; from the days of Broughton and Slack to the Heroes of the Present Milling Aera.* For years before that he had been writing about boxing for a sporting magazine called the *Weekly Despatch.* The unparalleled interest in the Sweet Science aroused by the two fights between Tom Cribb, the Champion, and Tom Molineaux, an American Negro, in 1811, inspired Egan to launch a monthly publication confined to milling.

He covered the historical portion of his self-assigned program in his first few numbers, and after that *Boxiana* became a running chronicle of the Contemporary Milling Aera. As the man with the laurel concession, he became a great figure in the making of matches, the holding of stakes, the decision of disputes, the promotion of banquets, and all the other perquisites of eminence.

"In his particular line, he was the greatest man in England," a memorialist wrote of him long after his death. "In the event of opposition to his views and opinions, he and those who looked up to him had a mode of enforcing authority which had the efficacy without the tediousness of discussion, and 'though,' says one who knew him, 'in personal strength far from a match for any sturdy opponent, he had a courage and vivacity in action which were very highly estimated both by his friends and foes.' . . .

"His peculiar phraseology, and his superior knowledge of the business, soon rendered him eminent beyond all rivalry and competition. He was flattered and petted by pugilists and peers: his patronage and countenance were sought for by all who considered the road to a prizefight the road to reputation and honor. Sixty years ago [that would have been 1809], his presence was understood to convey respectability on any meeting convened for the furtherance of bull-baiting, cock-fighting, cudgelling, wrestling,

boxing, and all that comes within the category of 'manly sports.'
If he 'took the chair,' success was held as certain in the object in
question. On the occasions of his presence he was accompanied
by a 'tail,' if not as numerous, perhaps as respectable as that by
which another great man was attended, and certainly, in its way,
quite as influential."

Egan brought out his first bound volume, comprising sixteen
numbers, in 1813, although the title page reads 1812. (It had
gone to the subscribers with the first installment.) He did not
put out another bound volume until 1818. There was a third in
1821, a fourth in 1824, and a fifth in 1828. By that time the
Sweet Science was entering one of its periodic declines. Too many
X (Egan's way of writing crooked) fights had disgusted backers
and bettors, and there was a lack of exciting new talent. The Science was not to reach another peak until the rise of Tom Sayers,
in the late 1850s, which would culminate in Tom's great fight
with the American, John C. Heenan, in 1860. Egan abandoned
Boxiana after the 1828 volume.

A great charm of *Boxiana* is that it is no mere compilation of
synopses of fights. Egan's round-by-round stories, with ringside
sidelights and betting fluctuations, are masterpieces of technical
reportage, but he also saw the ring as a juicy chunk of English
life, in no way separable from the rest. His accounts of the extra-
annular lives of the Heroes, coal-heavers, watermen, and butch-
ers' boys, are a panorama of low, dirty, happy, brutal, sentimental
Regency England that you'll never get from Jane Austen. The
fighter's relations with their patrons, the Swells, present that curious pattern of good fellowship and snobbery, not mutually ex-
clusive, that has always existed between Gentleman and Player in
England, and that Australians, Americans, and Frenchmen
equally find hard to credit. Egan is full of anecdotes like the one
about the Swell and his pet Hero, who were walking arm-in-arm
in Covent Garden late one night, when they saw six Dandies in-

sulting a woman. Dandies were neither Gentleman nor Players, and Egan had no use for them. The Swell remonstrated with the Dandies and one of them hit him. The Swell then cried, "Jack Martin, give it them," and the Hero, who was what we today would call a light-heavyweight, knocked down the six Dandies. From Egan's narrative it is impossible to tell which performance he considered more dashing, the Swell's or the Hero's.

That particular Hero, by the way, was known as the Master of the Rolls, because he was by trade a baker. "Martin is very respectably connected," Egan wrote, "and, when he first commenced prize pugilist, he had an excellent business as a baker; but which concern he ultimately disposed (or got rid) of, in order, it seems, to give a greater scope to his inclinations." Egan's cockney characters, and his direct quotes of how they talked, were a gift to Dickens, who, like every boy in England, read the author of *Boxiana*. In the New York Public Library catalogue there is listed a German monograph, circa 1900, on Egan's influence on Dickens, but I know of no similar attempt at justice in the English language.

Egan's pageant scenes of trulls and lushes, toffs and toddlers, all setting off for some great public, illegal prize-fight, are written Rowlandson, just as Rowlandson's print of the great second fight between Cribb and Molineaux is graphic Egan. In the foreground of the picture there is a whore sitting on her gentleman's shoulders the better to see the fight, while a pickpocket lifts the gentleman's reader (watch). Cribb has just hit Molineaux the floorer, and Molineaux is falling, as he has continued to do for a hundred and forty-five years since. He hasn't hit the floor yet, but every time I look at the picture I expect to see him land. On the horizon are the delicate green hills and the pale blue English sky, hand-tinted by old drunks recruited in kip-shops (flophouses). The prints cost a shilling colored. When I look at my copy I can smell the crowd and the wildflowers.

Egan could be stately when he wanted, as you can see from

the following sample taken from the dedication of the first volume of *Boxiana*:

> To those, Sir, who prefer *effeminacy* to hardihood—assumed *refinement* to rough *Nature*—and whom a *shower of rain* can terrify, under the alarm of their *polite* frames, suffering from the unruly elements—or would not mind Pugilism, if B OXING was not so shockingly vulgar—the following work can create no interest whatever; but to those persons who feel that Englishmen are not automatons . . . *Boxiana* will convey amusement, if not information . . .

I can think of nothing more to say in favor of the Present Extension of the G R E AT H I S T O R I A N 's Magnum Opus.

A. J. LIEBLING
Paris, 1956

The Big Fellows

Boxing with the Naked Eye

Watching a fight on television has always seemed to me a poor substitute for being there. For one thing, you can't tell the fighters what to do. When I watch a fight, I like to study one boxer's problem, solve it, and then communicate my solution vocally. On occasion my advice is disregarded, as when I tell a man to stay away from the other fellow's left and he doesn't, but in such cases I assume that he hasn't heard my counsel, or that his opponent has, and has acted on it. Some fighters hear better and are more suggestible than others—for example, the pre-television Joe Louis. "Let him have it, Joe!" I would yell whenever I saw him fight, and sooner or later he would let the other fellow have it. Another fighter like that was the late Marcel Cerdan, whom I would coach in his own language, to prevent opposition seconds from picking up our signals. *"Vas-y, Marcel!"* I used to shout, and Marcel always *y allait*. I get a feeling of participation that way that I don't in front of a television screen. I could yell, of course, but I would know that if my suggestion was adopted, it would be by the merest coincidence.

Besides, when you go to a fight, the boxers aren't the only ones you want to be heard by. You are surrounded by people whose ignorance of the ring is exceeded only by their unwillingness to face facts—the sharpness of your boxer's punching, for instance. Such people may take it upon themselves to disparage the principal you are advising. This disparagement is less generally addressed to the man himself (as "Gavilan, you're a bum!") than to his opponent, whom they have wrong-headedly picked to win. ("He's a cream puff, Miceli!" they may typically cry. "He can't hurt you. He can't hurt nobody. Look—slaps! Ha, ha!") They thus get at your man—and, by indirection, at you. To put them in their place, you address neither them nor their man but your man. ("Get the other eye, Gavilan!" you cry.) This throws them off balance, because they haven't noticed anything the matter with either eye. Then, before they can think of anything to say, you thunder, "Look at that eye!" It doesn't much matter whether or not the man has been hit in the eye; he will be. Addressing yourself to the fighter when you want somebody else to hear you is a parliamentary device, like "Mr. Chairman . . ." Before television, a prize-fight was to a New Yorker the nearest equivalent to the New England town meeting. It taught a man to think on his seat.

Less malignant than rooters for the wrong man, but almost as disquieting, are those who are on the right side but tactically unsound. At a moment when you have steered your boxer to a safe lead on points but can see the other fellow is still dangerous, one of these maniacs will encourage recklessness. "Finish the jerk, Harry!" he will sing out. "Stop holding him up! Don't lose him!" But you, knowing the enemy is a puncher, protect your client's interests. "Move to your left, Harry!" you call. "Keep moving! Keep moving! Don't let him set!" I sometimes finish a fight like that in a cold sweat.

If you go to a fight with a friend, you can keep up unilateral conversations on two vocal levels—one at the top of your voice, directed at your fighter, and the other a running *expertise* nominally aimed at your companion but loud enough to reach a modest fifteen feet in each direction. "Reminds me of Panama Al Brown," you may say as a new fighter enters the ring. "He was five feet eleven and weighed a hundred and eighteen pounds. This fellow may be about forty pounds heavier and a couple of inches shorter, but he's got the same kind of neck. I saw Brown box a fellow named Mascart in Paris in 1927. Guy stood up in the top gallery and threw an apple and hit Brown right on the top of the head. The whole house started yelling, 'Finish him, Mascart! He's groggy!' " Then, as the bout begins, "Boxes like Al, too, except this fellow's a southpaw." If he wins, you say, "I told you he reminded me of Al Brown," and if he loses, "Well, well, I guess he's no Al Brown. They don't make fighters like Al any more." This identifies you as a man who (a) has been in Paris, (b) has been going to fights for a long time, and (c) therefore enjoys what the fellows who write for quarterlies call a frame of reference.

It may be argued that this doesn't get you anywhere, but it at least constitutes what a man I once met named Thomas S. Matthews called communication. Mr. Matthews, who was the editor of *Time*, said that the most important thing in journalism is not reporting but communication. "What are you going to communicate?" I asked him. "The most important thing," he said, "is the man on one end of the circuit saying 'My God, I'm alive! You're alive!' and the fellow on the other end, receiving his message, saying 'My God, you're right! We're both alive!' " I still think it is a hell of a way to run a news magazine, but it is a good reason for going to fights in person. Television, if unchecked, may carry us back to a pre-tribal state of social development, when the family was the largest conversational unit.

Fights are also a great place for adding to your repertory of witty sayings. I shall not forget my adolescent delight when I first heard a fight fan yell, "I hope youse bot' gets knocked out!" I thought he had made it up, although I found out later it was a cliché. It is a formula adaptable to an endless variety of situations outside the ring. The only trouble with it is it never works out. The place where I first heard the line was Bill Brown's, a fight club in a big shed behind a trolley station in Far Rockaway.

On another night there, the time for the main bout arrived and one of the principals hadn't. The other fighter sat in the ring, a bantamweight with a face like a well-worn coin, and the fans stamped in cadence and whistled and yelled for their money back. It was thirty years before television, but there were only a couple of hundred men on hand. The preliminary fights had been terrible. The little fighter kept looking at his hands, which were resting on his knees in cracked boxing gloves, and every now and then he would spit on the mat and rub the spittle into the canvas with one of his scuffed ring shoes. The longer he waited, the more frequently he spat, and I presumed he was worrying about the money he was supposed to get; it wouldn't be more than fifty dollars with a house that size, even if the other man turned up. He had come there from some remote place like West or East New York, and he may have been thinking about the last train home on the Long Island Railroad, too. Finally, the other bantamweight got there, looking out of breath and flustered. He had lost his way on the railroad—changed to the wrong train at Jamaica and had to go back there and start over. The crowd booed so loud that he looked embarrassed. When the fight began, the fellow who had been waiting walked right into the new boy and knocked him down. He acted impatient. The tardy fellow got up and fought back gamely, but the one who had been waiting nailed him again, and the latecomer just about pulled up to one knee at the count of seven. He had been hit pretty hard, and you could see from his face that he was wondering whether to chuck it. Somebody in the crowd yelled out, "Hey, Hickey! You kept us all waiting! Why don't you stay around awhile?" So the fellow got up and caught for ten rounds and probably made the one who had come early miss his train. It's another formula with multiple applications, and I think the man who said it that night in Far Rockaway did make it up.

Because of the way I feel about watching fights on television, I was highly pleased when I read, back in June, 1951, that the fifteen-round match between Joe Louis and Lee Savold, scheduled for June thirteenth at the Polo Grounds, was to be neither televised, except to eight theater audiences in places like Pittsburgh and Albany, nor broadcast over the radio. I hadn't seen Louis with the naked eye since we shook hands in a pub in London in 1944. He had fought often since then, and I had seen his two bouts with Jersey Joe Walcott on television, but there hadn't been any fun in it. Those had been held in public places, naturally, and I could have gone, but television gives you so plausible an adumbration of a fight, for nothing, that you feel it would be extravagant to pay your way in. It is like the potato, which is only a succedaneum for something decent to eat but which, once introduced into Ireland, proved so cheap that the peasants gave up their grain-and-meat diet in favor of it. After that, the landlords let them keep just enough money to buy potatoes. William Cobbett, a great Englishman, said that he would sack any workmen of his he caught eating one of the cursed things, because as soon as potatoes appeared anywhere they brought down the standard of eating. I sometimes think of Cobbett on my way home from the races, looking at the television aerials on all the little houses between here and Belmont Park. As soon as I heard that the fight wouldn't be on the air, I determined to buy a ticket.

On the night of the thirteenth, a Wednesday, it rained, and on the next night it rained again, so on the evening of June fifteenth the promoters, the International Boxing Club, confronted by a night game at the Polo Grounds, transferred the fight to Madison Square Garden. The postponements upset a plan I had

had to go to the fight with a friend, who had another date for the third night. But alone is a good way to go to a fight or the races, because you have more time to look around you, and you always get all the conversation you can use anyway. I went to the Garden box office early Friday afternoon and bought a ten-dollar seat in the side arena—the first tiers rising in back of the boxes, midway between Eighth and Ninth Avenues on the 49th Street side of the house. There was only a scattering of ticket buyers in the lobby, and the man at the ticket window was polite—a bad omen for the gate. After buying the ticket, I got into a cab in front of the Garden, and the driver naturally asked me if I was going to see the fight. I said I was, and he said, "He's all through."

I knew he meant Louis, and I said, "I know, and that's why it may be a good fight. If he weren't through, he might kill this guy."

The driver said, "Savold is a hooker. He breaks noses."

I said, "He couldn't break his own nose, even," and then began to wonder how a man would go about trying to do that. "It's a shame he's so hard up he had to fight at all at his age," I said, knowing the driver would understand I meant Louis. I was surprised that the driver was against Louis, and I was appealing to his better feelings.

"He must have plenty socked away," said the driver. "Playing golf for a hundred dollars a hole."

"Maybe that helped him go broke," I said. "And anyway, what does that prove? There's many a man with a small salary who bets more than he can afford." I had seen a scratch sheet on the seat next to the hackie. I was glad I was riding only as far as Brentano's with him.

The driver I had on the long ride home was a better type. As soon as I told him I was going to the fight, which was at about the same time that he dropped the flag, he said, "I guess the old guy can still sock."

I said, "I saw him murder Max Baer sixteen years ago. He was a sweet fighter then."

The driver said, "Sixteen years is a long time for a fighter. I don't remember anybody lasted sixteen years in the big money. Still, Savold is almost as old as he is. When you're a bum, nobody notices how old you get."

We had a pleasant time on the West Side Highway, talking about how Harry Greb had gone on fighting when he was blind in one eye, only nobody knew it but his manager, and how Pete Herman had been the best infighter in the world, because he had been practically blind in both eyes, so he couldn't afford to fool around outside. "What Herman did, you couldn't learn a boy now," the driver said. "They got no patience."

The fellow who drove me from my house to the Garden after dinner was also a man of good will, but rather different. He knew I was going to the fight as soon as I told him my destination, and once we had got under way, he said, "It is a pity that a man like Louis should be exploited to such a degree that he has to fight again." It was only nine-fifteen, and he agreed with me that I had plenty of time to get to the Garden for the main bout, which was scheduled to begin at ten, but when we got caught in unexpectedly heavy traffic on Eleventh Avenue he grew impatient. "Come on, Jersey!" he said, giving a station wagon in front of us the horn. "In the last analysis, we have got to get to the Garden sometime." But it didn't help much, because most of the other cars were heading for the Garden, too. The traffic was so slow going toward Eighth Avenue on Fiftieth Street that I asked him to let me out near the Garden corner, and joined the people hurrying from the Independent Subway exit toward the Garden marquee. A high percentage of them were from Harlem, and they were dressed as if for a levee, the men in shimmering gabardines and felt hats the color of freshly unwrapped chewing gum, the women in spring suits and fur pieces—it was a cool night—and what seemed to me the prettiest hats of the season. They seemed to me the prettiest lot of women I had seen in a long time, too, and I reflected that if the fight had been televised, I would have missed them. "Step out," I heard one beau say as his group swept past me, "or we won't maybe get in. It's just like I told you—he's still one hell of a draw." As I made my way through the now crowded lobby, I could hear the special cop next to the ticket window chanting, "Six-, eight-, ten-, and fifteen-dollar tickets only," which meant that the two-and-a-half-dollar general-admission and the twenty-dollar ringside seats were sold out. It made me feel good, because it showed there were still some gregarious people left in the world.

Inside the Garden there was the same old happy drone of voices as when Jimmy McLarnin was fighting and Jimmy Walker was at the ringside. There was only one small patch of bare seats, in a particularly bad part of the ringside section. I wondered what sort of occupant I would find in my seat; I knew from experience that there would be somebody in it. It turned out to be a small, frail colored man in wine-red livery. He sat up straight and pressed his shoulder blades against the back of the chair, so I couldn't see the number. When I showed him my ticket, he said, "I don't know nothing about that. You better see the usher." He was offering this token resistance, I knew, only to protect his self-esteem—to maintain the shadowy fiction that he was in the seat by error. When an usher wandered within hailing distance of us, I called him, and the little man left, to drift to some other part of the Garden, where he had no reputation as a ten-dollar-seat holder to lose, and there to squat contentedly on a step.

My seat was midway between the east and west ends of the ring, and about fifteen feet above it. Two not very skillful colored boys were finishing a four-rounder that the man in the next seat told me was an emergency bout, put on because there had been several knockouts in the earlier preliminaries. It gave me a chance to settle down and look around. It was ten o'clock by the time the colored boys finished and the man with the microphone announced the decision, but there was no sign of Louis or Savold. The fight wasn't on the air, so there was no need of the punctuality required by the radio business. (Later I read in the newspapers that the bout had been delayed in deference to the hundreds of people who were still in line to buy tickets and who wanted to be sure of seeing the whole fight.) Nobody made any spiel about beer, as on the home screen, although a good volume of it was being drunk all around. Miss Gladys Gooding, an organist, played the national anthem and a tenor sang it, and we all applauded. After that, the announcer introduced a number of less than illustrious prizefighters from the ring, but nobody whistled or acted restless. It was a good-natured crowd.

Then Louis and his seconds—what the author of *Boxiana* would have called his faction—appeared from a runway under the north stands and headed toward the ring. The first thing I noticed, from where I sat, was that the top of Louis's head was bald. He looked taller than I had remembered him, although surely he couldn't have grown after the age of thirty, and his face was puffy and impassive. It has always been so. In the days of his greatness, the press read menace in it. He walked stiff-legged, as was natural for a heavy man of thirty-seven, but when his seconds pulled off his dressing robe, his body looked all right. He had never been a lean man; his muscles had always been well buried beneath his smooth beige skin. I recalled the first time I had seen him fight—against Baer. That was at the Yankee Stadium, in September, 1935, and not only the great ball park but the roofs of all the apartment houses around were crowded with spectators, and hundreds of people were getting out of trains at the elevated I.R.T. station, which overlooks the field, and trying to loiter long enough to catch a few moments of action. Louis had come

East that summer, after a single year as a professional, and had knocked out Primo Carnera in a few rounds. Carnera had been the heavyweight champion of the world in 1934, when Baer knocked him out. Baer, when he fought Louis, was the most powerful and gifted heavyweight of the day, although he had already fumbled away his title. But this mature Baer, who had fought everybody, was frightened stiff by the twenty-one-year-old mulatto boy. Louis outclassed him. The whole thing went only four rounds. There hadn't been anybody remotely like Louis since Dempsey in the early twenties.

The week of the Louis–Baer fight, a man I know wrote in a magazine: "With half an eye, one can observe that the town is more full of stir than it has been in many moons. It is hard to find a place to park, hard to get a table in a restaurant, hard to answer all the phone calls. . . . Economic seers can explain it, if you care to listen. We prefer to remember that a sudden inflation of the town's spirit can be just as much psychological or accidental as economic." I figured it was Louis.

Savold had now come up into the other corner, a jutty-jawed man with a fair skin but a red back, probably sunburned at his training camp. He was twenty pounds lighter than Louis, but that isn't considered a crushing handicap among heavyweights; Ezzard Charles, who beat Louis the previous year, was ten pounds lighter than Savold. Savold was thirty-five, and there didn't seem to be much bounce in him. I had seen him fight twice in the winter of 1946, and I knew he wasn't much. Both bouts had been against a young Negro heavyweight named Al Hoosman, a tall, skinny fellow just out of the Army. Hoosman had started well the first time, but Savold had hurt him with body punches and won the decision. The second time, Hoosman had stayed away and jabbed him silly. An old third-rater like Savold, I knew, doesn't improve with five more years on him. But an old third-rater doesn't rattle easily, either, and I was sure he'd do his best. It made me more apprehensive, in one way, than if he'd been any good. I wouldn't have liked to see Louis beaten by a good young fighter, but it would be awful to see him beaten by a clown. Not that I have anything against Savold; I just think it's immoral for a fellow without talent to get too far. A lot of others in the crowd must have felt the same way, because the house was quiet when the fight started—as if the Louis rooters didn't want to ask too much of Joe. There weren't any audible rooters for Savold, though, of course, there would have been if he had landed one good punch.

I remembered reading in a newspaper that Savold had said he would walk right out and bang Louis in the temple with a right, which would scramble his thinking. But all he did was come forward as he had against Hoosman, with his left low. A fellow like that never changes. Louis walked out straight and stiff-legged, and jabbed his left into Savold's face. He did it again and again, and Savold didn't seem to know what to do about it. And Louis jabs a lot harder than a fellow like Hoosman. Louis didn't have to chase Savold, and he had no reason to run away from him, either, so the stiff legs were all right. When the two men came close together, Louis jarred Savold with short punches, and Savold couldn't push him around, so that was all right, too. After the first round, the crowd knew Louis would win if his legs would hold him.

In the second round Louis began hitting Savold with combinations—quick sequences of punches, like a right under the heart and a left hook to the right side of the head. A sports writer I know had told me that Louis hadn't been putting combinations together for several fights back. Combinations demand a superior kind of coordination, but a fighter who has once had that can partly regain it by hard work. A couple of times it looked as if Louis was trying for a knockout, but when Savold didn't come apart, Louis returned to jabbing. A man somewhere behind me kept saying to a companion, "I read Savold was a tricky fighter. He's got to do something!" But Savold didn't, until late in the fifth round, by which time his head must have felt like a sick music box. Then he threw a right to Louis's head and it landed. I thought I could see Louis shrink, as if he feared trouble. His response ten years ago would have been to tear right back into the man. Savold threw another right, exactly the same kind, and that hit Louis, too. No good fighter should have been hit twice in succession with that kind of foolish punch. But the punches weren't hard enough to slow Louis down, and that was the end of that. In the third minute of the sixth round, he hit Savold with a couple of combinations no harder than those that had gone before, but Savold was weak now. His legs were going limp, and Louis was pursuing him as he backed toward my side of the ring. Then Louis swung like an axman with his right (he wasn't snapping it as he used to), and his left dropped over Savold's guard and against his jaw, and the fellow was rolling over and over on the mat, rolling the way football players do when they fall on a fumbled ball. The referee was counting and Savold was rolling, and he got up on either nine or ten, I couldn't tell which (later, I read that it was ten, so he was out officially), but you could see he was knocked silly, and the referee had his arms around him, and it was over.

The newspapermen, acres of them near the ring, were banging out the leads for the running stories they had already telegraphed, and I felt sorry for them, because they never have time to enjoy boxing matches. Since the fight was not broadcast, there was no oily-voiced chap to drag Louis over to a microphone and ask him stupid questions. He shook hands with Savold twice, once right after the knockout and again a few minutes later, when Savold was ready to leave the ring, as if he feared Savold wouldn't remember the first handshake.

I drifted toward the lobby with the crowd. The chic Harlem people were saying to one another, "It was terrific, darling! It was terrific!" I could see that an element of continuity had been restored to their world. But there wasn't any of the wild exultation that had followed those first Louis victories in 1935. These people had celebrated so many times—except, of course, the younger ones, who were small children when Louis knocked out Baer. I recognized one of the Garden promoters, usually a sour fellow, looking happy. The bout had brought in receipts of $94,684, including my ten dollars, but, what was more important to the Garden, Louis was sure to draw a lot more the next time, and at a higher scale of prices.

I walked downtown on Eighth Avenue to a point where the crowd began to thin out, and climbed into a taxi that had been stopped by the light on a cross street. This one had a Negro driver.

"The old fellow looked pretty good tonight," I said. "Had those combinations going."

"Fight over?" the driver asked. If there had been television, or even radio, he would have known about everything, and I wouldn't have had the fun of telling him.

"Sure," I said. "He knocked the guy out in the sixth."

"I was afraid he wouldn't," said the driver. "You know, it's a funny thing," he said, after we had gone on a way, "but I been twenty-five years in New York now and never seen Joe Louis in the flesh."

"You've seen him on television, haven't you?"

"Yeah," he said. "But that don't count." After a while he said, "I remember when he fought Carnera. The celebration in Harlem. They poisoned his mind before that fight, his managers and Jack Blackburn did. They told him Carnera was Mussolini's man and Mussolini started the Ethiopian War. He cut that man down like he was a tree."

Broken Fighter Arrives

When Louis knocked Savold out, I came away singularly re-
vived—as if I, rather than Louis, had demonstrated resistance to
the erosion of time. As long as Joe could get by, I felt, I had a
link with an era when we were both a lot younger. Only the great
champions give their fellow citizens time to feel that way about
them, because only the great ones win the title young and hold
on to it. There have been three like that among the heavyweights
in this century—Jim Jeffries, Jack Dempsey, and Louis. Jeffries
won the championship in 1899, when my father was a footloose
young sport, and was beaten, after a period of retirement, by Jack
Johnson in 1910, when Father was a solemn burgher with a wife,
two children, and three twelve-story loft buildings with second
mortgages on them. Dempsey beat Jess Willard in 1919, when I
was in short pants. He lost the second decision to Gene Tunney
in 1927 (I had believed that the first was an accident, and so I
had continued to think of him as champion), and by that time
I had written half a novel, spent a year at the Sorbonne, and
worked on two newspapers.

Louis was the champion, in the public mind, from 1935,
when he slaughtered Primo Carnera and Max Baer, until 1951.
Technically, his span was slightly shorter, because he didn't beat
Jim Braddock for the title until 1937, but everybody knew from
1935 on that he would beat Braddock whenever he got the
match. And he lost the championship by a decision to Ezzard
Charles in 1950, but Charles was subsequently knocked out by
old Jersey Joe Walcott, whom Louis had flattened a while back.
When the three were introduced from the ring before the bout
between Sugar Ray Robinson and Randy Turpin in September,
1951, the crowd left no doubt that it still considered Louis the
leading heavyweight.

At about that same time, I learned that Louis, who was

thirty-seven, had been "made" with a new heavyweight, Rocky Marciano, who was twenty-seven and a puncher. I didn't think much about it then, but as October twenty-sixth, the date set for the fight, approached, I began to feel uneasy. Marciano, to be sure, had never had a professional fight until shortly after Louis first announced his retirement, in 1948. (Joe had subsequently, of course, recanted.) In addition, Marciano had beaten only two opponents of any note, both young heavyweights like himself, who were rated as no better than promising. He was not big for a heavyweight, and was supposed to be rather crude. What bothered me, though, about the impending affair was that Marciano was, as he still is, steered by a man I know, named Al Weill, who is one of the most realistic fellows in a milieu where illusions are few. Marciano was already a good drawing card and would continue to be as long as he was unbeaten, and Weill, I was sure, would never risk the depreciation of an asset unless he felt he had a good bet.

Weill is at present the matchmaker of the I.B.C., which controls boxing here in New York and in a dozen other large cities, and his son, Marty Weill, is Marciano's manager "of record," which means he signs the contracts. The younger Weill has a job-lot commission business in Dayton, Ohio, and isn't properly a boxing man at all. When the elder Weill became matchmaker, he "gave" his son the fighter, much as a lawyer, upon becoming a public official, turns over his private practice to a partner. Marciano is, in effect, a kind of family enterprise, like Rockefeller Center. As the fight date drew near, I decided to go around to the headquarters of the International, above the Iceland Skating Rink in the Madison Square Garden building, and ask the elder Weill what was doing. I could have accomplished this less formally by giving him what he calls a bang on the telephone, but I wished to compare his facial expressions with his asseverations.

The matchmaker is of the build referred to in ready-made-clothing stores as a portly, which means not quite a stout. There is an implication of at least one kind of recklessness about a fat man; he lets himself go when he eats. A portly man, on the other hand, is a man who would like to be fat but restrains himself—a calculator. Weill has a Roman nose of the short, or budgereegah, variety, and an over-all grayish coloration that is complemented by the suits he generally wears and the cigar ashes he frequently spills on them. On his home block—86th Street between West End Avenue and Riverside Drive—he blends perfectly with the tired 1910 grandeur of the apartment houses; he looks like one more garment manufacturer worried by a swollen inventory. This does not stop him from knowing more about the fight business than any of the flashier types who wear long beige jackets and stay downtown after dark.

Weill is a frugal man, and he likes frugal fighters. Every kind of serious trouble a fighter can get into, he says, has its origin in the disbursement of currency—rich food, liquor, women, horse-race betting, and fast automobiles. Once a fighter starts gambling, Weill doesn't want him. "A gambler thinks he can get money without working for it," he says. Weill had a big string of fighters before the war, and used to quarter them all in a lodging house near Central Park West, where the housemaster would issue to each boy a weekly meal ticket with a face value of five dollars and fifty cents, redeemable in trade at a coffeepot on Columbus Avenue. The tickets cost Weill five dollars each, cash. A fighter could get a second ticket before the week was out, but only if he showed that the first one had been punched out to the last nickel. None of those fighters ever suffered a defeat that could be attributed to high living. Mere frugality, however, may prove a boomerang, for the fighter sometimes gets to like it. There was once an old colored heavyweight named Bob Armstrong, who, when asked his utmost ambition, said, "To wake up every morning and find a dollar under my pillow." Naturally, he never got to be champion. Weill wouldn't want a fighter like that. What he really loves is an avaricious fighter.

When I asked Weill about Marciano he looked happy. "He is a nice boy," he said. "The dollar is his God. That is to say, he is a poor Italian boy from a large, poor family, and he appreciates the buck more than almost anybody else. Them type guys is hard to get outa there. You want to look out for them young broken fighters." By "broken fighter," Weill, who is a purist, meant a fighter who is broke. "He only got two halfway decent purses— with LaStarza and Layne—and it was like a tiger tasting blood," Weill went on. "So you know how confident he is when he will take a fight like this for fifteen per cent of the gate. Louis gets forty-five. Why, Marciano will bring more money into the Garden than Louis. Connecticut, Rhode Island, and half of Massachusetts will be empty that night." Marciano hails from Brockton, Massachusetts.

Having considered the morale factor, which with him always comes first, Weill passed to the tactical level. He said Marciano would never be a clever boxer; he wasn't made for it, anyway, being short for a heavyweight, and wide, with short, thick arms. "But he knows what he has to do," Weill said. "Get in close enough to hit and then keep on hitting. And he don't come walking in straight, like Savold. Anybody would look good punching a punching bag that comes straight to you. This kid will fight out of a crouch. How I got him"—he changed the subject abruptly—"is three years ago a fellow I know used to promote around Boston wrote me there was a hell of an amateur he would like me to take. So I sent up the carfare for them to come down. They come, and we took Rocky to the C.Y.O. gym and put him in with a young heavyweight from Staten Island, a big blond guy belonged to a friend of mine. We had to stop him or he'd killed that Staten Island guy. I seen right then Rocky had the beginning of it. So I sent him up to Manny Almeida, a friend of mind promotes in Providence, which is near where he is out of Brockton, but Brockton is too small to have fights. And I asked Manny to put him in with the same kind he was, but no setups.

Because you got a guy knocking over setups, you don't know what you got. He come along good. When I come over here, I give him to Marty. Who should I give him to if not my own flesh and blood?"

A day or two after my talk with Weill, I went out to Louis's training quarters at Pompton Lakes, New Jersey, and it was like going back to the first administration of Franklin D. Roosevelt. There was about all Louis's habits a majestic continuity, as there was about his style in the ring, which is basically classical. His style has diminished in speed of execution but has never varied in concept. Pompton was his lucky camp; he trained there for his first New York fight, against Carnera, in 1935, when he was twenty-one, and he trained there for all his succeeding fights but four—"way more than twenty," he told me when I talked with him later that day. I hadn't been out there since the summer of 1938, when Louis was preparing for his return fight with Max Schmeling, the only man who had up to that time knocked him out. (That return fight was his happiest victory; he destroyed the German in less than a round.) Incidentally, Louis has knocked out six men who at one time or another held the heavyweight championship—Schmeling, Jack Sharkey, Carnera, Baer, Braddock, and Walcott—a record possible because the championship changed hands so often in the short period between 1930 and 1937, leaving so many mediocre ex-champions simultaneously extant.

The camp, like Louis himself, was essentially the same but much older-looking. Part of the difference, I suppose, was due to the fact that the Schmeling fight had been in the summer, and now the leaves were turning on the sides of the Ramapos, and the air was chill. But that wasn't all of it. Before the war, the camp was operated by a bright and energetic couple named Dr. and Mrs. Bier, who had ambitions about turning it into a health farm for millionaires. On days when Louis was to spar, the grounds were always packed with charabancs from Harlem bringing people to see him work. The money pouring in at the gate, at a dollar a head, made training actually a profitable activity, and the hot-dog concession alone—there was also a bar—brought in enough to pay the sparring partners. The place has since been bought by a man by the name of Baumgartner, and there is no longer a bar, or even a hot dog, on the premises, although I heard that Coca-Cola can be bought on Sundays. The day I was there, there were perhaps a dozen automobiles on the grounds when sparring was scheduled to begin, and no more than twenty-five paying customers, at sixty cents a head, despite the fact that the fight was only a week off. And, except for me, the press was represented only by Colonel John R. Stingo, who writes a column called "Yea Verily" for the New York *Enquirer*, a newspaper always dated Monday but published only on Sunday afternoon. Colonel Stingo is a small, agile man who helped cover the Corbett-Sullivan fight for the New Orleans *Item* in 1892. A Boston newspaperman named Gilhooley had ridden out with us from New York in a car hired by the I.B.C., but had gone on to Marciano's training camp at Greenwood Lake, New York, seventeen miles farther along. The car was to wait there for him, and then pick us up after the workouts were over.

One of the first things I saw on getting out of the car was a familiar sweatered figure sprawled in a lawn chair in front of the red frame building that in livelier days housed the bar. It was Mannie Seamon, Louis's trainer, a white man who stepped into the job after the death of Jack Blackburn, the old colored fighter who formed Louis's style. Seamon is more of a conditioner than a boxing coach—a jovial, rosy-cheeked man who sometimes discourses learnedly on "bone juice" and keeping the air out of his charges' bones. He hadn't changed at all in the intervening years, I noted enviously, but I winced when I thought of how many thousand medicine balls he must have thrown at Louis's and other fighters' stomachs since 1938. All the sparring partners of thirteen years ago were gone—working on the docks, most of them, Seamon said—and so were Louis's managers then, John Roxborough and Julian Black, the two colored sporting men who brought Joe out of the Middle West, and Mike Jacobs, the quondam ticket scalper who once controlled boxing through his control of that great new favorite, Louis.

"Joe's looking the best he has in four years," Mannie said. (It was in 1947, in his first match against Walcott, that Louis first showed he was slipping badly.) We talked a while about fellows we had known in the thirties, and I asked Mannie if the terrible monotony of training wasn't beginning to tell on Louis. Joe made his pro debut in 1934, and he had boxed amateur before that, and the Army meant no letup, for his duty there consisted of boxing exhibitions for other soldiers. So he had been at it for nearly twenty years—light bag, heavy bag, pushups, belly bends, roadwork, and shadowboxing. It is hard to stay interested in your own shadow for twenty years. Even an old race horse gets so he won't extend himself in works.

"We keep his mind off it as much as we can," Seamon said. "We got a rule here, we never talk fight. Anything but that. We listen to phonograph records, or we play cards, or handicap horses. I tell him funny stories, and the best is different people come in and talk to him."

Seamon walked over to the gymnasium to get the fighter ready for his sparring exhibition, and after a while Colonel Stingo and I followed him. When we got to the dressing room, Louis was sitting on the rubbing table while Seamon prepared his hands—bandages, gauze, and flat sponge-rubber pads over the knuckles, and then adhesive tape to hold the structure in place. Seamon said, "Joe, this is Colonel Stingo. He is seventy-eight years old and he wants to work a couple of rounds with you." Louis looked down at the Colonel and couldn't at the moment think of anything to say except "Glad to meet you." I reminded

Louis that he and I had last met in Frisco's, a drinking club on Sackville Street, in London, during the war, and he said, "That man once charged me sixteen dollars for a pint of gin." With us in the dressing room was a slender colored man named Reed, a friend of Louis's who had evidently been a patron of Frisco's at the same time, and he joined in the conversation to say he had once paid a cabby three pounds and six shillings to drive him to Frisco's from a few streets away. " 'Three-and-six,' the man said," Reed recalled. "So I gave him three pounds and six shillings, and then I reached in my pocket and all I had left was a ten-shilling note, so I gave it to him for a tip. I didn't know if it was enough. That was my first time on leave in London." Louis began to laugh. "That was a pretty good tip," he said. "Two dollars for a seventy-cent ride that you already paid him nearly fifteen bucks for."

Louis, Reed, and I began telling stories about prices we had paid in London, straining the elastic of credulity with each tale—a kind of auction. Louis stuck closest to plausibility; Reed and I were just trying to be funny. Fruit had been fantastically dear in London by American standards, and Louis said he had once paid thirty shillings for a pound of hothouse grapes, as a present for an English family he knew. "Then I saw just a small apple there for six shillings," he said. "So I bought that, and bit into it outside the store. Man, it was sour! I give the rest of it to an old dog that come along, and he took one bite and took off." Louis also told about going up on a roof to watch an air raid his first night in London. "The tracers was the most beautiful thing I ever saw," he said.

By the time Seamon had finished with his hands, Louis was in high good humor. "I'm sorry we got no boxing shoes to fit you, Colonel," he said to Stingo just before he went into the gymnasium. "So I guess I won't be able to work with you today. You worked with me wearing those shoes, you might step all over my feet and disable me."

There was nothing showy about the workout. Two of Louis's three partners were light heavyweights, much smaller than the old champion, and they worked fast, to speed up his reflexes. He didn't punch hard at either, since the idea wasn't to discourage them. One of them, a brown boy from Bermuda, hit Louis pretty freely, but it was reasonable to suppose the Bermudian was a lot faster than Marciano could possibly be. That's the point of working with a light, fast man. The only partner on hand of the big, rough type that used to staff Louis's camps was a heavyweight named Elkins Brothers, whom I had seen fight in the semifinal on the Robinson–Turpin card. Brothers, a squat, powerful fellow, played the part of Marciano when he sparred with Louis. He came in crouching, and threw overhand rights at Louis's jaw. The overhand right, thrown in a rising arc like an artillery shell, was supposed to be Marciano's best punch. Louis kept jabbing at Brothers' head, trying to hit him just as the right started coming and keep him off balance. When he succeeded, he stepped in with a right uppercut. It was a pattern of battle, but neither man pressed it to its ultimate implication. They were methodical rather than fierce. Louis's body looked good—leaner, if anything, than it had in 1938—and the jab was as sweet as ever.

Stingo and I were sitting out on the lawn after the workout, waiting for the car from Greenwood Lake to pick us up, when Louis came along, on his way from the gym to his living quarters. He looked younger with his snap-brim hat on. It hid the bald spot. And in street clothes, after all, a superbly conditioned man of thirty-seven is still young. It's when he gets into a ring that age comes on him. Louis hovered over us for a while, but none of us could think of much to say. It was no use asking him how he felt, or whether he thought he could win this one, because clearly he was as good as anybody could get him now, and he had never had a match in his life that he didn't think he was going to win, and sixty-nine times out of seventy-one he had been right. So why would he change his mind this time?

Louis gave a small shiver and said, "Well, I guess I better go in, or I might get a chill." We shook hands all around, and he went along to play cards with the sparring partners who belonged to a younger generation.

The camp at Greenwood Lake, which I visited three days before the fight, was more lively. Marciano looked like the understander in the nine-man pyramid of a troupe of Arab acrobats. He was bull-necked and wide-shouldered, and even when he was merely walking around in the ring, he kept rippling the muscles of his arms and back, as if afraid that if he let them set they would tie up. He looks as if he should be muscle-bound, but he isn't. He worked with a big, rangy young heavyweight named Jimmy DeLange, who had the Louis role, and they fought as if they wanted to transcend the limitations of the leather head guards and the huge sparring gloves and knock each other out. Marciano moved around briskly on his stubby legs and threw punches well, especially to the body, but DeLange had no trouble reaching his head with left jabs, and the spar-mate's right uppercuts to the body came off well in close. Marciano was working in a head guard that was a cross between a gladiatorial helmet and race-horse blinkers, with long leather wings at the sides of his eyes. He wouldn't have that, at any rate, when he fought Louis, I told myself. He finished the third, and last, round with a big burst of punching.

During the workout, I sat alongside the ancient featherweight champion Abe Attell, and after it was over and the trainers had pulled Marciano's gloves off, Abe called up to the fighter, "Take it easy, Rocky! He's only a sparring partner!" The fighter held up three fingers and called back apologetically, "Only tree days!"— signifying that, with but three days to go, he was in too good shape to restrain himself.

"I had five hundred on him," Attell said to me. "And after

what I seen today I'm making it a thousand." Attell, who was himself one of the greatest of boxers, is a knowing man about fights, but he is famous for having an intricate mind. I consoled myself with the thought that he might, in fact, be betting on Louis and speaking favorably of Marciano only to get the odds up.

"Louis is all through," Attell went on, with what I considered a deplorable lack of sentiment in an old champion who had himself felt the sharp tooth of time. But Attell, who looks at you with cold eyes around his huge beak that is like a toucan's with a twisted septum, is not a sentimental man. "If they get a referee who don't let Louis hang on, the kid will knock him out," he said. He then put a handful of BB shot in his mouth and started to pick his teeth. He uses bamboo toothpicks, which he has tailored for him at a novelty shop on Broadway. From time to time, by means of his toothpick, he propels the pellets, one by one, through gaps between his teeth, hitting with perfect accuracy any object up to ten feet away. A nightclub hostess with a plunging neckline is his favorite target, but a busy bartender in a dimly lighted joint will keep him almost equally happy. *En ville - giature*, he will take targets of opportunity, like the back of a stranger's neck. "I got hit with an automobile a couple years ago and got three new choppers on the right side, with no holes between then," he told me. "So now I developed a curve out the left."

Leaving the unfeeling Mr. Attell, I went over to wait outside the dressing room for Charlie Goldman, Marciano's trainer, an old bantamweight who has coached Weill's fighters for years. Goldman is a fine pedagogue, because he brings out his pupil's qualities instead of trying to change them. "The great thing about this kid is he's got leverage," he told me when he came out of the dressing room. "He takes a good punch and he's got the equalizers. He had leverage from the start, and when you teach a fellow like that, you have to go slow, because you might change the way he stands or the way he moves, and spoil his hitting. Everything new you show him, you have to ask him, 'Does it feel natural?' 'Can you hit from there?' So naturally he'll never be a flashy boxer. But he's in the improving phase. He's still six months—maybe a year—away. But whether he beats Louis or not, he's going to be a lot better next summer."

Goldman is a soft-spoken, merry little man with a large head, buffed to a plane surface in front, and a pair of hands that look as if they had been trampled on. "Looka the bum, how many times he broke his hands!" Attell says loftily. His own magnificent fists carried him through three hundred and sixty-five fights with only one break. Goldman's more friable maulies prevented him from knocking out many of the four hundred opponents he fought, but they made him a thoughtful kind of boxer.

"Most fighters at twenty-seven have been boxing eight, nine years, and they are as good as they ever will be," Goldman told me. "But Rocky has only had about the equivalent of one year's experience. So he's still learning. Every time we made a fight for him up in New England, we would bring him down to New York for a week and get him a room at the C.Y.O., and then he would work out four or five afternoons at Stillman's," he said. "But he didn't do as much boxing in the three years as one of the boys who's at Stillman's every day would do in a year. So he's just beginning to come along. He'll knock them all out."

When I entered Madison Square Garden on the night of the fight I couldn't help hoping that Marciano was still too far away to demolish Louis. His day was bound to come anyway, if Goldman was right, and I wanted to see Louis get by once more. My seat was about where I had sat when I watched Louis beat Savold. I was sitting well forward in the mezzanine on the 49th Street side, midway between the east and west ends of the ring, at a point where I could watch crowd as well as fighters.

There were the usual introductions from the ring of white and colored men in knee-length jackets with flaring shoulders—

rough, tough Paddy DeMarco, Philadelphia's undefeated Gil Turner, Sugar Ray Robinson, former heavyweight champion Ezzard Charles, and, finally, Jersey Joe Walcott, the reigning champion, as old as Louis by his own statement, several years older by popular report. ("I'm not old," he told a sports writer in 1947. "I'm just ugly.") The names of the judges and referee were announced: Joe Agnello, Harold Barnes, Ruby Goldstein—no surprises. And then the two factions were in the ring—Louis's in the northwest corner, Marciano's in the southeast. Mannie Seamon and a couple of fellows I didn't know were with Louis; Goldman and Marty Weill were with Marciano, together with a fellow New Englander named Al Columbo. Weill, a thin, pale young man with rumpled hair, seemed more awed than his fighter. Marciano was bouncing on his thick legs and punching the air to warm up. A tall, ash-blond woman near me was saying, "I hate him! I hate him! I think he's the most horrible thing I've ever seen." This struck me as being hard on Rocky; he didn't look particularly repulsive. Husky as he was, he looked slight compared to Louis, who was three inches taller and, according to the announced weights, twenty-five pounds heavier. When the fighters were introduced, it was evident that if Connecticut, Rhode Island, and half of Massachusetts were not completely empty, their populations were at least substantially depleted for the evening. The Marciano supporters were cheering him as if he were a high-school football team. But Louis got an even bigger welcome.

And then, as the immortal historian of the British ring, Pierce Egan, wrote of the third fight between Dan Mendoza and Dick Humphries, in 1789, "The awful set-to at length commenced—when every eye beamed with anxiety—the moment was interesting and attractive, and each party was lost in suspense." I had a pair of pocket binoculars, 6 × 15s, and I kept them trained on Louis for the first half minute. His face was impassive, as usual, but his actions showed that he wasn't taking the strong boy lightly. Instead of moving relentlessly forward, as in his great days, he seemed to be waiting to see what he was up against. In the first clinches, it was he who shifted Marciano, and not the other way about; Louis was stronger than the strong boy—at the beginning, anyway. He could outbox him at a distance, and if he could continue to smother him in close, I thought he would get by. Up to the last five seconds of the round, I noted, glancing at the ringside clock, neither of them had done anything remarkable, and that was all right with me. I had had a feeling that Marciano might rush out of his corner throwing punches and try to take Louis by storm. Then Marciano threw one of those rights, and it landed, it seemed to me, just under Louis's left ear. Louis had dropped his left shoulder after jabbing—an old fault, which brought about most of the bad moments of his career. This was the kind of punch that addles a man's brains, and if it had happened thirty seconds earlier and Marciano had pressed his advantage, he might have knocked Louis out in the first round.

I think that punch was the one that made Joe feel old. Between the rounds, I could see Seamon pressing an ice bag against the back of Louis's neck, and when I turned my binoculars on Charlie Goldman's face, he was grinning. Louis was apparently clearheaded when he came out for the second, but he didn't do much. I thought he won the next three rounds, jabbing Marciano's face and jolting him with rights in close. But the rights didn't sicken Marciano, as they had sickened Louis's opponents from 1935 to 1940; he reacted as if he were being hit by just an ordinary fighter. Marciano was missing almost all his own swings, and Goldman, between the rounds, was looking very serious as he talked to his pupil. Also, he was working on Rocky's brows with cotton-tipped toothpicks that had been steeped in some astringent solution. The jabs had cut. But Rocky came out for each new round very gay, as Egan would say, and went across to Louis as if to ask for a light.

When the fifth round ended, marking the halfway point of

the fight, I felt that it would be a long way home but that Louis would make it. He had hardly used his left hook, which was now his best punch. Critics had been saying for years that his right had lost its authority, but the hook had existed in all its pristine glory as recently as the Savold bout, and he had had it in the training camp when I was watching him. ("It would take a Goliath to withstand a couple of those," old Colonel Stingo had said solemnly.) The way I figured it, Louis was being so careful about that crazy Marciano right that he was afraid to pull his own left back to hook. He would just jab and drop his forearm onto Rocky's right biceps, so he couldn't counter. Sooner or later, Joe would throw the hook, I thought, and that would end the fight. It looked like a fight between two men with one good hand apiece.

In the sixth, things started to go sour. It wasn't that Marciano grew better or stronger; it was that Louis seemed to get slower and weaker. The spring was gone from his legs—and it had been only a slight spring in the beginning—and in the clinches Marciano was shoving him around. A man can be as strong for tugging and hauling at thirty-seven, or for that matter at forty-seven, as he was in his twenties, but he can't keep on starting and stopping for as many minutes. And even grazing blows begin to hurt after a while. Near the end of the round, Marciano hit Louis another solid one.

The seventh was bad for Louis. Marciano didn't catch him with one big punch, but he was battering at his body and arms, and shoving him around, and Joe didn't seem to be able to do anything about it. Then, toward the end of the round, Joe threw the hook. It was beautiful. It hit Marciano flush on the right side of the jaw, but it didn't seem to faze him a bit. I knew then that Joe was beaten, but I thought that it might be only a decision. Three rounds don't seem forever, especially when you're just watching.

Then, in the eighth round, as you probably read in the daily press, Marciano, the right-hand specialist, knocked Louis down with a left hook that Goldman had not previously publicized. When Louis got up, Marciano hit him with two more left hooks, which set him up for the right and the pitiful finish.

Right after Marciano knocked Louis down the first time, Sugar Ray Robinson started working his way toward the ring, as if drawn by some horrid fascination, and by the time Rocky threw the final right, Robinson's hand was on the lowest rope of the ring, as if he meant to jump in. The punch knocked Joe through the ropes and he lay on the ring apron, only one leg inside.

The tall blonde was bawling, and pretty soon she began to sob. The fellow who had brought her was horrified. "Rocky didn't do anything wrong," he said. "He didn't foul him. What you booing?"

The blonde said, "You're so cold. I hate you, too."

Two weeks later, I stopped by the offices of the International Boxing Club to ask Al Weill how he felt about things now. "What did I tell you?" he said. "You want to look out for them broken fighters. The way things look now, the kid could make a fortune of money."

The Melting Middleweight

Sugar Ray and the Milling Cove

Part of the pleasure of going to a fight is reading the newspapers next morning to see what the sports writers think happened. This pleasure is prolonged, in the case of a big bout, by the fight films. You can go to them to see what *did* happen. What you eventually think you remember about the fight will be an amalgam of what you thought you saw there, what you read in the papers you saw, and what you saw in the films.

The films are especially insidious. During the last twenty seconds or so of the fight between Sugar Ray Robinson and Randy Turpin, for example, it seemed to me from where I sat, in the lower stand at the Polo Grounds, that Robinson hit the failing Turpin with every blow he threw—a succession of smashing hits such as I had never before seen a fighter take without going down. The films show that Robinson missed quite a few of them, and that Turpin, although not able to hit back, was putting up some defensive action until the last second—swaying low, with his gloves shielding his sad face, gray-white in the films. It was the face of a schoolboy who has long trained himself not to cry under punishment and who has had endless chances to practice, like an inmate of Dotheboys Hall. That's the way I now catch myself remembering Turpin's face in the last seconds, although I couldn't see it at the Polo Grounds because Robinson was between us and both were a good distance from me anyway. The face isn't gray-white in real life, but a kind of dun.

The films of the first nine rounds of the fight upset my original impressions in the same way. Those rounds seem exciting now, because I look for hints of what is to come in the tenth, which contained all the fight's excitement. I forget that when they were being fought I saw them only as nine very bad rounds, almost a hoax on the 61,370 spectators, who, in the consecrated formula, had paid $767,630 for the privilege of watching them. All they seemed likely to lead to was six more bad rounds and a decision that would be sure to provoke an argument, since the boxers were going nowhere at the same pace. In the third, or maybe the fourth, round, the fans in the general-admission seats began to clap in unison, as they do at small clubs when two preliminary boys either can't or won't fight. I wondered if either Robinson or Turpin had ever before been treated so disrespectfully. Their styles seemed just made to reduce each other to absurdity. But years from now, when I reminisce about the fight, I'll probably say it was tense all the way, and I'll believe it.

I still think the referee, Ruby Goldstein, was right to stop the fight; no referee should take it upon himself to gamble on a man's recuperative powers. One more punch like the ones Robinson was throwing might have ended the boxing days of any fighter— even Turpin, who is what *Boxiana* would have called "a prime glutton." *Boxiana* is one of my favorite books, and, because of the international nature of the fight, I had a refresher glance at it before going up to the Polo Grounds.

On the night of the fight I started out early, in the true Egan tradition. In his time, the migration to a fight would begin days in advance, when the foot-toddlers (fellows who couldn't afford horse-drawn transportation) would set out on the road for the rumored meeting place. Rumors were all they had to go on because in England at that time prizefighting, although patronized by the Prince Regent, was illegal. A day or so later, the milling coves and the flash coves (fighters and knowing boys) would set out in wagons or hackneys, with plenty of Cyprians and blue ruin (sporting girls and gin) to keep them happy on their way. The Cyprians counted on making new and more profitable connections later. Last of all, the Corinthians (amateurs of the fancy and patrons of pugilists) would take the road in their fast traps and catch up with the others in time to get their bets down before the fight. But blue ruin stopped many a wagon before it got there; milling coves and flash coves both were lushing coves.

Attendance at an old-time British fight was preceded, for all classes, by a visit to the pubs of the contending heros, to wish them success. In accordance with this tradition, at six o'clock on the evening of the Robinson–Turpin fight I made my way to Sugar Ray's, which is Robinson's pub, on the west side of Seventh Avenue between 123rd and 124th Streets. Improvements in transportation have made it unnecessary to start for a fight days in advance, unless one is to foot-toddle. I approached the pub by taxi, the equivalent of a hackney, but sans Cyprian, and disembarked on the northeast corner of Seventh Avenue and 124th Street, in front of the Citadel of Hope Mission, which was not getting much of a play. I got out there because if I'd got out on the Robinson side of the street I'd have had to step on somebody's feet. With the time to go to the fight drawing near, the sidewalk in front of his bar-and-grill had vanished. The sidewalk in front of the Hotel Theresa, which extends from 124th to 125th Street on the west side of Seventh Avenue, was similarly jammed with Harlemites, and the narrow traffic island in the middle of the avenue was also filled with Negroes, who were gazing up at the hotel.

A small colored boy, presumably from the Citadel of Hope, handed me a throwaway preaching class war. "There are two classes of people in the world—the righteous and the wicked," it read. "You belong to one of these two classes. Which?"

"Let me ask you a question," I said to the boy. "Who is up in that hotel?"

"Randy," the boy answered. "He's resting until the fight."

I looked about me and imagined the trade consequences of a Turpin victory. I could visualize the thousands of shoulders draped in British tweed, and the equal number of feet, now impacted one on another, encased in shoes by Maxwell of Dover Street. In Harlem, fashion follows the brave. It seemed to me I could already detect a slight premonitory change, in the accent of the first man who spoke to me, but he may have been a West Indian. "Randy is superior," he said. "He's overconfi*dence*. I mean he feel no fear."

I crossed the street and worked my way into the lobby of the Theresa, which is the largest hotel under Negro management in America and about the busiest hotel anywhere—a contrast to its moribund last twenty years in white hands. Joe Louis was standing, almost unnoticed, with a group of friends near the door. He's still a favorite, but no novelty. Everybody was waiting for a look at Randy.

Coming out of the Theresa, I stood on the inner edge of the sidewalk and allowed myself to be propelled slowly half a block downtown, being carried past the Golden Glover's Barbershop and the store-front office of Ray Robinson Enterprises. (Robinson is in almost as many businesses in Harlem as Father Divine was before that divinity moved to Philadelphia.) I detached myself from the current just in time to duck into Sugar Ray's, which is a narrow but deep saloon with walls of blue glass chips tastefully picked out with gold. The bar was as crowded as the street outside, but at the back of the place, where the bar ends, Sugar Ray's widens out enough to permit three parallel rows of tables, one row against each side wall and the third between them, and there were a few empty seats. Since I could find no place to stand up, I sat down at a table.

This rear section of Sugar Ray's is decorated with four huge photomontages, two on each side wall. Two show him making a fool of Kid Gavilan, the Cuban fighter, who is a competitor of his for local fame. Another shows Robinson bringing an expression of intensely comic pain to the face of the French middleweight Robert Villemain, a muscle-bound, pyknic type with a square head. The fourth shows him standing above Georgie Abrams, a skillful pugilist who is so hairy that when knocked down he looks like a rug. Abrams got up after his knockdown, but from the picture it doesn't seem as if he ever would.

I asked a man at the table next to mine, who looked like an old colored milling cove, whether the boss was around, and he said he wasn't. "He left about an hour ago," he said. "He's taking this one serious. He was carrying his bag, and I told him, 'Now, don't you stop on the way to do any training.' " Some women at the cove's table laughed, and so did I. I dined on bourbon and the largest, pinkest pork chops I have ever seen, priced at a dollar-sixty-five. "They're mighty good," I said to the cove, who seemed to be regarding me with interest. "They ought to be," he said. "I once fought a man eight rounds for not much more than that."

I approved of Robinson's decision to leave early. Drinking with customers just before a battle was a practice deprecated by Egan. There was, to give you an example from *Boxiana*, Dan Donnelly, an Irish heavyweight, who was never beaten but who fell dead in his own bar after drinking forty-seven whiskey punches with well-wishers. His epitaph read:

O'ERTHROWN BY PUNCH,
UNHARMED BY FIST,
HE DIED UNBEATEN PUGILIST!

A slim, earnest black man with a briar pipe in his right hand walked down between the tables, saying in a peremptory voice, "A hundred to seventy-five. A hundred to seventy-five." "*What* you betting?" another man asked him. "I bet Robinson," the man with the pipe said. "Everybody here betting him," the second man said. "That ain't no odds." The man with the pipe walked away, and I asked the second man, "Who do you think will win?" "Ray," he said. "Ray, sure. He always win when the chips are down." I did not tell him about the statement of Colonel Stingo, whom I had encountered the day before and who had seen the films of the London bout in which Turpin defeated Robinson for the middleweight championship. The Colonel said Turpin appeared to be a very strong boxer, and had kept crowding Robinson from the beginning of the bout. "Ray has never looked too good against a crowding fighter," the Colonel said, "and now he's getting old. He's got to make a different kind of a fight to win this one." He added that he had just been talking to Jack Kearns, the former manager of Jack Dempsey. Kearns had been out to Pompton Lakes to watch Sugar Ray train, and had said that he was "dry"—not sweating well—which is considered an indication of poor condition. "It'll take him a year to get back in shape," Kearns had told the Colonel. "Paris licked him."

When I arrived at the Polo Grounds, a short time before the first preliminary bout, the place was only half full, but the people running the show had already effected an almost complete strangulation of movement as far as the customers were concerned. By setting up wire gates between various sections of the stand, probably to prevent ticket holders from "creeping" forward to better seats than they had paid for, they had made long detours necessary for anyone trying to get anywhere. Since even the ushers, of whom there were few, didn't know where the temporary barriers were, they couldn't tell people how to avoid them. A lane so narrow that it could be threaded only in single file had been left between the lower-stand boxes and the first row of lower-stand seats, and customers coming in through runways at the ends of this lane had to struggle against each other to reach the aisles leading up into the stands. Once I had made it to my own seat, in the first row of the lower stand, the struggle provided a sort of preliminary to the preliminaries.

The "ringside" seats, which covered the baseball diamond and reached well into the outfield, were for the most part empty at that stage of the evening. They filled slowly; many of the people who buy them do not much like boxing but go to big fights so that they can talk about them afterward, and they seldom arrive before the main bout. But I knew they would be along; this was something you had to see, like *Guys and Dolls* or a van Gogh show at the Metropolitan. Midway through the preliminaries, hundreds of young hoodlums in Hawaiian shirts, all of whom had clearly come in on general admission—unless they had scaled the fence—dashed down the aisles of the stands in back of third base, vaulted the wire barriers with admirable ease, and hurtled onto the field, racing to occupy empty ringside seats. It was a concerted break, and there weren't nearly enough special cops to stop them. Once in a seat, each of these fellows would try to avoid attention until the rightful ticket holder arrived, upon which, after a conversational delaying action, the interloper would move to another empty seat, continuing to move until the lights went out for the main bout. Then, if evicted again, he would squat in an aisle. The specials were flushing them all through the show, in a succession of comedy chases. The rush, because it was so concerted, did not amuse me; in a previous decade and in other circumstances, the louts might have been wearing black or brown shirts, I thought, and a time might come when they would be again. The night was sweating hot.

I could identify one ticket holder who was already in his seat. He was a man who looks like Ethel Waters, especially when he has his mouth open, and who calls himself Prince Monolulu. He says he is an Ethiopian prince, and wears a bright-red jacket embroidered with the Star of David and the signs of the zodiac, as well as headdress of ostrich plumes and a set of flowing skirts.

These make him fairly easy to recognize if you have seen him once, and I had seen him several times in England—once at Epsom, plying his regular trade as a race-track tout, and on endless Sundays at Hyde Park Corner, where he preaches Zionism. I had read in the morning paper that he'd come over on a chartered plane with fifty other Turpin supporters. When working, Prince Monolulu shouts, at unpleasantly frequent intervals, "I got a 'orse!" and then, to those who gather around in response to his shouts, he tells about the dialogue between the camiknickers and the nightgown, winding up by selling his horse, on a folded slip of paper, for a modest half crown. I bought Black Tarquin from him at Epsom, and it beat twenty-four other horses, finishing eighth. At the Polo Grounds, I noticed, he was silent. He may have been molting.

In the very first preliminary, one boy knocked the other down for a count of nine in the first round, and the referee stopped the fight. This apparently exaggerated solicitude, I felt sure, could be attributed to the death of a preliminary fighter named Georgie Flores, who had been fatally injured when knocked out in Madison Square Garden a couple of weeks earlier.

In another preliminary Jackie Turpin, an older brother of the champion's and a featherweight, defeated a boy named Wamsley in six rounds. Jackie is a light tan, like his bigger brother, but on the night of this fight the resemblance ended there. I thought he boxed a bit like Jackie (Kid) Berg, an English lightweight of the thirties, getting inside fast and throwing dozens of punches, most of which landed but none of which seemed solid. Still, the other boy went down for short counts twice, and Turpin earned the decision. I knew that somewhere in the stands there were five hundred members of the Queen Elizabeth's crew, and the cheering for the featherweight Turpin showed where they were sitting—behind the third-base line.

The semifinal was between two big Negro heavyweights, one of whom, apparently beaten, knocked the other out in the last thirty seconds. "How do you like that?" one of two Garment Center Corinthians on my right asked his companion. "Just before he landed the winning punch, he was supremely out."

Then the ring was full of fighters, the majority of them colored, being introduced to the crowd, and the belated ringside-seat holders were pouring in, a number of pretty women with them. Jersey Joe Walcott, then the heavyweight champion; Ezzard Charles, his predecessor; and Joe Louis entered the ring together and were introduced, one at a time; Louis got an ovation, although he was then just the champion-before-last. (When he walked out on the field to his seat before the semifinal, he was given a bigger hand than General MacArthur, who preceded him.) Louis looks like a champion and carries himself like a champion, and people will continue to call him champion as long as he lives.

The two seats at my left, which had been vacant all evening, were now occupied by a couple. The girl, a smashing blonde in a backless black evening dress, must have expected that she was going to sit out in ringside, where people could see her. A woman somewhere behind her said, but not to her, "I call that a vulgar way to dress." It seemed to cheer the blonde, but the man with her looked uncomfortable.

Everybody stood up for a long recorded version of "God Save the King," with a vocal chorus. It reminded me of the time they played the "Marseillaise" for Marcel Cerdan before he knocked out Tony Zale in Jersey City, and the machine wouldn't stop. "God Save the King" received polite applause. The applause for "The Star-Spangled Banner," which followed it, was tumultuous.

The principals came into the ring. Robinson, the challenger, was first—tall, slender, and dark brown, wearing a blue-and-white robe. He discarded the robe, revealing white trunks with a blue stripe, and jigged furiously up and down to limber his leg muscles. Turpin followed, in a yellow bathrobe over black trunks with a white stripe, sat down in his corner, and remained seated,

even during the introduction, while Robinson stood and waved
to the crowd. Robinson acted like a young, nervous fighter;
Turpin, eight years his junior and fighting for the first time in
this country, was calm as a Colchester oyster. When the bell rang,
it was the same way. Robinson was making the play. Turpin
wasn't crowding this time; he was taking it easy, as if sure Robinson would slow down. Jimmy Cannon, of the New York *Post*,
wrote afterward that Turpin "moved with a clumsy spryness and
appeared to be serenely anticipating Robinson's collapse." The
trouble with this policy was that it gave the much older Robinson a chance to make his own pace, fighting in spurts and then
resting. He was still about the fastest thing in the world for
thirty seconds or so, as Turpin was to find out.

Turpin stood more like some of the illustrations of boxers in
Boxiana than a modern fighter. He had his left knee far forward,
the leg almost straight out, and all the weight of his body back.
It made him hard to get at, but it also made it hard for him to
get at Robinson. (I had often wondered, looking at those illustrations, how men could hit from that position. Now I understand
why *Boxiana* lists so many fifty- and sixty-round fights.) When
Turpin did hit—with marvelous speed, most of which was
wasted in coming such a long way around—it was always at
some curious angle. One punch for the body looked like a man
releasing a bowling ball; another, a right for the head, was like a
granny boxing a boy's ears. His jab was like a man starting his
run for the pole vault. If he hit conventionally, from the shoulder,
he would be less disconcerting, but he might also be one of the
hardest hitters in history. For he is the strongest middleweight I
have ever seen—built like a heavyweight, and tall, too. I haven't
figured yet how he can be so big all around and still make a hundred and sixty pounds.

Turpin was so strong that his unconventional blows shook
Robinson when they landed, although Robinson knew that, according to the book, they shouldn't. When the warning whistle

blew ten seconds before the beginning of the second round, Robinson stood up. I thought it a rash gesture, because it meant that now he would have to spend an extra ten seconds on his feet at every interval. If he stayed down, it would be a public confession that he was tired. Turpin sat the full minute.

"The kid's got nothin', nothin', absolutely nothin'," one of the fellows next to me began saying during the fifth or sixth round, meaning Turpin, and he continued to repeat it, like an incantation: "Nothin', nothin'." He must have had a good bet on Robinson, because he sounded worried.

"If Turpin hasn't got anything, what's Robinson got?" I finally asked him. "It's even, isn't it?"

"Even?" He looked at me as if I were mad. "Turpin ain't took a round," he said.

The referee's card had four rounds for each fighter and one even, up to the tenth round.

A stout colored man in back of me was wearing a bright-green suit, a Tattersall waistcoat with a green stripe, a yellow tie, and a maroon silk shirt with two-inch white polka dots. If he had taken off jacket, waistcoat, and about forty pounds, he would have been dressed to ride for the Woolford Farm Stable, of Kansas City, Missouri. Every time Sugar Ray started a punch, this man would grunt like a bullfrog and then softly moan, as if enduring the agony of a shattered Turpin, even when the punch didn't land.

I was beginning to resent my neighbors bitterly by the time the tenth round came and Robinson, with his eye cut, either by a butt or by a blow, put together the really amazing attack that finished poor Turpin off—or didn't quite, according, next day, to Turpin's manager and to some of the British boxing writers, who hadn't been hit. When the referee stepped between the fighters and grabbed Turpin in his arms, I thought I had never seen a man so game or so beaten as the mulatto from Leamington Spa. Within a minute, the ring was full of policemen, who lined the ropes; I don't exactly know why, since there appeared to be no danger of a riot. There seemed to be nothing to argue about.

On the way down the ramp to the exit, I saw a sight that struck the proper note—a tall, grave, fair-haired man, with a pipe in his mouth, walking silently beside an equally grave blond boy of around fifteen, who was carrying a furled Union Jack. By contrast, as I got out onto Eighth Avenue, under the "El," I nearly bumped into three men who turned out to be sailors from the Elizabeth, and though they were wearing Turpin buttons in the lapels of their land-going clothes, they were all laughing. "I feel like 'iding my fice," one of them was saying. "What a 'iding 'e took!" "What I'm laughing at," said another, "was old Bill, 'ere. 'Go right in, Randy,' 'e says. 'What are you afraid of?' " They were, I felt, devoid of proper patriotic sentiment.

Since there were no taxis to be had and the subway entrances, choked with struggling human bodies, looked slightly less inviting in that heat than gas chambers, I started to foot-toddle down Eighth Avenue, hoping to encounter a cab along the way. After I'd gone a block or so, I was stopped by another British seaman, a square-faced bloke who looked as if he might once have boxed a bit himself. He wanted to know the way to the entrance to the Eighth Avenue subway I had just passed up. I told him, and added consolingly, "I never saw a gamer man than your fellow." "Oh, 'im," the seaman said. " 'E's a good lad, sir, but no experience. No defense. No class, sir. Forget about 'im." This, too, seemed hardly right.

Eighth Avenue, from the Polo Grounds south, is Harlem, but it's poor Harlem, unrelieved by bright lights or jive. I walked past store fronts fetid with the smell of old vegetables, and dismal houses that never were much and now are less, where ill-dressed Negroes sat on the doorsills. Other people walking from the fight, or perhaps a radio bulletin, had carried the news ahead of me. (The fight itself, of course, hadn't been broadcast or televised—for New York audiences, at any rate.) All along the way, the people in the doorways knew that Sugar Ray had won, but they didn't seem excited. Perhaps it was the heat.

I stopped in at a bar at 145th Street for a drink—it was not festive there, either—and then switched over to Seventh Avenue, still looking for a taxi. At 143rd and Seventh, two men in their twenties were bullying a boy of about eighteen. They had him backed up against an automobile, and whenever he turned on one, the other would kick him. A crowd of women had gathered around, at a safe distance. The men had been drinking and looked rough. "You let him alone!" a woman cried. "He's only a young boy!" In a nearby saloon, there was another row going on. Just then, I sighted a cab headed uptown empty, and I stopped it and got aboard. "Drive me downtown, past Sugar Ray's," I said.

As we approached the Theresa, the avenue was so jammed up with traffic that we could barely move. People were packed around the safety islands and overflowed onto the street. Somebody was beating an oilcan like a tomtom, and a tall, limber man was dancing in the street. Any idea I may have had of stopping at Sugar Ray's for a nightcap left me when I saw the crowd in front of the door.

My maid walked by Sugar Ray's a couple of days after the fight, and she said there were twenty-five Cadillacs parked in front of the place. "Any that weren't 1951 had to double-park," she said. "His is a big pink one. He was standing outside, with just a small patch over his eye, and everybody that came by shook hands with him."

I went up to Sugar Ray's myself on the following Sunday, but it was very quiet, with only a girl about five feet tall behind the bar, and a monumental cash register and a sign that read, "Try Sugar Ray's Bolo, 55 cents." The bolo, which is named after one of Robinson's favorite punches, is made of rum. There were enough customers to keep the girl busy, but they all looked tired, as if they had been celebrating for several nights in a row and had just come in for pick-me-ups.

Kearns by a Knockout

The division of boxers into weight classes is based on the prem-
ise that if two men are equally talented practitioners of the Sweet
Science, then the heavier man has a decided advantage. This is
true, of course, only if both men are trained down hard, since a
pound of beer is of no use in a boxing match. If the difference
amounts to no more than a couple of pounds, it can be offset by a
number of other factors, including luck, but when it goes up to
five or six or seven, it takes a lot of beating. The span between the
top limit of one weight class and the next represents the margin
that history has proved is almost impossible to overcome. Between middleweight and light heavyweight, for example, that
gap is fifteen pounds. A middleweight champion may weigh, at
the most, a hundred and sixty, and a light heavy a hundred and
seventy-five. But some champions are more skillful than others,
and every now and then one comes along who feels he can beat
the titleholder in the class above him. That was what made it interesting to anticipate the match between Sugar Ray Robinson,
the middleweight champion, and Joey Maxim, the champion
of the light heavyweights, in June, 1952. As soon as I heard the
match had been arranged, I resolved to attend it. I had seen
Robinson in four fights, not including television, and knew that
he was a very good fighter. I had heard that Maxim, whom I had
never seen, was merely pretty good. But there was that fifteen
pounds. It was the smaller man who appealed to the public's
imagination, and to mine. Goliath would not have been a popular champion even if he had flattened David in the first round.
Robinson is such a combination of skill and grace that I had a
feeling he could do the trick. For exactly the same reason, the
London fancy, back in 1821, made Tom Hickman, the Gas-Light
Man, who weighed a hundred and sixty-five, a strong favorite
over Bill Neat, at a hundred and eighty-nine. The Gas-Light

Man, according to Egan, was "a host within himself—his fist possessing the knocking-down force of the forge-hammer—his brow contemptuously smiling at defeat—*to surrender* not within the range of his ideas, even to the extremity of perspective—and VICTORY, proud victory, only operating as a beacon to all his achievements." Neat was a mere plugger, but he "turned out the Gas."

One man who did not share the public's sentimental regard for Robinson was an old-time prizefighter, saloon-keeper, and manufacturer of fire extinguishers named Jack Kearns. This was not surprising, because Kearns, who in more glorious eras managed Jack Dempsey, the Manassa Mauler, and Mickey Walker, the Toy Bulldog, now happens to be the manager of Maxim. Not even Kearns hinted that Maxim was a great champion, but he said he had a kind nature. "All he lacks is the killer instinct," Jack maintained. "But he takes a good punch. When he's knocked down he always gets up." He once told a group of fight writers, "Maxim is as good a fighter as Dempsey, except he can't hit." Since that was all Dempsey could do, Kearns wasn't handing his new man much.

Kearns is as rutilant a personality as Maxim apparently isn't, and from many of the newspaper stories that appeared in the weeks leading up to the fight one would have thought that Kearns, not Maxim, was signed to fight Robinson. This was an impression Kearns seemed to share when I met him six days before the date set for the fight, in the large, well-refrigerated Broadway restaurant operated by his former associate Dempsey. The old champion and his manager quarreled spectacularly back in the twenties, but are now friendly. "This is my big chance," Kearns said, buying me a drink and ordering a cup of coffee for himself. He was one of the big speakeasy spenders but says he has been on the wagon for eight years. "Up to now, I had to stuff myself up and fight heavyweights," he said. "Me, the only white guy with a title. But now I got somebody I can bull around." By this he meant, I gathered, that, in order to obtain what he considered sufficiently remunerative employment in the past for Maxim, he had had to overfeed the poor fellow and spread the rumor that he had grown into a full-sized heavyweight. Then, after fattening him to a hundred and eighty, he had exposed him to the assault of more genuine giants, who had nearly killed him. But now, he implied, Maxim had an opponent he could shove around and control in the clinches. I said I hoped it would be a good fight to watch, and he said, "I got to be good. I can't afford to lay back. I got to keep moving him, moving him." As he said this, he picked off imaginary punches—Robinson's hooks, no doubt— with both hands and shoved straight out into space, to show how he would put on the pressure.

Most managers say "we" will lick So-and-So when they mean their man will try to, but Kearns does not allow his fighter even a share in the pronoun. He is a manager of the old school. His old-school tie, on the day I met him, was Columbia blue covered with sharps and flats in black, green, and cerise. The weaver of his shirt had imprisoned in it the texture as well as the color of pistachio ice cream. It was a wonder children hadn't eaten it off his back in the street, with the weather the way it was outside. He was wearing a pale-gray suit and skewbald shoes, and his eyes, of a confiding baby blue, were so bright that they seemed a part of the ensemble. He has a long, narrow, pink face that widens only at the cheekbones and at the mouth, which is fronted with wide, friendly-looking incisors, habitually exposed in an ingenuous smile. The big ears folded back against the sides of his head are not cauliflowered. They are evidence that in his boxing days he was never a catcher. Kearns is slim and active, and could pass for a spry fifty-five if the record books didn't show that he was knocked out by a welterweight champion named Honey Mellody in 1901, when he must have been at least full-grown.

In the course of his boxing career, which was not otherwise distinguished, Kearns had the fortune to meet the two fighters

who in my opinion had the best ring names of all time—Honey
Mellody and Mysterious Billy Smith. Smith was also a welterweight champion. "He was always doing something mysterious,"
Kearns says. "Like he would step on your foot, and when you
looked down, he would bite you in the ear. If I had a fighter like
that now, I could lick heavyweights. But we are living in a bad
period all around. The writers are always crabbing about the
fighters we got now, but look at the writers you got now themselves. All they think about is home to wife and children, instead
of laying around saloons soaking up information."

He told me in Dempsey's that he played nine holes of golf
every day to keep his legs in shape. Since Kearns was obviously in
such good condition, I saw no point in taking the three-hour ride
to Grossinger's, in the Catskill Mountains, to see Maxim train.

I did go out to look at Robinson next day, however. He was training at Pompton Lakes, New Jersey, which is only an hour's drive
from town. I got a free ride in one of the limousines chartered by
the International Boxing Club, which was promoting the fight.
There were four newspapermen with me, including a fellow
named Frank Butler, from the *News of the World*, of London, who
had seen both Robinson and Maxim fight in England and said
Maxim could bash a bit when he liked. "He took all Freddie
Mills' front teeth out with one uppercut," he said. "I rather think
he'll do Robinson."

Any effect Mr. Butler's prediction might have had on me was
dissipated by the atmosphere of the camp. When we arrived, a
crowd had already gathered around George Gainford, Robinson's
immense, impressive manager, on the lawn between the sleeping
quarters and the press building. It was a mass interview. The
topic of discussion was what Robinson was going to do with *two*
championships after he whipped Maxim. Since Robinson would
indubitably weigh under a hundred and seventy-five pounds for

the fight, the light heavyweight title would be his if he won. But since Maxim would certainly weigh more than a hundred and sixty, he could not take the middleweight championship, no matter what he did to Robinson. The chairman of the New York State Athletic Commission, someone said to Gainford, had announced that if Robinson won the heavier championship, he would have to abandon the lighter one. It sounded to me like the kind of hypothetical problem harried publicity men so often cook up as fight day approaches. But Gainford, a vast ebon man, broad between the eyes, played it straight. "The Commission do not make a champion," he intoned. "Neither may the Supreme Court name him. The people of the world name him; that is democracy. And if Robinson emerge victorious, he will be champion in both classes until somebody defeat him."

"How about the welterweight championship?" somebody asked. Robinson was the welterweight champion (one hundred and forty-seven pounds) until he entered the middleweight class. He was never beaten at that weight.

"I do not want to make that weight," Gainford said majestically, using the first person singular as if he were Jack Kearns. He must weigh two hundred and forty.

While Gainford propounded, the fighter and three camp-mates were sitting around a table, unperturbed by the jostling visitors. They were playing hearts, and all shouting simultaneously that they were being cheated. Robinson put an end to the game by standing up and saying he had better get ready for his workout. He was wearing a green-and-white straw cap and a red-and-white Basque shirt and cinnamon slacks, and he looked as relaxed and confident as a large Siamese tomcat. Sam Taub, the I.B.C. press agent at the camp, led him into the press shack to be interviewed by "just the bona-fide newspapermen," and he sprawled gracefully on a narrow typewriter shelf, one leg straight out and the other dangling. Robinson is about six feet in length, very tall for a middleweight, and on casual inspection he seems more like a loose-limbed dancer than a boxer. A long, thin neck, the customary complement of long arms and legs, is a disadvantage to a boxer, because a man with his head attached that way doesn't take a good punch. The great layer of muscle on the back of Robinson's neck is the outward indication of his persistence. It is the kind that can be developed only by endless years of exercise—the sort of exercise no shiftless man will stick with.

"Have you ever fought a man that heavy?" a newspaperman asked him.

"Never a *champion* that heavy," Robinson said, smiling.

"Do you think you can hurt him?" the man asked.

"I can hurt anybody," the boxer said. "Can I hurt him enough is the question. I'll be hitting *at* him, all right."

"Have you a plan for the battle?" another fellow asked.

"If you have a plan, the other fellow is liable to do just the opposite," Robinson said.

"How are your legs?" somebody else asked.

"I hope they all right," Robinson said. "This would sure be a bad time for them to go wrong."

The interview broke up and the fighter went along to get into his ring togs. He worked four easy rounds with two partners, who didn't seem to want to irritate him. They sparred outdoors, in a ring on a kind of bandstand under the trees. Around the ring were bleachers, occupied by a couple of hundred spectators— Harlem people and visiting prizefighters and a busload of boys brought out from the city by the Police Athletic League. "We had three hundred paid admissions at a buck here last Sunday," Taub told me. "Sugar gave a dinner for sixty-five. 'My friends and relatives,' he said. They ate fifty-five chickens."

The newspapermen agreed that tepid sparring was all right, since Sugar Ray was as sharp as a tack already, and this was almost the end of his training. The thing about Robinson that gets you is the way he moves, even when shadowboxing. He finished off with a good long session of jumping rope, which he enjoys.

Most fighters jump rope as children do, but infinitely faster. Robinson just swings a length of rope in his right fist and jumps in time to a fast tune whistled by his trainer. He jumps high in the air, and twists his joined knees at the top of every bound. When he jumps in double time to "I'm Just Wild About Harry," it's really something to see.

On the way back to town we all said he had never looked better.

The fight itself, as you have probably read, was memorable, but chiefly for meteorological reasons. It was postponed from the night of Monday, June twenty-third to that of Wednesday, June twenty-fifth, because of rain. Wednesday was the hottest June twenty-fifth in the history of the New York City Weather Bureau. I rode the subway up to the Yankee Stadium, where the fight was to be held, and the men slumped in the seats and hanging to the straps weren't talking excitedly or making jokes, as fight fans generally do. They were just gasping gently, like fish that had been caught two hours earlier. Most of those who had been wearing neckties had removed them, but rings of red and green remained around collars and throats to show the color of the ties that had been there. Shirts stuck to the folds of bellies, and even the floor was wet with sweat.

My seat was in a mezzanine box on the first-base line, and I felt a mountain climber's exhaustion by the time I had ascended the three gentle inclines that lead to the top of the grandstand, from which I had to descend to my seat. A fellow in a party behind me, trying to cheer his companions, said, "And you can tell your grandsons about this fight and how hot it was." The preliminaries were on when I arrived, and two wretched forms were hacking away at each other under the lights that beat down on the ring. I could see the high shine on the wringing-wet bodies, and imagined that each man must be praying to be knocked out as speedily as possible. They were too inept; the bout went the full distance of six rounds, and then both men collapsed in their corners, indifferent to the decision. A miasma of cigarette smoke hung over the "ringside" seats on the baseball diamond, producing something of the effect you get when you fly over a cloud bank. There was no breeze to dispel it, and the American flags on the four posts at the corners of the ring drooped straight down. It was a hundred and four degrees Fahrenheit in there, we were to learn from the newspapers next morning.

I missed the next two preliminaries because I was up at the top of the stand, waiting in line for a can of beer. The venders who usually swarm all over the place, obstructing your vision at crucial moments in a fight, had disappeared, on the one night when their presence would have been welcome. So the customers had to queue up—a death march to get to a bar tended by exactly two men. Meanwhile, the fights were invisible, but once one was locked in the line, the thought of giving up one's place unslaked became intolerable. Our line inched along toward a kind of Storm Trooper with a head like a pink egg. Rivulets of sweat poured from the watershed of his cranium, and his face appeared behind a spray, like a bronze Triton's in a fountain. At every third customer, he would stop the line and threaten to pack up and call it a day. We would look at him beseechingly, too thirsty even to protest, and after enjoying our humiliation for a while he would consent to sell more beer.

By the time I got back to my seat, Robinson and Maxim were in the ring and the announcer was proceeding with the usual tiresome introductions of somebodies who were going to fight somebody elses somewhere. Each boy, after being introduced, would walk over and touch the gloved right paw of each principal. The last one in was old Jersey Joe Walcott, the heavyweight champion, and the crowd evidenced torpid good will. I could see the vast Gainford in Robinson's corner, over toward third base, and, with the aid of binoculars, could discern that his face still wore the portentous, noncommittal expression of a turbaned bishop in a store-front church. Kearns had his back to me, but I could tell him by his ears. He was clad in a white T shirt with "Joey Maxim" in dark letters on the back, and he seemed brisker than anybody else in the ring. Maxim had his back to me, too. When he stood up, I could see how much thicker and broader through the chest he was than Robinson. His skin was a reddish bronze; Sugar Ray's was mocha chocolate.

Fighting middleweights, Robinson had always had a superiority over his foes in height and reach, together with equality in weight. Against Maxim he had equality in height and reach but the weight was all against him. His was announced as a hundred fifty-seven and a half and Maxim's as a hundred and seventy-three. The first ten rounds of the fight weren't much to watch. Maxim would keep walking in and poking a straight left at Robinson's face. Robinson would either take or slip it, according to his fortune, belt Maxim a couple of punches, and grab his arms. Then they would contend, with varying success, in close. Some of the fans would cry that Robinson wasn't hurting Maxim at all in these interludes, others that Maxim wasn't hurting Robinson at all. There seemed to be some correlation between their eyesight and where they had placed their money. Because of the nature of the combat, most of the work fell upon the referee, Ruby Goldstein, a former welterweight then in his forties, who had to pull the men apart. In consequence, he was the first of the three to collapse; he had to leave the ring after the tenth round. I have never seen this happen in a prizefight before. Old-time photographs show referees on their feet at the end of twenty-five-round fights, and wearing waistcoats and stiff collars. It is a bad period all around.

Robinson had been hitting Maxim much more frequently than Maxim had been hitting him, but neither man seemed hurt, and both were slowing down from a pace that had never been

brisk. Now the relief referee, Ray Miller, a snub-nosed little man
with reddish hair, entered the ring, bringing with him more
bounce than either of the contestants possessed. He must have
been sitting on dry ice. Miller, also an old fighter, enjoined the
fighters to get going. The crowd had begun clapping and stamping, midway in the fight, to manifest its boredom. Miller broke
clinches so expeditiously in the eleventh and twelfth that the
pace increased slightly, to the neighborhood of a fast creep. Up to
then, it had been even worse than the first ten rounds of the previous year's fight between Sugar Ray and Randy Turpin, the
milling cove. But that fight had ended in one wildly exciting
round that made the fancy forget how dull the prelude had been.

This fight was to produce excitement, too, but of a fantastically different kind. In the eleventh round, Robinson hit Maxim
precisely the same kind of looping right to the jaw that had
started Turpin on the way out. The blow knocked the light heavy
clear across the ring, but he didn't fall, and Robinson's legs, those
miracles, apparently couldn't move Ray fast enough to take advantage of the situation. It may have been as good a punch as the
one of the year before, but it landed on a man fifteen pounds
heavier. Maxim shook his head and went right on fighting, in his
somnambulistic way. Now all Sugar Ray had to do was finish the
fight on his feet and he would win on points. But when he came
out for the thirteenth, he walked as if he had the gout in both
feet and dreaded putting them down. When he punched, which
was infrequently, he was as late, and as wild, as an amateur, and
when he wasn't punching, his arms hung at his sides. He had,
quite simply, collapsed from exhaustion, like a marathon runner
on a hot day. Maxim—at first, apparently, unable to believe his
good fortune—began, after a period of ratiocination, to hit after
him. He landed one or two fairly good shots, I thought from
where I sat. Kearns must have been yelling to Maxim.

And then Robinson, the almost flawless boxer, the epitome of ring grace, swung, wildly and from far back of his shoulder, like a child, missed his man completely, and fell hard on his face. When he got up, Maxim backed him against the ropes and hit him a couple of times. The round ended, and Robinson's seconds half dragged, half carried him to his corner. He couldn't get off the stool at the end of the one-minute interval, and Maxim was declared the winner by a knockout in the fourteenth, because the bell had rung for the beginning of that round.

Sugar Ray, according to the press, was pretty well cut up over his defeat, and in his dressing room, after enough water had been sloshed on him to bring him to, he raved that divine intervention had prevented his victory. This refusal to accept the event is also an old story in the ring, but in the words of John Bee, a rival of Egan, it is "a species of feeling which soon wears out, and dies away, like weak astonishment at a nine days' wonder." On the day after the fight many of the sports writers took the line that Robinson had been beaten by the heat alone, and some of them even sentimentally averred that he had been making one of the most brilliant fights of his life right up to the moment when his legs gave out. They tried to reconcile this with their assertions that Maxim was a hopelessly bad fighter and had made a miserable showing until his unbelievable stroke of luck. It would have required no brilliance on anyone's part to outpoint the Maxim they described. But Goliath never would have been popular anyway.

The heat was the same for both men. This much is sure, though: Whenever a man weighing a hundred and fifty-seven has to pull and haul against a man weighing a hundred and seventy-three, he has to handle sixteen pounds more than his own weight. The other fellow has to handle sixteen pounds less than his. And when you multiply this by the number of seconds the men struggle during thirty-nine minutes of a bout like this, you get a pretty good idea of why they weigh prizefighters. The multiplication is more than arithmetical, of course; a man who boxes four rounds is more than four times as tired as if he had boxed one. I had no idea, from watching the fight, whether Maxim was pacing himself slowly, like Conn McCreary, the jockey who likes to come from behind, or whether he just couldn't get going any faster, like even Arcaro when his horse won't run. But I talked to Kearns a couple of days after the fight, and he left no doubt in my mind about what he wanted me to believe had happened. The nine holes of golf a day, he said, had kept him personally in such condition that he could exercise all the natural alacrity of his perceptions during the conflict. "The heat talk is an alibi and an excuse," he said. "Robinson was nailed good in the belly in the tenth round, and again in the twelfth, and he got a left hook and a right to the head at the end of the thirteenth, when he was on the ropes. If the bell hadn't a rang, he'd be dead. I didn't move Maxim until the twelfth round. I didn't have to. I knew I could win in any round when I got ready. The only reason I shoved Maxim in at all was because I wanted to win with a one-punch knockout. Robinson escaped by luck."

I paused to commit this to memory, and then asked Dr. Kearns, who seemed in high good humor, to what he attributed his victory. "Oh, I don't know," he said modestly. "Anybody who was around those old-time fights we used to have in the hot sun on the Fourth of July knew you had to rate any athalete according to what the heat was. Robinson figured he had any one of fifteen rounds in which to win in. He was going to try for a knockout in every round he fought. But I just told Maxim, 'Just keep this fellow moving, moving. Then he'll have to clinch and hang on.' After that, it just depended how quick I decided to move Maxim. It was up to me to pick the round. Next time I'll knock him out quicker."

"And who do you want next?" I inquired.

"I'd like that Walcott or Marciano," Dr. Kearns replied bravely. "I'll fight anybody in the world."

Since then Robinson has come back, at least as far as being middleweight champion again. After the Maxim fight he retired, and a fellow named Bobo Olson won the title after an elimination tournament among the inept left-overs. Robinson returned to the ring and stopped Mr. Olson in two rounds at Chicago, which was nice going, and the Cadillacs are back at his door. One fight writer, reporting the victory, said Olson was a "burned-out hollow shell," which is like merging Pelion and Ossa, or Ford and General Motors, in the cliché business. He must have meant the shell of a broiled lobster after a shore dinner.

Maxim lost his title to a great man, who will be introduced in a later chapter of this book, named Archie Moore, but Dr. Kearns did not say after the bout, "Moore licked me." He said, "Moore licked Maxim."

The Big Fellows Again

New Champ

Before Marciano fought and beat Louis, Charlie Goldman told me that Rocky was in what he called "an improving phase." "He's still six months—maybe a year—away," Goldman told me. Almost a year passed before Marciano was matched to meet Jersey Joe Walcott for the heavyweight championship. "The great thing about this kid is he's got leverage," Goldman kept saying in the time between. "He takes a good punch and he's got the equalizer." By this last, he meant that Marciano had the ability to equalize—or cancel out with one solid punch—the advantage in points piled up by a more skillful opponent in the rounds preceding equalization.

Marciano knocked Louis out in the eighth round after wearing the older man down. But there was a trace of intellection in the way he finished off the former champion. His right hand had received all the advance publicity, and during the fight he threw it so often, usually missing, that Louis paid less and less attention to the left. Then, in the eighth, Marciano knocked him out with three left hooks and an almost redundant right. The progress of an education, whether that of a candidate for the Presidency or that of a candidate for the heavyweight championship, always interests me. So when I read in a newspaper that Marciano had been matched to fight Jersey Joe Walcott for the title in the Philadelphia Municipal Stadium on the night of September 23, 1952, I went.

A boxer solidly constructed, intelligently directed, and soundly motivated is bound to go a long way. I had not seen Marciano since the Louis bout, but I knew that in the interim he had knocked out several lesser heavyweights to keep his hand in. In the first of these bouts, against Lee Savold, he had seemed to some of the experts to be regressing. I ran into Goldman after that one, and he said, "Yeah, we let him lay off a couple months after Louis, and he went back. He's the kind you got to keep working. We won't make that mistake again." Mr. Goldman added, "After all, they call him crude because he misses a lot of those punches, but it's his style. I could teach him to punch short—across his chest—but to tell the truth it wouldn't be very effective. So let him throw them old Suzi-Qs." In his subsequent fights, Marciano, I noted in the newspapers, finished his chaps off in fast time, winding up with a fellow named Harry Matthews, a clever sort, whom he knocked out in the second round. Matthews' manager, Jack Hurley, had predicted a contrary result, basing his forecast on a mysterious strategy he said he had imparted to his fighter. "Hurley wanted to be a Swengali but the strings broke," Al Weill said to me later.

As soon as I learned that Rocky had been made with Jersey Joe, I went in quest of Weill, to hear how his fighter's education was getting on.

Weill's office then was on the third floor of the Strand Theatre Building, and he had worked out of it for nearly thirty years, retaining it even when he was the Garden matchmaker, as if he knew he would be back there someday. It was impregnated with the smell of the cigars he smokes and decorated with framed photographs and cartoons of boxers he has managed at one time or another. The wide window across the front of the room looked out on Broadway, a street fraught with temptations for fighters to spend money. For this reason, Weill kept his boxers as far from it as possible, usually within earshot of Goldman. He knew he could resist the temptations all right himself. Also, a fighter learns more when sufficiently secluded. Out of sheer boredom, he may listen to some of the pearls of wisdom Goldman casts in his direction, such as "If you're ever knocked down, don't be no hero and jump right up. Take a count," or "Always finish up with a left hook, because that brings you into position to start another series of punches." Goldman frequently voices less technical advice, too, such as "Never play a guy at his own game; nobody makes up a game in order to get beat at it," and "Never buy anything on the street, especially diamonds." Weill now has an office in the Hotel Lexington, on the more fashionable East Side, as befits the manager of the heavyweight champion of the world, but it doesn't smell right yet. It takes a heap of smoking to give a hotel suite the atmosphere of a humidor.

On the morning of my call, I found Weill looking out the window and smoking a cigar while waiting for, he at once informed me, telephone calls from Pittsburgh, Providence, Honolulu, and Salt Lake City. A prizefight manager will never admit he is waiting for a telephone call that costs less than a dollar. "People all over the country are going crazy about this fight, and everybody expects me to get them a good seat," he said. "I already sold fifteen thousand dollars' worth personally." Looking like a kind of gray-haired Napoleon, he wore a white-on-white shirt, fresh that morning—an evidence of prosperity—while his chief assistant was in not-so-white-on-not-so-white, out at the elbows. A prizefight manager's assistants assist him in waiting for telephone calls, especially when he goes out for a cup of coffee. Sometimes they inherit his shirts.

Mr. Weill, aware that I don't smoke, offered me a cigar and then said, with a romantic intonation, "You know, this fight means a lot to me. I've had three champions—a feather, a lightweight, and a welter—but never a heavyweight champion. I had Godoy, who fought Louis twice, and gave him a lot of trouble, but he didn't make it. And I had a good young prospect named Marty Fox, but he went wrong. He was fighting Unknown Winston in Hartford, and he was stabbing Unknown to death. The referee waves to him to go in and fight, because they were stinking out the joint, and you know what the damn fool done? He done what the referee told him. Winston knocked him cold. When I heard what he done, I told him, 'You are too dumb to be a fighter.' So I retired him."

The manager threw to the floor a cigar only four-fifths smoked, for him an evidence of great emotion, and ground the stub with his right heel, as if obliterating an evil memory. "I can't fight for them," he said. "They got to help me." But he brightened when I asked about Marciano. "He come a long way since you seen him," he said. "You wouldn't know him. I got him up at Grossinger's." Grossinger's is a legendary and dietary resort hotel in the Catskills. With its attached golf courses and airfield, it is only slightly inferior in area to the King Ranch, in Texas. A prizefighter training for a big match is one of the attractions at Grossinger's, giving the guests something to talk about between meals and getting the hotel publicity every time a fight writer files a dispatch datelined Grossinger, New York. It was a mark of Rocky's advancement that in the course of one year he had come to be considered an attraction of Grossinger magnitude.

I flew up to Grossinger's on the Tuesday just two weeks before the fight, in a plane chartered by the I.B.C., which had arranged the match, and freighted mainly with photographers going up to take pictures of the challenger posing with Jack Dempsey, the old heavyweight champion and restaurateur, who was scheduled to watch him spar and then make the customary Delphic prediction. On the next day, Dempsey and the photographers were booked to visit Walcott, in Atlantic City. I found Rocky and Charlie Goldman and the rest of the camp, including Rocky's father, sprawled on cots in the sun in front of the training quarters, which were on the rim of the airfield, a couple of miles from the hotel and its potential distractions. The fighter and his faction had a rather large cottage and an annex to live in, and an old airplane hangar had been fitted up as a gymnasium, with benches for spectators, who paid a dollar a head to watch workouts. The airfield is used only by occasional small planes, and at night the quiet is mountainous. In between Rocky and Charlie was Al Columbo, the fighter's friend, contemporary, and assistant trainer, who is from his home town. All three were wearing blue-and-yellow checked peaked caps with red pompons; it is part of a trainer's role to provide small sources of amusement for his fighter, and Goldman thinks there is something particularly funny about headgear. (In town, he usually wears either a bowler or a beret. "It takes a handsome man to carry them off," he says.)

Marciano isn't a hard man to keep in a good humor; he doesn't go in for the rough practical jokes with which some fighters both enliven their camps and get rid of their apprehensions. His outline has a squareness and his skin a terra-cotta tint that make you think of an Etruscan figurine. His body has no Grecian grace; he has big calves, forearms, wrists, and fingers, and a neck so thick that it minimizes the span of his shoulders. He is neither tall nor heavy for a heavyweight—he weighs around a hundred and eighty-five in fighting trim—but he gives the impression of bigness when you are close to him. His face, like his body, is craggy—big jaw, big nose (already askew from punching), high cheekbones—and almost always, when he is outside the ring, has a pleasant asymmetrical grin on it. It is the grin of a shy fellow happy to be recognized, at last, as a member of the gang in good standing. His speech doesn't fit the type caster's idea of what a prizefighter's should be; he speaks with that southern New England accent in which the "a" in "far" is sounded as New Yorkers sound the "a" in "hat," and the "a" in "half" is sounded as we sound the "a" in "far." Grammatical constructions are more carefully worked out there than in most parts of the country, and Marciano (whose name in this dialect becomes "Masiano," with two short "a"s) sometimes sounds more like former Senator Lodge than like one of his own professional colleagues working on the New York–Chicago–California axis. He is, in fact, as much of an exotic, in his way, as was Luis Angel Firpo, the man in the celluloid collar. Weill, mindful of the pitfalls of Broadway, is anxious to keep him that way. Marciano goes back to Brockton after every fight. Each expedition into the outside world has for him the charm of an overnight trip with the Brockton High School football team, on which he once played center, and, like the team, he is accompanied by hundreds of home-town rooters. When I asked him, for lack of a more original question, how he felt, he replied, with an accent I remembered from my days on the Providence *Journal*, "Peufict." He is not exactly gabby.

The workout in the hangar that day was not spectacular. Marciano boxed two rounds with a colored light heavyweight from California named Tommy Harrison, a fast, shifty fellow who kept stabbing and going away while Rocky slid along after him. It was logical to expect evasive action from Walcott, a celebrated cutie who had never, as far as anyone could remember, made a standup fight with any opponent. Against Rocky, who was notoriously slow afoot, the champion might be expected to circle and move in and out even more than usual. But the test was inconclusive, since Harrison, who weighed a hundred and seventy and was in his early twenties, was certainly faster than Walcott, who was by his own admission thirty-eight and weighed nearly two hundred. And Rocky would have fifteen rounds, not two, in which to catch up with the old fellow.

Then Marciano did two rounds with Keene Simmons, a colored heavyweight every bit as big and rugged as Walcott, and much younger. Simmons had once given Marciano a pretty good fight in public. His imitation of Walcott was good—he would throw quick sneak punches, some of them right-hand leads, and slide away. When he didn't slide away, he clinched. He even did the kind of jig-step shuffle Walcott uses to disconcert his opponents, although there is no particular reason it should. Marciano, I noticed, wasn't throwing as many long, looping punches as he threw the previous year. He couldn't afford to be caught off balance by a sharpshooter like Walcott, who could move in fast on any mistake. But I remembered what Goldman had said about Rocky's ineffectiveness with short punches. I wondered what he would use against Walcott in place of "them Suzi-Qs." His boxing had improved vastly—from terrible to mediocre—but I couldn't imagine him outpointing Walcott. He would have to keep crowding—pushing him around until the spring went out of the old man's legs and arms and it was safe to revert to the Suzi-Q.

After the workout, a fellow drove Rocky back to the house— a distance of a few hundred yards—and Goldman and Columbo and I followed on foot. When we got there, the boxer was already lying on a bed in a second-floor room, warmly covered to keep him sweating. "This is the best part of boxing," he said. Goldman talked to him about old fighters; I noticed that, unlike veterans, who want to talk about anything but boxing, Marciano was intensely interested. He seemed to be trying to build up background for the position he felt he had been called to. When Marciano went downstairs for his shower, Columbo told me how they had come out of the Army together when they were both twenty-two, and how Rocky had started boxing in amateur tournaments in New England. "He was crude, but there was one move he would wait for the other fellow to make, and when he made it, Rocky would swing and knock him out," Columbo said. "He must have knocked out a hundred. Half the time he would hit them on top of the head. One time he broke his right thumb on a bird with a hard head, and they laid him off at the shoe factory where he worked. So he knew he would have to make up his mind—either give up boxing or the shoe factory. By that time,

Weill had seen him, and he offered to carry him along for the first year or so if he would turn pro, until he started to earn real money. So he turned."

The fighter came back and Goldman rubbed him down. I asked him again how he felt, and he said, "Peufict."

Rocky's father, addressed as Pop by the trainers and sparring partners, ate supper with us, at five-thirty. His name is Pietro— or, affectionately, Pietrone—Marchegiano. ("Marciano" is a contraction adopted for the convenience of fight announcers.) He is a small, thin man, gravely polite, with a heavy Italian accent and a most un-Italian reserve. From the day of his arrival in America until recently, he cobbled shoes in his own one-man shop in Brockton. Only in his large, strong hands does he resemble his son. While we ate—a good-sized steak apiece, with bread and butter, string beans, and potatoes—the telephone rang almost continuously. Most of the callers were well-wishers in Massachusetts and Rhode Island, asking for blocks of good tickets to sell to friends. One said the Mayor of Brockton was coming to the fight and was bringing the Governor of Massachusetts and Adlai Stevenson as his guests.

While waiting for an automobile to pick me up—the plane had long since gone back to New York with the photographers and their undeveloped plates—I stood on the lawn for a moment with Charlie Goldman. "The shoe factory that laid him off sends him a new pair of boxing shoes before every bout," he said. "They done it for his last ten bouts, and every pair has his name inside. Everybody rides with a winner." The little man looked up at me and said, "You know, there are two kinds of friends—the ones who are with you when you are winning and the ones who stick when you are losing. I prefer the second kind. But you got to take advantage of the others while you got them. Because they won't be with you long."

A fortnight later I boarded the five-o'clock train to Philadelphia at Pennsylvania Station with a twenty-five-dollar ticket in my wallet and a small but good pair of binoculars in my pocket. There were six Brocktonians across the aisle from me. They made no secret of their civic identity. Florid men with small, merry eyes, all in clothes slightly tight for them—probably, like trees, they added a circumferential ring each year—they might have been either union officials or downtown businessmen, types hard to distinguish between in their part of the world. They were organizing a two-dollar pool among themselves on which round Rocky would win in. One, addressed by the others as Mac, caused indignation, which I judged to be not entirely feigned, by saying that for his two dollars he would take Walcott by decision.

"Then we'll be laying you five to one," one of his townsmen said.

"You don't think Walcott has a chance, do you?" Mac asked. "I'm doing you a favor." I could see he had raised a doubt in their minds, and at the same moment he saw he was losing popularity. "I just said it for laughs," he added lamely.

But their journey to Philadelphia had been spoiled. Mac had opened up a possibility they had shoved resolutely into the back of their minds. In forty-two fights, Rocky had never even been knocked from his feet.

On arrival, I took a subway to the center of town and walked about for a while, looking for Lew Tendler's restaurant. Tendler is an old Philadelphia fighter who has remained a Philadelphia idol because, I think, he embodies the city's sense of being eternally put upon. He once had Benny Leonard beaten when Leonard was lightweight champion; Leonard was on the floor but got up before "ten," and it was a no-decision bout. I thought I knew where Lew's restaurant was, and wouldn't ask anybody the way. I soon got tired of walking, though, and ate in a place called Mike Banana's. A minute after I had finished and left, I found Tendler's, but I saw I couldn't have eaten there anyway. I couldn't even have got as far as the bar, it was so packed. The sidewalk on Broad Street in front of the restaurant was jammed right out to the curb, and gentlemen with embossed ears were struggling to keep from being pushed under taxicabs. Everybody (I use the word in its Ward McAllister sense) who goes to Philadelphia for a fight meets at Tendler's and tries to put the lug on somebody for a free ticket. On the night of the twenty-third of September, the people with the free tickets had apparently sold them to scalpers. Some, in their enthusiasm, had even sold their own seats, and were now looking for friends to put the lug on. It was a scene of great confusion. Joe Walcott, in a car preceded by a police escort, passed by on his way to the fight. The main bout would not go on until ten-thirty, but he wanted to get there in plenty of time. Walcott is from Camden, New Jersey, across the river from Philadelphia, and the crowd in the street cheered. I had thought I could put the lug on somebody for a ride to the stadium, but the only acquaintance I met who had a car had to wait for somebody who had promised him a ticket. I was lucky to get a seat in a taxi.

The Municipal Stadium, situated in a kind of Gobi Desert at the end of all transportation lines, can, it is said, seat a hundred thousand. The crowd of forty thousand in attendance filled one end of the oval grandstand and, of course, a great carpet of "ringside" seats on the grass inside the running track. I found that my fifteen inches of concrete in the stand afforded a good view, with the aid of binoculars, except for a minute segment of the ring that was masked by one of a number of tall steel masts that were disposed around its circumference. I suppose they had something to do with the public-address system, since they all had capitals of entwined horns, like morning-glories. However, I had an aisle seat, and by stretching far out, like a runner with a lead off base, I could take this obstacle in enfilade in a matter of seconds. The preliminaries gave me a chance to adjust my lenses and perfect my moves to the right and the left of the post. They had no other interest for me.

When the main-bout fighters entered the ring with their factions, I saw that Weill had decided to act as Marciano's chief second. He had four subordinates, of whom the smallest, and consequently the hardest to see, was Goldman. One of Weill's strongest points of resemblance to Napoleon—or, for that matter, to Mr. Pickwick—is what he calls his "built." He worked from a standing but bending position directly in front of his seated fighter and facing him. As Marciano was in the corner diagonally across from my perch, my only memory of what happened there between rounds centers on the seat of my old friend's white flannel pants. All I could see of Walcott was the back of his head.

The fight was, as you probably read, one of the stubbornest matches ever fought by heavyweights. When all the lights except those over the ring went out and the bout started, I began to be aware there had been a mistake, and I soon recognized what it was. Walcott, a great, earthen-hued man, mature but sprightly, has a cylindrical torso and a smaller cylinder of a head rising directly out of it. He weighed a hundred and ninety-six pounds, twelve more than Rocky. And the mistake was that he was not imitating Keene Simmons' imitation of him. Instead he was walking forward, hitting at Marciano and moving him back. In just about a minute he landed a beautiful left hook to the jaw, and the hope of Brockton went down on his left side. Walcott started to walk away, assuming, I suppose, that anything human so hit would take the longest permissible count—nine seconds. But Rocky jumped up at three. (This was the only thing Marciano did all night that Goldman complained of after the fight.) Walcott turned, unable to believe his good fortune, but didn't get back to him soon enough. The way Marciano came up made me think the hope of Brockton was out of his head. I learned afterward that what had made him bounce was a combination of indignation and inexperience. The remainder of the round was not reassuring to the Brockton rooters, and when the old fellow continued to batter Charlie's pupil in the second, I was reminded of the remark of a trotting-horse man I know, made in similar circumstances: "The cow got loose and killed the butcher."

There was a colored man to my right, entirely surrounded by whites. I could hear him yelling, and what he was yelling hardly sounded sensible—though, come to think of it, it may have been. "Don't get mad, Joe!" he was hollering. "*Please* don't get mad!" But Walcott continued to act mad, walking right out to meet Marciano in the third. Half a minute later it was Marciano who was shaking the champion, knocking him back with body blows and punches that did not land clean on the jaw but hit him on the side or the back of his bobbing head. The old fellow gave way slowly, hitting all the time, not breaking away and circling, as he had in other fights. Pierce Egan would have called his tactic "milling in retreat." The match now seemed to be following the script more closely. Rocky was slowing him down. The old man would go in a couple more rounds. If he started running he might last a little longer. The young fellow kept pounding in the fourth and fifth. At the end of several rounds they continued after the bell, and Marciano usually got in the last punch. At the end of the fifth I couldn't understand how Walcott stood up.

Then, in the sixth, there was blood all over Walcott's white trunks and Marciano's matted chest. It didn't show on Marciano's trunks, which were black, or Walcott's torso, which was nearly so. Walcott, I could see with the glasses, had a cut over his left eye. Marciano was bleeding, too, but from an unlikely place—the top of his head. You could figure how head and eye must have come together. Marciano, an inch or so shorter than Walcott, accentuated the difference by fighting out of a crouch; his game was to get his head in against the bigger man's chest, where Walcott couldn't hit it, and then punch up, and when he stepped back out of one clinch, his head had come up hard. This accident, the crowd thought, would hasten Walcott's end. In the seventh, though, it was, unaccountably, Marciano who began to flounder. He wavered and almost pawed the air, although he had not been hit by any one particular big punch. He seemed to be coming unstuck, and in the eighth it was the same. Walcott's seconds had closed his cut after the sixth round, using one of those mysterious astringent solutions trainers treasure. And Marciano's corner had closed the wound on his scalp. But now Marciano's right eye had been cut by a punch. (Late that night, or early next morning, at a party given by a man called Jimmy Tomato, who had won a good bet on Marciano, I was told by Weill and Goldman that Rocky, nestling his brow against Walcott's chest early in the seventh round, had got a liquid in both eyes that blinded him. They did not know whether it was some of the astringent solution, dripping from the cut above Walcott's eye, or just liniment, well spiked with capsicum, which Walcott's seconds had sloshed on their man as a form of chemical warfare. "He fought four rounds that he couldn't see the guy," Weill said. I thought this an exaggeration, because in the ninth Marciano had recaptured the lead, which was pretty good going for a blind man.)

In nine rounds the lead changed hands three times—Walcott to Marciano in the third round, Marciano to Walcott in the seventh, Walcott to Marciano in the ninth. You don't see many fights like that. In the tenth, which was the hardest-fought round of all, Marciano stayed on top. But somehow the calculations had gone awry; the old fellow looked further from collapse now than he had six rounds earlier. It might go to a decision, after all. I thought with pity of my Brocktonians on the train. If it was close, I felt, Walcott would get the decision. It is traditional not to take a championship away on a close one, and Philadelphia was virtually his home.

Then Walcott, as if bolstered by the certainty that he could last, came out for the eleventh and had his best round of the fight, except for the opener, when he had floored Rocky. It was the fourth switch in the plot. In the twelfth, he looked not only more effective but stronger than the challenger. Up to then I had had the feeling that if Marciano did land flush on the jaw, he could take the champion with one punch. Now his arms and legs seemed a trifle rubbery. He was swinging wildly, and missing by absurd margins. At the end of the twelfth, Walcott was well ahead and looked stronger than ever.

In the thirteenth the fighters disappeared momentarily from my view behind that steel mast. They were doing nothing particularly exciting. Walcott was giving ground slowly, backing toward the ropes, as he had done repeatedly. Whenever he reached the ropes, he would start a rally; it was a habitual tactic of his. Marciano was following—hopelessly, it seemed. He had to keep moving in, because if he stayed away Walcott, who had a much longer reach, could hit him without return. I wasn't as quick going into my own crouch with the binoculars as I had been in the early rounds; perhaps I was feeling slightly rubbery myself. Then I heard one of those immeasurable shouts that follow a ball over the fence in a World Series. And I could see Walcott's legs protruding to the right of the mast. The fellow next to me, who thought he had seen what happened, yelled, "I can't believe it! He knocked him cold with a left hook. Who said he could hit with a left?" This miserable creature, who by sheer luck had been looking when I wasn't, invited my contempt, and I shouted back, "Who said he couldn't? He knocked Louis crazy with lefts! He belted Matthews cold with a left!" Actually, as I learned later, Rocky had knocked Walcott out with a right that traveled at most twelve inches, straight across his chest to the champion's jaw. The guy next to me hadn't seen the punch at all; Marciano had had his back toward our side of the ring. But Marciano had grazed Walcott with a left hook as the champion fell, already dead to the world. "He trun it for insurance," a fellow who had been in his corner told me later. The fan could be excused, of course. The sports writer of the Philadelphia *Inquirer*, sitting at ringside, wrote that Rocky had hit Joe with a "roundhouse right, swung from his hip and his heart." The punch was the antithesis of a roundhouse; it was a model of pugilistic concision. The newsreel film of the fight shows that both men started right leads for the head at the same moment. Walcott, the sharp, fast puncher, figured to get there first in such an exchange. But Marciano hit sharper, faster, and, according to old-timers, about as hard as anybody ever hit anybody. Walcott, the film shows, flowed down like flour out of a chute. He didn't seem to have a bone in his body. And so, after old Jersey Joe had piled up a lead by fighting the way he wasn't supposed to, Rocky knocked him out with the kind of punch he wasn't supposed to know how to use. "In other words," Charlie Goldman said to me at Jimmy Tomato's party in the Hotel Warwick after the fight, "he equalized." Mr. Tomato, whose real name few of his acquaintances remember, is a businessman and patron of the arts who has been known to bet on Marciano. From the scale of the party it was safe to conclude his investment had been more than nominal.

When the referee, a Pennsylvanian named Charlie Daggert, had counted Walcott out—a hollow formality—all the ringside-seat holders from Brockton, Swansea, Taunton, New Bedford, Attleboro, Seekonk, Pawtucket, Woonsocket, East Providence, Providence, and even Hopkinton, Hope Valley, and Wakefield climbed over the shoulders of the sports writers, kicked them under the typewriter benches, stamped on their typewriters, and got up into the ring to shake hands with Rocky. It seemed that they might pluck his arms off like petals from a daisy, but somehow he escaped and came shooting through the crowd, propelled by the long line of admirers pushing along behind him. A group of police cleared the way and the fellows from his corner locked arms behind him to keep the jubilious from pawing him over. He disappeared under the stand almost at a dead run.

As for Walcott, I can't even remember seeing him leave.

Long Toddle, Short Fight

The spectator who goes twice to a play he likes is pretty sure of getting what he pays for on his second visit, especially if the cast is unchanged. If it is a three-act melodrama when he first sees it, he can be reasonably sure it won't have turned into a bit from the repertory of burlesque the next time he drops in. This is not true of the form of entertainment that the Herodotus of the London prize ring denominated the Sweet Science. For one thing, a prize-fight contains within itself the seeds of its own abrupt termination, a possibility of which the members of the fancy are well aware but which they push back into a neutral corner of their unconscious when they set out for the scene of a return match. For another, it is always possible that there has occurred, subsequent or consequent to the first encounter, a change in the emotional relationship of the two principals.

This last was the case with the pair of combats between Tom Oliver the Gardener, the hero and champion of Westminster, weighing a hundred and seventy-five pounds, and Ned Painter, whom the great Egan describes as "a customer not easily to be served," weighing a hundred and eighty. Their first fight, at Shepperton-Range, near London, on May 17, 1814, moved Egan to rapture. Writing of the third round of their battle, he exclaimed, "Such a complete determined *milling* round is not to be met with in the Annals of Pugilism, and there was more execution done in it than in many fights of an hour's length. It was enough to *finish* any two men. By a correct stop-watch, it continued FOUR MINUTES AND A HALF AND TWELVE SECONDS!" (A round by the rules of those days lasted until one man or the other went down, and half a minute separated the rounds. A round now lasts three minutes.) In the eighth round, "Painter was quite done up, and Oliver finished the contest in prime style." As evidence of their sincerity, the historian noted, "they were both *punished* in the extreme, and Painter was quite blind, and his nose beat flat upon his face. Oliver's body was terribly beaten, his head much disfigured, and one of his eyes nearly closed."

At the end of six years—things went more slowly then—the men were rematched to fight in the village of North Walsham, twenty miles from Norwich, Painter's home town. Egan says that the contest "excited an unusual degree of interest in the sporting circles; and numerous parties, for a week previous to the fight, left the Metropolis daily, to be in time to witness this combat." After a mere fifty-five minutes of rather dull milling—"the *pun - ishment* that both the combatants received," Egan skeptically records, "was so truly light for such heavy men that they were up at an early hour the next morning to breakfast"—Painter floored Oliver with "a tremendous blow upon his temple." Half a minute elapsed—he would have had a minute at the end of one of our rounds—and Oliver didn't come to. He passed the time sitting on his second's knee, the custom in an age when stools were not permitted within the ropes. But when Painter had been proclaimed the victor, Oliver "rose (as from a trance) from his second's knee, and going up to Painter said, *'I am ready to fight.'* 'No,' said Painter, *'I have won the battle.'* " And that was that. "It is true," says Egan, concluding his account of this ambiguous ending, "that many ill-natured remarks have been made upon the termination of this battle; nay more, that it was positively a X between the combatants. It is the duty of an impartial writer to mention this circumstance; indeed, he could not pass it over. But it is equally his duty to observe that nothing like P R O O F has been offered to substantiate it was a X. . . . At all events, no man possesses a higher character for a deserving well-behaved man in society, whether in Lancashire, London, or Norwich, than N E D PAINTER." By "a X," Egan meant "a cross." A "cross fight" was a bout in which one of the combatants had agreed to lose. A "double cross" was one in which the man who had agreed to lose didn't.

To complete the discomfiture of the fight fans who had traveled all the way from London to see this mystery—and who had mostly bet on Oliver—it was followed by a great downpour of rain. "The hedges were now resorted to, and hundreds sought for shelter even under the slightest sprig or a bush; and those who *scampered* off to North Walsham had not a dry thread about them long before they reached it. The *daffy* and *eau de vie* [gin and brandy] were tossed off like milk, to put the *toddlers* (who were as exhausted as drowning rats) in *spirits*." By "*toddlers*" Egan meant pedestrians. "In short, the road beggared all description—it was a fine *finish* to the fight—and the *Bonifaces* never had such liberal customers before, that they might very fairly exclaim, 'It is an ill wind that blows nobody good.' "

The annals of the modern ring are not lacking in anecdotes about fights that ended prematurely. Most of them follow the same pattern. Arrived at the ringside, the man who has traveled great distances to get there lowers his head for some trivial reason. He looks up and the fight is over. Practically every ancient who ever told me that he was at the fight between Bob Fitzsimmons and Peter Maher, in 1896, across the Mexican border from Langtry, Texas, was lighting a cigar when Fitzsimmons knocked Maher out in a minute and thirty-five seconds. A Norwegian ship broker on whose integrity banks have ventured millions in pounds has assured me that after a trip from Oslo just to view the fight at the London National Sporting Club, in 1913, between Georges Carpentier and Bombardier Wells, he was verifying the number of his seat when Carpentier dispatched Wells in the first round. My friend Colonel Stingo, who in 1908 took the then heavyweight champion, Tommy Burns, a Canadian, to Dublin to fight an Irishman named Jem Roche on St. Patrick's Day, is exceptional in that he had his eyes fixed on the principals when

Burns leveled Roche in a minute and twenty-eight seconds. "He dazed him with a grazing left to the chin," the Colonel told me, "and then, while Roche stood there as if frozen, he struck him a blow that would have felled an ox. He fell like an avalanche instead, and I could see on Honest Tom's face a puzzled expression that denoted, 'How long has this been going on?' Only blind chauvinism could have induced those people to think Roche had a chance."

I should have had in mind all these gloomy precedents before I took the plane to Chicago to see the return bout between Rocky Marciano and Jersey Joe Walcott. No unpleasant thoughts marred my journey, however. In the words of Colonel Stingo, I "let disinclination limit the horizon of my anticipation"—always a dangerous procedure. I like going to fights.

When I awoke in my Chicago hotel room on the morning of May fifteenth, the date set for the championship match, the sun was already high in the heavens, although, since my chamber gave upon a court, I was not immediately aware of it. I was reminded of where I was by the sound of the police whistles, which in that city sound like sea gulls' cries, except that they have two syllables. Instantly remembering the occasion of my presence, I arose and called room service for two three-and-a-half-minute eggs—they arrived hard-boiled—and the newspapers, from which I learned that the combatants were to weigh in at noon at the Chicago Stadium, the scene of the fight that night. I had been of the opinion, ever since the previous fall, that Marciano probably would repeat his victory, because he was of an age when a conscientious fighter is still capable of improvement, while Jersey Joe was of an age when most boxers have long retired from competition and the best any fighter can hope for is a slow rate of deterioration. But the lapse of eight months since their Philadelphia go seemed hardly enough to make the return bout one-sided. Marciano would have the advantage of added confidence, but he had always had plenty of that. Since one thing I couldn't find in the papers was an advertisement saying where tickets were on sale in downtown Chicago, I decided to go out to the Stadium for the weigh-in and buy my ticket there. I could have bought one in the hotel lobby, I suppose, but the prices were quite steep enough without paying a commission. And, besides, it was a lovely morning and I had nothing else to do.

Most of the sports writers in the papers seemed to take roughly my view of the probabilities, although they phrased them more elegantly than I would have thought possible before I boarded the plane. "Bald on top but smart inside, old Jersey Joe Walcott is razor sharp and ready to shear boxing's gold-crusted heavyweight crown off champion Rocky Marciano's proud, un-bowed head tonight at the Chicago Stadium," a figure-of-speech man named Wendell Smith, of the Chicago *American*, began his piece. "The most amazing, durable antique in the museum of mayhem, the thirty-nine-year-old challenger intends to cut the rugged champion down with his slashing, powerful tools of de-struction as quickly as possible and become the first fighter in history to regain the heavyweight title. Tradition says he can't do it. Seven others have had the same opportunity and failed. The gods of chance are against him, too. They've made old Joe the 3–1 underdog. They're heaping their affections and blessings on the young man—the bull-like king of clout from Brockton, Mass., who strikes with the terrifying might of Thor and light-ning suddenness of Ajax. The experts, too, believe Walcott is about to be sacrificed upon the altar of futility." This was just about the way I saw things.

But another fellow on the same paper took a diametrically op-posite view of the situation. His name was Tom Duggan, and he spoke with an authority I had previously associated with only one other name in Chicago, that of Colonel Robert Rutherford McCormick. "Jersey Joe Walcott is going to win back his heavyweight boxing title out at Octopus Palace tonight," Mr.

Duggan said, without qualification of any variety. "I think he'll win it by a knockout within seven or eight rounds. . . . The press-rows for this fight will be filled to the scuppers with self-appointed experts on the manly-art-of-self-defense. You would do well to remember that most of these guys are familiar with fight-ing only to the extent of their wives taking a belt at them for sneaking in past curfew time with a load on, garnished with lip-stick on their collars. . . . I have never been in favor of running benefits for anyone, but, in Marciano's case, I would like to make an exception. After this fight, I think we should all pass the hat for him. . . . He not only is giving his title away but forcing Wal-cott to take most of the money along with it. . . . I'm astonished at the odds the professional gamblers are maintaining on the fight." This put a different light on the match. As I started for the street, I wondered how Al Weill, ordinarily a shrewd fellow, had allowed himself to be caught in such a trap.

The Stadium, which, as I knew, is not a stadium but a large shed, is about two and a half miles from the center of the Loop, but I had a full hour to spare, so I walked out along West Madi-son Street, past the Morrison Hotel, which was headquarters for Marciano and the visiting press; past the Civic Opera House, with a sign on it proclaiming the imminent arrival of Louis Arm-strong and Benny Goodman; across the Madison Street draw-bridge over the piddling Chicago River; past the soot-blackened Northwestern Railroad station; and then along the most readable thoroughfare in America, the part of West Madison that has the flophouses and the signs—"Second Shot Your Favorite Whiskey 1/2 Price," "Mamie's Day Old & Fresh Broken Bakery Goods," "We Dare Them! The Largest and Best Bowl of Soup in Town," "Our 20-Ounce Schooner, 15 cents," "Jesus Saves—Are You Saved?" "Pants $1.00 Up," "2 Strickly Fresh Eggs Tost and Buter, 25 cents."

Before a shack bearing signs that read, "Shine 25c" and "First

Class Shine 20c," I stopped. I knew from the street numbers that I was now at about the three-quarter pole, and any kind of chair looked good. "I want a first-class shine," I said. "Twenty cents."

"We sold the last first-class shine yesterday," the shoeshine man said. "Got only twenty-five-cent shines left."

Like Mr. Duggan, the shoeshine man picked Walcott. He was a clay-tinted man in a pink shirt. "I think Joe'll whup the kid," he said. "I bought two tickets for me and my wife. I also got a hundred dollars up against a hundred fifty that Joe will go twelve rounds. The bell rings for the end of the twelfth round, I win." I figured he was going to lose four hundred shoeshines.

I got to the Stadium in plenty of time for the weigh-in, which was held in the ring in the center of the arena, before a small mob of cameramen, of all varieties—newspaper, newsreel, 3-D, and publicity-department. The working-press seats were almost as full as they would be at fight time. Either out of good nature, which seemed unlikely, or with a vague idea of stimulating ticket sales, the I.B.C., which was promoting the bout, had opened the doors to anybody who wanted to see the weighing-in rites. At least a thousand of the seats that would be worth fifty dollars that evening were occupied by the otherwise unemployed males of the quarter, mostly colored.

Marciano, perhaps unaware of the fate Duggan had predicted for him, looked friendly and invulnerable, more heavily muscled than a boxer is supposed to be and whiter than he had been in September, which was natural, since he had trained for the Phila-delphia fight under the summer sun. He doesn't verbalize his cockiness, but he has a kind of negative confidence, like a sleepy bulldog. Walcott was massive, elephant-colored, and preoccu-pied. Some of the journalistic eyewitnesses later wrote that he had the air of a doomed man, but he has never been renowned for gaiety. I attributed his air to the slow, pleasurable digestion of a hearty breakfast. A chap at a microphone announced the weights as each fighter stood on the scale—Marciano a hundred and eighty-four and a half, Walcott a hundred and ninety-seven and three-quarters. That meant that the champion was eight ounces heavier than at their first fight; Walcott had put on a pound and three-quarters.

Directly in front of me sat a delegation of Marciano's home-town friends—four young men in green silk windbreakers whose backs were prophetically lettered, in red, "And Still Champion, Rocky Marciano." They were accompanied by four young women of a southern New England small-town high-school freshness never previously observed in a fighter's entourage. I would have laid a bet that none of the eight had ever seen a fight before Rocky turned professional. The girls looked at Walcott with a hauteur generally reserved for members of the visiting basketball team.

There had been some of the usual synthetic acerbity between the fighters' managers during the training period. Walcott's manager, an acidulous little character named Felix Bocchicchio, from Camden, New Jersey, had accused Marciano of butting Walcott in their Philadelphia fight and blinding him so he couldn't see the fatal punch. (The official program for the Chicago fight described him as "smiling, good-natured, and soft-spoken Felix Bocchicchio, who, among many other enterprises, handles Jersey Joe Walcott.") In cultured circles, these charges were recognized as strictly publicity stuff, but to the girls with the boys in the green silk jackets they must have been as bad as saying Brockton High played dirty football.

The advance sale of tickets had not been particularly brisk, I had read in the newspapers, but on the morning of the fight the management reported three hundred and eighty-five thousand dollars already in hand, a statistic that later proved to have been purely imaginary. To judge from the failure to advertise on fight day, the Stadium must be operated by book publishers. Television rights—for regions outside the Chicago district, which was blacked out—were supposed to have been sold for another three hundred thousand dollars, and a 3-D feature-length movie of the fight was to bring in unknown sums. Bocchicchio and Walcott had been guaranteed a flat sum of two hundred and fifty thousand dollars, regardless of the amount taken in at the gate, along with thirty per cent of the 3-D rights. The champion was to have thirty per cent of the gate, thirty per cent of the television and radio take, and thirty per cent of the 3-D rights.

I bought a thirty-dollar ticket, which entitled me to a seat in Row F of the first balcony, overlooking the ring. This essential preliminary disposed of, I took a streetcar back to the Loop and walked to Mike Fritzel's restaurant, where I had a date with a friend. Fritzel's is a kind of Chicago Lindy's, and as I went in I met a New York comedian named Jack E. Leonard, who told me he was playing at the Chez Paree, a Chicago night club. Leonard was sad because he wouldn't be able to see the fight. The headliner at the Chez was Tony Martin, the singer, and Martin also was a fight fan. Somebody had to do the early show, and Martin had pulled rank on Leonard, who would therefore miss the fight. He is probably still laughing.

The fellow I was lunching with told me a bit about Mr. Duggan. Duggan, he said, had had a sports program on N.B.C. television, in the course of which he had needled the identical ownership of the Stadium and the International Boxing Club, and had predicted that the fight would never be held in Chicago. N.B.C. had dropped him—yielding to outside pressure, according to Duggan; nothing of the sort, according to N.B.C.—and the Hearst *American* had picked him up as a sports columnist. He had christened the Stadium Octopus Palace because it is the home of the boxing octopus that controls professional fighting all over the country. He was already famous even to the outmost suburbs as a champion of free speech, a fearless iconoclast, and an exponent of the locally popular thesis that everybody in the world is trying to put one over on Chicago. I ventured the thought that Duggan's prestige might be damaged by the fact that the fight was going to be held in Chicago after all, but my informant said I didn't understand how the Chicago mind works. "They'll say the fight *wouldn't* have been held here unless Duggan had blown the whistle," he said. "It'll make him bigger."

After lunch, I went back to my hotel to rest. This is always a good idea before a big fight, because you are going to have to battle crowds going in, you can never find a taxi coming out, and you often have to toddle home without benefit of daffy unless you are willing to battle more crowds to get to a bar. The spectators sometimes take as much *punishment* as the fighters, and on this particular evening, as it turned out, we were to take considerably more.

At eight o'clock I took a taxi to within a third of a mile of the Stadium, and dismounted when my vehicle could no longer advance. The first preliminary bout was to go on at eight-thirty, as it usually does in big shows, but the main bout was to begin at nine instead of ten, because it would have to be on the air at ten in the Eastern time zone. One result was that the hordes of people who customarily stream in between nine and ten were for once hurrying to get to their seats early. To extract the maximum amount of fun from this situation, the Stadium management had decided to admit ticket holders at my gate only in single file, like candidates for a crap game, each one squeezing by the belly of a large special policeman, who half blocked the interstice through which we were eventually admitted. Now and again, he would stop the whole line to permit the egress of someone governed by a premonition; I can think of no other reason why so many people would want to come away from a fight before it started. When we had finally been allowed to proceed to the point where a guard was waiting to snatch our tickets, we were turned onto the first of six flights of concrete stairs and at length run down a ramp to our seats. The layout had evidently been designed by the same chap who built the stockyards, but fight followers have been a hardy lot since Egan's day. I arrived at my perch, which was as exiguous as a racing saddle but harder, full of that exhilaration that always precedes what old Pierce would call a contest of heroes. I could not sit back. The customers adjoining me had already arrived, and both of them overlapped their thirty dollars' worth of space by several inches. But by adopting a forward crouch, which I modeled after my recollection of how Eddie Arcaro rides a finish, I was able to maintain a kind of equilibrium and enjoy a good view of the ring. While we were thus wedged in, venders of binoculars and hot dogs, who merely block your vision as they walk down the aisles in other cities, walked over our feet and crawled over our laps.

I took to reading the biographical notes in the official program. The one I liked best was about Walcott. It began, "If public support was the decisive yardstick in Jersey Joe Walcott's bid to become the first boxer ever to regain the heavyweight championship, the popular 39-year-old Negro would be assured of the distinction when he encounters Rocky Marciano tonight. Few fighters have won the heart of the public as has this wholesome, deeply religious father of six children."

There were two preliminaries before the main bout, and they fitted into the half hour with several minutes to spare, since both ended in quick knockouts. Neither presented any semblance of competition. Then Walcott and Marciano and their handlers came into the ring, hurriedly. Television time schedules have taken the old dragging dignity from the overture to a championship match. There were a number of garbled introductions of visiting prize-ring celebrities, the announcer never seeming to know the name of the fighter in the ring but always announcing the name of a fellow who had just left or one who was still making his way up through the crowd. Of the former champions introduced, only Tony Zale, the middleweight, got a big hand. Ezzard Charles, who lost the heavyweight title to Walcott, and

Jim Braddock, who lost it to Joe Louis, were present too, but the old champions with the greatest names, Jack Dempsey and Joe Louis, weren't.

Then the ring was cleared. As the hour hand of the big clock on the balcony facing us neared nine, the principals went to the center of the ring to hear the referee make his brief speech, and then returned to their corners. Marciano jumped up and down in his—he was trying to warm up for a fast start—and Walcott sat quiet, waiting for the bell. In a moment, the fight started. Because all these anterior events had been crammed into a half hour, it was still very early in the evening. There were great blocks of empty seats at the ends of the vast shed, both on the arena floor (euphemistically called ringside), and in the mezzanine and first balcony. All the empties were fifty- and thirty-dollar seats. In retrospect, the judgment of the people who didn't buy them seems excellent. (After the bout, the I.B.C. announced that the fight had been attended by around sixteen thousand people, of whom a bare thirteen thousand were paid admissions. It drew a gross gate of $331,795, which included the federal and state taxes on each ticket.)

Marciano had a whole swarm of handlers in his corner— Weill; Charlie Goldman, described in the program as "an elf from Brooklyn with a broken nose"; Columbo; Freddie Brown, a fight handler good at stopping cuts; and Marty Weill. When they left the ring and the bell rang, the champion looked lonely. He sought the company of the only other human up there with him, Walcott. But the wholesome, religious father of six children was not in a sociable mood.

A small colored man far off to my left cried encouragingly, "Come on, Satchel!"—a reference to Satchel Paige, a big-league-baseball pitcher, who was even older than Walcott but sometimes came through in tight spots. There was no great conviction in his voice, and none at all in the way Walcott handled himself. In September, I had seen Walcott walk out and beat Marciano to the punch. But this time he neither punched nor skipped; he just backed away. And Marciano, never a fast starter, couldn't think of much to do but walk after him. When he got close, Walcott grabbed his arms. It appeared to be the kind of fight we could all settle down to. The excitement, if any, would not come until the late rounds. The pace was so slow that I looked a couple of times at the big clock that measures off each three-minute round. Walcott flicked a couple of left jabs at Marciano as he retreated, but he was going away so fast that they fell short. Marciano missed a couple of right swings that were so clumsy I thought they were feints, designed to draw some counteraction. If so, they failed. Then, while the two men were groping about in Marciano's corner, the champion with his back toward our side of the house, I saw Rocky throw a high left hook, and Walcott hit the floor. I learned afterward that Marciano had thrown a rising right to the jaw immediately after the left, but I couldn't see it land from where I sat. So I simply assumed Jersey Joe had been knocked down with a left hook.

It wasn't a crashing knockdown, the kind that leaves the recipient limp, like a wet hat, or jerky, like a new-caught flatfish. This appeared to be a sit-down-and-think-it-over knockdown, such as you might see in any barroom on a night of full moon. Jersey Joe must have begun the process of ratiocination right away. But the conclusion at which he was arriving was not instantly apparent. Like the drowning men in stories, he may have been reviewing his whole life, with a long pause on what had happened to him in Philadelphia. The dramatic significance of the fleeting seconds was lost upon the crowd, because everybody present, with the possible exception of Mr. Walcott himself, took it for granted that he would get up within ten seconds. And maybe he thought so, too, for a while, but if he did, he dismissed the thought. Sprawled on the canvas floor covering, his right arm hooked over the middle strand of the ropes, he waited for the referee to count ten, and arose. Even then it was not clear to us in the balcony that the fight was over. Unable to hear the count, we assumed that he had risen on nine. But when the referee, a slight man named Frank Sikora, spread his arms wide to indicate that all was ended, Walcott walked calmly over to the ropes on our side of the ring, evincing a commendable independence of public opinion. If he had maintained this attitude, I would have admired him. The spectators were resentful, and their resentment was based on the suspicion that he had not been hit hard enough. This is a decision every man must make for himself, and of all the sixteen thousand persons under the big shed, Walcott was in the best position to make it. But as he heard the boos, he changed his mind. He mimed outrage, batting his gloved hands together and stamping like a wrestler. Wrestling is classed as a species of exhibition by the New York State Athletic Commission, and the acting is part of the show. Jersey Joe made it plain that he had not been knocked out at all. The crowd, with a forlorn hope that the fight might be resumed—after all, it had got precious little action for its money—increased its booing, but it was now booing *for* Walcott. Jersey Joe had stolen the scene from the man who had knocked him out. (And yet no man possesses a higher character for a deserving well-behaved man than ROCKY MARCIANO.) The whole fight had lasted two minutes and twenty-five seconds. The Kentucky Derby this year lasted two minutes and two seconds, and nobody cried, "Stop thief!" But fight fans are accustomed to more protracted pleasures.

Like the toddlers of North Walsham long ago, I made for the nearest lushing crib to restore my spirits. Going down the concrete stairs of the Stadium in front of me were three men, one of whom shouted, with what sounded like immense satisfaction, "This will kill boxing in Chicago!" One of his companions said indignantly, "I thought they were going to work it the opposite, so there'd be a bigger gate next time." It was evident he felt hurt because "they" had disappointed him. The third said, with a bitter laugh, "Write Duggan a letter."

In the Stadium Tavern, the closest dispensary of daffy and *eau de vie*, I caught one of the bartenders tying on his apron. "I sneaked off to watch the fight and I had to run like hell to get back here for the rush," he said. I had one Scotch, which I tossed off like milk, and headed for a streetcar. There were plenty of cars, because a good part of the crowd had remained behind to watch the rest of the minor bouts on the card, hoping to salvage a few nickels' worth of amusement. I found myself sitting next to a knowing drunk, a pale old man who was the shade and shape of a fat, soft clam. "Waidle you read the papers tomorrow," he said exultantly. "Duggan'll burn up the paper."

"What for?" I asked. "Duggan said Walcott would kill him."

The old drunk winked and snorted. "But he knew sumpm was up, dint he?" he said. "He couldn't write all 'at stuff if it wasn't true, could he? They'd soom."

A man with a flashlight gun and camera—a newspaper photographer who had been at ringside—was telling anybody who cared to listen what had really happened. "It was a right uppercut that did it," he said. "He tried to get up, but he couldn't make it in time." (The moving pictures of the count, however, show that Walcott didn't start until it was all over.) "Read Duggan!" the photographer yelled as he swung off the car. I think he meant to be funny, but a stout man sitting with a woman shouted a protest after him, "But Duggan predicted—"

I stopped briefly in the lobby of the Morrison, where friends and admirers of Marciano were giving a party to celebrate his victory. A couple of the kids in green jackets were standing there when Al Columbo breezed in, straight from the Stadium. "He didn't butt him this time!" Mr. Columbo yelled.

I decided I didn't want to go to a party, and went on to my hotel and bed.

Next morning, I bought an armful of Chicago newspapers at

the airport and read them on the plane going home. The first columnist I turned to, naturally, was Duggan, and he was as omniscient as if he had been right. "If the Illinois Boxing Commission has the guts God gave a lazy white dog," he began, "they'll hold up those purses till they get a look at the films of last night's fiasco to determine what knocked out Jersey Joe Walcott. . . . Out here in a hick town like Chicago, I guess anything can happen. Everybody knew the fight had no business here in the first place. It was a natural for New York in June. But say what you want about New York, you can be sure they wouldn't stand for the exhibition we put up with last night." I have never seen the man, but I make him no worse than even money to wind up as mayor. He had proved that, like everything else that goes wrong in Chicago, it was New York's fault. We had planted that fight on them like a road company of *The Student Prince*.

Charles I

In my study I have a print by Thomas Rowlandson of a milling match between Tom Cribb, the champion of England, and Tom Molineaux, an American Negro, at Thistleton Gap, in the County of Rutland, on September 28, 1811. This was a return fight; Molineaux had very nearly won the first, and Pierce Egan, the Froissart of the London prize ring, wrote concerning the second match, "It is supposed that near 20,000 persons witnessed this tremendous *mill*"—which, since it was an illegal event and all the customers had to dodge the constabulary to get there, denoted a high intensity of interest. Cribb won the fight at Thistleton, and there were bonfires in the streets when the news reached London. Rowlandson's picture was turned out with journalistic speed to profit by the public excitement. Cribb has just landed a mighty right to the jaw, stepping in with the punch in smashing style, and Molineaux is falling. There have been few artists like Rowlandson for catching action without arresting it. But the detail I recall first when I think of the picture is the face of Bill Richmond, one of Molineaux's seconds and also an American Negro, as he sees his man go. He is following Molineaux down with his eyes, bending as the challenger falls, and his face is desolate.

I sat in the fourth row behind Ezzard Charles's corner when he fought Rocky Marciano at the Yankee Stadium on the night of June 17, 1954, and what I shall remember about that fight longer than anything else, I imagine, is also a face. It was not Charles's—although that became a memorable sight in itself as the fight wore on—but the face of a plump, light-colored man named Jimmy Brown. Charles, like Molineaux long ago, is a Negro, and Brown, like Richmond in my print, was a second. There is much about Marciano, with his square torso, short, heavily muscled arms, and granite jaw, that recalls the Cribb of the picture, and he is as appallingly discouraging to fight. Each time Charles came back to his corner after a round, his seconds took the same positions about him, to save time and eliminate confusion. Brown was in front of him, facing the crowd as he bent over the seated fighter. Before Charles went out for the first round, Brown pressed his hand reassuringly on the challenger's left knee, and when Charles came back to his corner after drawing first blood from Marciano's nose, there was a look on Brown's wide, oval ecru face that said, "There, now, it wasn't so bad after all, was it?" It seemed to me—and, as it turned out, to both judges, the referee, and all the press—that Charles had outboxed the champion in that first round, as well as bloodied him. As Charles got past the second and third rounds, still leading, Brown's face relaxed, and after the fourth, when Charles opened a dangerous cut on the champion's left eyelid with a right, Brown grinned over the fighter's shoulder like one who saw before him a rosy future as the traveling companion of a world's champion. (I have no doubt that he had a good bet on, too, and the gamblers' odds on Marciano were 18 to 5.)

It was another Brown—Freddie Brown, the white "cut man" in Marciano's corner—who was worrying then. He used adrenalin to check the bleeding, a mineral jelly over the surface, and a quick-hardening plastic shield over all, but he knew a good punch would wreck his repair job; the cut was two inches long and an inch deep. "With a cut like that, you got to be nervous," he said afterward. "A quarter of an inch further in and it would of run like a faucet."

Marciano kept on swinging in the fifth; as the bell rang, Charles hit Marciano one punch, and the champion came back with a couple of determined swings, both launched well after the round ended. Charles looked very gay, to use an Eganism, when he came back to his corner; you could see that he felt he had the champion flustered. And there was always the cut to work on, a deep and promising little gold mine. There is a difference of a couple of hundred thousand dollars between the champion's and the challenger's share of a million-dollar gate. If Charles could work his vein properly, the return match would be sure to draw that. Jimmy Brown was still looking happy, as a man looks at Belmont when he sees his horse in good position and running easy. Both corners covered their men with robes of Turkish toweling between rounds; the night was cool, and a sweating fighter stiffens if the chill gets to him. Standing behind Charles and with his back toward me was one of his managers, a big Greek, who kept a hand on the fighter's left shoulder, as if to steady him, while he talked into his right ear. Charles is a temperamental boxer and sometimes has emotional blocks. Ray Arcel, a trainer who handled him in an exasperating failure, once said, "He is like a good horse which won't run for you." Arcel is severe and decisive, like a teacher in a Hebrew school. This time, Charles's corner was trying sweetness. The Greek's hand was soft and manicured, and a large diamond on his middle finger refracted the ring lights. As the ten-second klaxon warned the seconds to leave the ring, the hand gently urged the fighter forward, taking the robe as Charles stepped out of it.

Then came the sixth round. It was a round in which Marciano's apparently clumsy blows began to rock the challenger. The blow that really started Charles's decline, though, was a short, jarring left hook to the jaw that wasn't clumsy at all. One of the things that make Marciano a disconcerting opponent for a good boxer like Charles is that even his awkwardness is inconsistent; every now and then he does something highly skilled. Abruptly, Charles began to go slack, like every other fighter I have seen after Marciano's punches have begun to tell; they have a cumulative effect that asserts itself suddenly. When Charles sat down in his corner after that round, Jimmy Brown's face was grave, and the Greek's fingers beat a brief tattoo on the toweled shoulder before they remembered that they were there to soothe. I thought the finish would come in another round or two. It had been quite as good a fight as I had expected. I had not taken too seriously the reports from the training camp that this was a "new Charles," determined to do or die, but even if I had, I shouldn't have thought he was strong enough to take Marciano's blows for fifteen rounds. The spring came back into his legs after the bad round, though, and he went out and fought savagely, never avoiding the issue, in the seventh and eighth. This was the Indian summer of Charles's fight.

The bounce and snap had left him for good now, but what the sports writers had said about his determination was true. As for his endurance, it was unbelievable. His face—rather narrow, with a high, curved nose—changed in shape to a squatty rectangle as we watched; it was as though he had run into a nest of wild bees or fallen victim to instantaneous mumps. He moved, hung on, twisted his body, rolled his head on his columnar neck, which was now a cable between aching body and addling brain. He broke to his right, away from Marciano's swinging rights, but he didn't run. He even punched—straight but without power. He was doubtless admonished in his corner that he still had a chance to win on points if he could just keep going. But between rounds his toweling was getting soaked with blood, and Jimmy Brown's face—concerned, anxious, horrified, and finally despairing—was like Bill Richmond's in my picture. Some of the newspaper experts (trying, it seemed to me, to make too much of a good thing) said the next day that it was still a close fight in the late rounds, because the men were almost even in rounds won; Charles had taken five of the first six, by some counts. If he had rallied and won the last three, they said, he could have earned the decision. But there was no possible chance that he could rally, since the strength was out of him; there was a much better chance that he would collapse. That he didn't is great credit to his gameness, but if, like Cribb and Molineaux at Thistleton Gap, he and Marciano had been fighting to a finish, Marciano must have finished him off. After the announcer, Johnny Addie, who looks like a younger and plumper Billy Rose, had read the decisions of the two judges and of the referee, Ruby Goldstein, all agreeing on Marciano, Jimmy Brown achieved a histrionic triumph. He managed to look indignant.

It had been a hard fight but not great, in my opinion, because there were none of the sudden changes of fortune that mark a great one, as in the first Walcott–Marciano match. This time, Charles's success in the early rounds was expected, since he is a faster, better boxer than Marciano. The cut he inflicted on Marciano in the fourth round gave the champion's backers, including his vociferous fellow townsmen from Brockton, only temporary anxiety. The one true surprise was the loser's capacity for punishment. As Egan said of the Thistleton Gap mill, "The hardiest frame could not resist the blows of the *Champion*; and it is astonishing the Moor stood them so long."

It was a mighty crowd—paid admissions 47,585, and, counting deadheads like me, a total attendance of more than fifty thousand. There were fifteen hundred occupants of working-press seats alone, including a major general in uniform and Joe Louis. As is usual at big outdoor fights nowadays, platoons of young hooligans from the bleachers stormed down on the field in successive waves, to take over better seats than they had paid for. Legitimate ticket-holders who arrived late managed as best they could. In some cases, with the aid of ushers and special cops, they expropriated the squatters. These, however, made it a point of pride always to move forward instead of back, so that by the time the star bout began, they were standing all over the poor devils who had paid forty dollars for the use of a folding chair. The goal of the game, apparently, is to get to literal ringside, with the press photographers. This proved impossible during the big fight, but after it was over and the photographers went away, a swarm of adenoidal lummoxes came clambering over reporters' shoulders to get to ringside for the four-round bout that always follows a main event. "We're in fifty-dollar seat zat last!" one boy brayed as he dropped down by my side after a hurdle race over the backs of chairs. I was happy to note that the lagniappe bout ended with a sudden knockout while he was still breathing hard.

After the fights, I walked up to 167th Street to get a seat on a subway train before it reached the Stadium, which is at 161st. Several hundred other people seemed to have thought of the same stratagem, and it worked for all of us; the squares who got on at the Stadium found no seats and had to stand all the way downtown. They may well have been the seat-stormers. This provided a happy ending to the excursion.

Charles II

Pierce Egan, the Sire de Joinville of the London prize ring, characterized the immortal Tom Cribb as "placid, condescending, and obliging." "If not possessing the volubility of an orator," Egan wrote, "the C H A M P I O N, in company, is facetious, and endeavours to render himself pleasant and sociable to those around him, with a modest and unassuming deportment." Dr. J. L. Moreno, described by the Associated Press as a noted psychiatrist and author, visited the training camps of Ezzard Charles and Rocky Marciano before their recent fight at the Yankee Stadium, and gave Marciano even higher marks. Marciano, like Cribb, is a forthright, outgoing type in the ring. "He has poise, charm, sensitivity, imagination, a remarkably retentive memory, and a rugged handsomeness," Dr. Moreno wrote in the second article of a series of three sent out to all A.P. member papers, but, unfortunately, not used by any of the New York dailies. I was wised to Dr. Moreno by a member of the staff of the Newark *Evening News*, which had better editorial judgment. "He is friendly, warm, winning, and appeals to women, especially when he smiles," the analysis continued. Dr. Moreno is not a woman, but he took his wife along to the training camps to supply feminine reactions. "Marciano has presence of mind," he wrote. "That is a most important thing—a most decisive factor in the ring. Absence of mind is most devastating to a pugilist. Marciano has the ability to concentrate immediately on the crisis. . . . He is not calculable. His concentration is intense. . . . Unlike Ezzard Charles, Marciano has no inhibitions. Charles is the dreamer type."

I suppose the A.P. sent a psychiatrist to the two camps because when Marciano and Charles fought for the first time, Charles, who was in the estimation of the fancy a timid fighter, stood up to the champion for fifteen rounds, thus confounding the lay analysts who hang out in Stillman's gymnasium. It was the general opinion of these unlicensed practitioners that Charles's brave fight had been a temporary flight from reality, or fugue, which was not to be expected in the return match. "That kind of beating stays with a guy" was how one of them explained his prognosis.

The schema, or main idea, of the training-camp series was that Dr. Moreno would visit Charles and analyze him in his first article, visit and analyze Rocky in his second, and then, in his third article, for release on the day set for the fight—Wednesday, September 15, 1954—tell who was going to win. But for an old psychiatric buff like me, that line about inhibitions blew the gaff. I knew a day in advance that Dr. Moreno was touting Marciano. It was not a highly negotiable piece of information, because so was everybody else.

From the first article, however, I could see that Charles was really the one who interested Dr. Moreno. He probably wished he had had time to work on those inhibitions before they calcified. An inhibition is a challenge to a psychiatrist, like a leaky faucet to an amateur plumber, and, seeing Charles on the rubbing table, Dr. Moreno must have felt tempted to get out his notebook and have a try, even at the eleventh hour. "Charles is a dreamer," he wrote. "In his dreams, he is a mighty, invincible fighter, who sweeps all before him in a reckless, savage, destructive fashion. In the ring, however, he loses the spontaneity he has in his dreams." It was almost a miracle, he went on, that Charles had got as far as he had in the ring. "Can a 'miracle' happen again?" he asked himself point-blank. "Yes," he answered himself. "If Charles can wipe out his inhibitions in a frenzy—for just thirty seconds—if he is as spontaneous as he is in his dreams, he might knock out Marciano or anyone else. He would be irresistible. He would be like a tiger fighting for his mate. If the dream man can loose the tiger from within him, then Marciano had better watch out. There are several mental blocks, however, that have held back the tiger. Charles is an intelligent, cultured, well-mannered, sensitive person. He intuitively resents that part of his primitiveness which he loathes at times in other fighters. . . . Because of this conflict, Charles is neither a primitive slugger nor is he a classic boxer. [Here the Doctor may have stumbled on the explanation of switch hitters in baseball.] He is part puncher and part boxer."

The Wednesday piece appeared in the Newark *Evening News* under a headline contributed by a member of the staff who is probably an extrovert, like Rocky:

DOC PICKS ROCK
BY A KNOCKOUT

"After making a psychological study of Rocky Marciano and Ezzard Charles, and weighing all the factors involved," Dr. Moreno said, "I pick Marciano to knock out Charles tonight in one of the middle rounds, probably the seventh or eighth. Charles, a split personality, has to fight himself as well as the champion. . . . Ezzard, the way I see it, has but one way to win— a slim one at best. If he can rid himself of his emotional blocks in a frenzy, if he should cut or hurt Rocky and then turn loose the 'tiger' of his dream personality, then he could stop Marciano. But he must knock out Marciano to win. As the rounds go by, the possibility of a wild onslaught by Charles decreases. . . . Psychologically, the chances for this to happen are extremely small. Rocky is positive and supremely confident. He has no fears to hold him back. He is of one piece."

After that, the Doctor began to sound like an old A.P. sports writer. "I expect to see them both start slowly tonight," he wrote, "with Marciano permitting Charles to meet him halfway. Charles will be cautious. He will retreat and counter. In the second or third round, Marciano, who generally warms up slowly, will suddenly take over the offensive and begin to crowd Ezzard. In the fourth and fifth, Charles may break loose once or twice in short spurts, but something will hold him back from letting loose to the fullest. Then Marciano, supremely assured and confident, will assert himself. He will move in with short, punishing blows and begin to wear Ezzard down. Rocky may knock Charles down in the seventh and finish him in the eighth round."

Having read Dr. Moreno day by day, I felt *au courant* with the psychological situation when I walked over to Madison Square Garden at noon on Wednesday to see Charles and Marciano weigh in. In addition, I had acquired a pretty good notion of the somatic prospects from a piece in *Sports Illustrated* by Dr. Paul Peck, an anatomist, who had furnished drawings of both men stripped of their skins, like the charts in patent-medicine shows. Dr. Peck had labeled all the muscles from the zygomaticus to the gastrocnemius. (The zygomaticus is the muscle under the cheekbone; the gastrocnemius is way down in the leg.) "If the fight were held in a swimming pool, with both boxers treading water," Dr. Peck said, "Rocky wouldn't be able to hit very hard. Charles would." As it was already raining when I set out for the Garden, I thought this might be worth pasting in my chart book.

The weighing-in before a heavyweight fight is completely irrelevant, since the men do not have to make any stipulated weight. It provides photographs and new leads for the afternoon newspapers, however, and has a social function. Admission is by card (police) or badge (a tin ear), giving all visiting journalists and milling coves, active or retired, a place of rendezvous where they can exchange autobiographical notes since the last fight. It also gives you a chance to see who is in town. This time, I noticed, none of the British boxing writers who had covered the June fight were present—an indication that the London editors didn't think Charles would loose that tiger. The weighing of Marciano and Charles seemed particularly unimportant because it was plain from the weather that there would not be any fight in a New York ball park that night. Marciano weighed a hundred and eighty-six and a half and Charles a hundred and ninety-two and a half—a gain of seven pounds over his ring weight in June; with my new psychiatric orientation, I attributed it to compulsive eating, caused by anxiety. The champion looked as placid, pleasant, and unassuming as ever. His placidity, it appeared, had in the course of years spread to all his faction. Al Weill, who in the past had been a fuming, worrying kind of man, wore a fat, paternal smile. Charlie Goldman, who three years before, when Marciano was training for Louis, had acted like a tutor trying to teach a boy the whole of mathematics in time for a college-entrance examination three days away, now had the relaxed air of a professor emeritus. Charles, taller than Marciano and of a fashionable charcoal shade, looked about as excited as a man waiting for a subway train. The weather forecast for the next day, Thursday, was unfavorable, and it occurred to me that a forty-eight-hour prolongation of the dreaming period might accentuate Charles's internal conflict, if Dr. Moreno was right in diagnosing one. I voiced this thought to Mr. Jimmy Brooks, a Harlem *boulevardier* and associate of pugilists, who chanced to be at my elbow, and he agreed. "It does not pay for a fighter to be too intellectual, brainy—you get my meaning?" Mr. Brooks said. "They get to laying awake and thinking too much about their physical body—what might happen to it, you know?"

Mr. Brooks did not attend the second weighing-in, which was held on Friday, September seventeenth, when the weather cleared. Neither did any of the other people who had come to the first one for purely social reasons, since nothing to talk about had developed in the intervening two days. Just the newspapermen and photographers showed up, to repeat the routine of the first ponderation. This time Marciano weighed a hundred and eighty-seven, a gain of an inconsiderable half pound (he had been doing enough gymnasium work to hold his edge), and Charles registered no change. After the weighing-in I had lunch in Gilhuly's saloon, near the Garden, with a fellow who said that a movie producer had wanted to bet him thirteen hundred dollars to two hundred on Marciano, but that he didn't see how Charles could win.

"Oh, I don't know," I said. "He is a very complex MacTavish. If he could wipe out his inhibitions for just thirty seconds, he would be like a tiger fighting for his mate."

"I never thought of that," the fellow said. "Excuse me while I give this wise guy a bang on the telephone." He came back and said he had taken the bet.

Late that evening, I made my way up to the Yankee Stadium by subway. The curtain for the main bout was to be fashionably late—at eleven o'clock. It was practically a supper show. This was in order to avoid a conflict with a baseball game at the Polo Grounds, half a mile away, where the Giants were playing the Phillies; the game had begun at eight-fifteen. On Wednesday night, when the fight had been rained out, the Giants had not been scheduled to play. The late hour of the match made for a long, straggling evening, with the crowd assembling slowly.

The preliminaries were, if possible, worse than usual, to judge from the three I saw. The six principals in these three had all appeared on the Marciano–Charles card in June, and none had improved over the summer. This time, I sat behind the corner that was to be Marciano's—in June, I had landed behind Charles— and during the next-to-last preliminary Al Weill sat down in front of me, to root for a moderately belligerent hundred-and-seventy-five-pound man in whom he had a proprietary interest. "Stop hoppin'!" Mr. Weill would shout at him, and then "Stick, stick!" meaning stick him with your left hand. "I know what they should do," he said when he happened to turn around and see me, "and it hurts me when they don't do it." Since Mr. Weill's champion was going to defend the world's heavyweight title within twenty minutes, his preoccupation with such a trivial performance indicated to me that he wasn't worried.

The notorious dreariness of the preliminaries at championship fights is due to a feudal arrangement whereby the managers of the main-bout fighters get berths for all their fighter's stablemates and sparring partners on the preliminary card. The promoter fills in the remaining spots with the cheapest boxers obtainable. Sparring partners are endowed with habitual consideration and forbearance, and they find it hard to change character. A kind of guild fellowship holds them together, and they pepper each other's elbows with merry abandon, grunting with pleasure like hippopotamuses in a beer vat. Mr. Weill left to change into the form-fitting garments he wears in the ring as Marciano's second, and his man floundered through to a decision.

After the last preliminary Whitey Bimstein, the trainer of one of the participants in it and an old friend of mine, came down from the ring, his face wearing an expression designed to apprise the world that there had been a miscarriage of justice; the officials had called it a draw. Whitey's fighter, less experienced in mimesis, looked as if he were glad to have escaped with his life.

Now Marciano's faction began pushing its way toward the ring along a narrow path left between the massed undertaker's chairs on which the International Boxing Club mounts its patrons. Cops and bodyguards cleared a passage, and then the fighter appeared, wrapped in a blue bathrobe with a cowl over his head. He would have four men in his corner: Columbo, Weill, Goldman, and Freddie Brown. Weill would handle the strategy, Goldman the tactics, and Brown the surgery. Columbo was there just because he couldn't live if he weren't. Goldman and Brown are old fighters—small men with mashed noses and quick eyes. Columbo is young, and in his white sweater he looked like a college cheerleader. Weill is onion-shaped and authoritative; Marciano, when I first met him, used to call him "Mr. Weill." The demeanor of all was confident, but what was especially impressive was Marciano's back when he had seated himself on the stool in his corner. It looked as wide and as immovable as a blue wall. There was a brief fashion show as Floyd Patterson, a young light heavy who is coming along, and Sugar Ray Robinson were introduced from the ring. They were both sharp, but I thought Robinson, in yellow haberdashery and a black suit, had it.

At about six minutes after eleven the fight began, and it was lucky I had Dr. Moreno's scenario with me, because from where I sat I missed occasional fractions of action. In the June fight, Charles had moved out faster than Marciano, stepping in and hitting him away with rights. This time, however, he was acting like an intelligent, cultured, well-mannered, sensitive person, gracefully poised. I could but recollect the time-honored Egan's description of Richard Humphries, the Gentleman Boxer, in his second contest with Dan Mendoza, at Stilton in 1789. "Humphries had lost that commanding style which was so prominent in his last attack; and he seemed to labor under an impression that he had a superior to encounter with; he did not maintain his ground with his usual confidence, but suffered his opponent to drive him, and even, upon some occasions, there was a sort of shrinking from the blows of his adversary." Marciano, forcing the fighting, missed most of his punches, but he came back to his corner grinning. For him it was a pretty good start.

Meanwhile a considerably more acrimonious round had been contested behind Marciano's corner, where his seconds, coming down from the ring, had found themselves with nothing to sit on but photographers and account executives' friends. Columbo, hopping up and down with excitement—he was probably the only person in the Stadium so affected by that round—had aroused the wrath of an Athletic Commission inspector sitting to my right. The inspector ordered Columbo to sit down, so that he, the inspector, could see; if Columbo had sat down, *he* couldn't have seen. The function of a second during action is, as Freddie

Brown says, "to see if he can see anything" worthy of communication to his principal between rounds. Weill said to the inspector, "He got a right." Columbo started to say something, too, but Weill cuffed him on the back of his head. Marciano, blissfully unaware of all this ill-feeling, was the calmest man in the corner when he returned at the bell.

In the second round—to my amazement and, apparently, to Charles's—the champion began to use a straight left, jabbing to the face with jolting force and then crossing a right, exactly as they teach in boxing school. ("He is not calculable," as Dr. Moreno had it.) For years little Charlie Goldman had refrained from trying to teach Rocky anything so fancy, on the ground that it might "spoil his natural leverage." It was as fancy as A B C. Goldman must finally have decided it was safe. Before Charles could react to this treacherous attack of orthodoxy, Rocky landed a right to his zygomaticus, and he went sprawling down, forgetting to tread water, until he hit the bottom of the pool. The referee, Al Berl, counted to two, and Charles got up. ("In the second or third round, Marciano . . . will suddenly take over the offensive.") When Charles went down, I had a feeling he would stay there, like Walcott in Chicago, but he didn't. He had too much self-respect. However, he didn't take the count of nine, to which he was entitled, and this may have been because he didn't trust his self-respect that far. Marciano, moving in and swinging, the fancy stuff forgotten, appeared to have him headed for a quick knockout, but Ezzard rid himself of his emotional blocks for a fleeting second. He hit Marciano two dazzling left hooks, which, coming from a fighter apparently on his way out, gave the only intimation, however brief, that this could be a good fight.

Between the second and third rounds, inhibitions coagulated in Charles. In the third round, Marciano plodded after him, sometimes landing and more often missing, but Charles's intuitive resentment of violence had set in like ice on a pond. Understanding the psychiatric problem, Marciano concentrated intensely. Meanwhile the battle of Al Columbo continued, but the inspector couldn't get at him without climbing over Jack E. Leonard, the fat comic who missed the fight at Chicago. In the fourth round, my score card recalls, Marciano feinted a left beautifully and followed with a right hard enough to rearrange anybody's emotional pattern, and, sure enough, in the fifth Charles displayed a pinch of spontaneity. I thought he won the round, but I also thought it was academic.

The sixth round brought Freddie Brown his chance to operate. Marciano, for all his toughness, cuts easily, and in the first Charles fight got a long cut over the left eye. In this fight, Charles's right elbow collided with the champion's nose, inflicting a deep, wide cut along its bridge. Marciano came back to his corner with an embarrassed grin, as if asking to be excused for putting his seconds to so much trouble. Brown, after stopping the chink with a quick-setting plastic called Thromboplastin, topped it off with a generous handful of Vaseline, which made the champion look as though he were wearing a Halloween false nose. Even this, however, failed to unleash the tiger in Charles. Once, when Marciano stuck out that rudimentary jab again, Charles countered with a fine right to the champion's head, delivered over Marciano's arm. But this was an intellectual rather than an emotional response. He wasn't weak—once he grabbed Marciano by the back of the neck and spun him—and he wasn't entirely unresentful; when Marciano hit him after the bell, he hit back. I remember thinking, as I looked at him in his corner after the sixth round, that he was strong and unmarked, but I was perfectly sure he would be knocked out, and sure that he was sure of the same thing.

The two men wallowed through the seventh round—Marciano slugging away, the Vaseline dissolving in blood, and Charles intuitively resenting the primitiveness of it all. Early in the eighth, Marciano caught Charles with a series of blows that knocked him down. He took four this time, rose, and reeled away, with Rocky hitting at him. The knockdown was on the side of the ring to the left of the champion's corner; Charles staggered across the base of the triangle, and there Rocky hit him again, this time using a sweeping left, like a man swinging a brush hook. Charles went down, and Marciano nailed him with a right as he fell. We were all on our feet, watching, and at four Charles pulled himself up to one knee. It was the better part of discretion to take the count of nine, and I expected him to rise when Al Berl, counting in his ear, reached that numeral. Instead, he stayed a second more—a very long second—and Berl said "Ten." Maybe he had just forgotten to get up; as Dr. Moreno says, absence of mind is most devastating to a pugilist. The Doc, as a matter of fact, had called the round.

After the fight I shared a cab with a friend, and we rode all the way down to the Artists' & Writers' Restaurant, formerly Club, on 40th Street, and had a beer. On the way, he said that Marciano was a travesty of a champion, but that it was all right; one great champion was all a man could expect in a lifetime, and he had seen Joe Louis at his best. I said that Marciano was so good, in his peculiar way, that there should be a law against allowing him to fight return bouts. "He takes it out of them," I said. Neither of us was happy. It just hadn't been a good fight.

It wasn't until I dropped in at Stillman's the next day that I got a reasonable non-Freudian explanation of Charles's conduct. Freddie Brown and Whitey Bimstein were sweating a number of their future champions between calls on what is known in Stillman's as the long-distance phone. Hurricane Tommy Jackson, the colored heavyweight with the double uppercut, was hitting the big bag on the gymnasium balcony. Mr. Jackson, a temperamental young man while on a winning streak, had been a model pupil ever since the unfortunate termination of a bout with a Cuban heavyweight named Nino Valdes; the referee stopped the bout and awarded it to Valdes at a moment when, according to Hurricane, "that man was so tired he was staggling."

Mr. Bimstein was, as usual, bemoaning the effect of television on the development of new talent. At nine-tenths of the boxing shows nowadays, he said, you might as well be fighting in a telephone booth, and only the feature bout is televised. Fighters in the preliminaries, therefore, labor practically in private, unremarked even though they perform prodigies.

I congratulated Mr. Brown on his job on Marciano's nose, which had at least remained attached to the champion's face, and he said it had been an unusual kind of injury but one that had not found him unprepared. When I propounded Dr. Moreno's theory of the caged tiger within Charles's breast, it met with polite skepticism from Mr. Brown. "Why did he fight that way, then?" I asked.

Mr. Brown looked at me with placid, obliging condescension. "He fought the way he fought because Marciano fought the way *he* fought," he said. "Charles come in in a good mental condition, and he started right in to execute—biff!" Mr. Brown here took the stance of a confident, standup boxer. "But Rocky is coming in." Mr. Brown here came in, and I stepped back. "It is very hard to think when you are getting your brains knocked out," Mr. Brown said. "So Charles withdraws back to consider the situation." Mr. Brown withdrew. "That puts him further from a position where he can execute. Meanwhile, Marciano is still coming in. He is cruel. Charles hits him a good right to the jaw, and Rocky hits him with a left hook *and* a right. First thing Charles knows, he is grabbing, and then he is just trying to hang on. Why? He don't know why. It is not like football," he said, kindly, like one trying to convey truth to little children. "Rocky never gives you the ball."

Other Fronts

The Boy from South Main Street

Like every American city, the capital of Rhode Island cherishes its sporting celebrities. When I worked as a reporter on the Providence *Journal* and *Evening Bulletin*, in the late twenties, one of the walking monuments of the town was Norman Taber, a trustee of Brown University, who soon after graduating from Brown had set the world's record for running a mile—4:12⅗, I think it was. Another monument—and quite a nice one, too—was Glenna Collett, the National Women's Amateur golf champion. Brown's Iron Men had just gone undefeated through the football season of 1926, and the Providence Steamrollers won the professional-football championship in 1927. Gus Sonnenberg, the Steamrollers' star tackle, was flattening visiting wrestlers every week in the Arcadia Ballroom by a tactic of almost miraculous simplicity—butting them in the belly. But the town had never produced a world's boxing champion. It was not for lack of aspirants; the weekly amateur tournaments at the Arcadia dance hall drew crowded entry lists. Nor was it for lack of scheming—there were more old fighters around than you could shake a towel at, all saturated with good counsel and looking for a likely young ear to pour it into. There was a shining example of ringcraft to observe; a Providence boxer called Young Montreal—his real name was Maurice Billingkoff—who had boxed six world's bantamweight champions and, according to local belief, beaten them all. He had beaten three even according to the record book, and had boxed no-decision bouts with two of the others; unfortunately, he had never been able to beat one of these fellows at the precise moment when the fellow was holding the championship. When I saw Young Montreal, he was past his prime but still a most elusive, exasperating man in the ring. He was bald and had red freckles and pipestem arms, and in his pugilistic old age I saw him make a fool of Bud Taylor, one of the hardest punchers who ever lived. I was on the city side then, but I could usually get a free ticket from the sports department. It has always seemed to me a historic injustice that Monty never held a title—something like Gustave Flaubert's failure to receive an invitation from the Académie Française. While I was in Providence, a young featherweight named Ernie Mandell showed promise—he was a good, graceful boxer—but he got knocked out by a Filipino from Cleveland, and never did much after that. And in the twenty-six years that have passed since my departure from that tranquil town, it has produced perhaps a dozen fair fighters, but never one who went all the way to a title.

A few years ago a cellist and former journalistic confrere of mine who still lives in Providence told me there was a lightweight boxer up there who showed signs of real virtuosity. The boy's name, he said, was George Araujo, and since the cellist himself had been an amateur boxer of some technical capacity when I first knew him, I made a mental note of it. From time to time after that, I saw wire-service stories about Araujo on the sports pages, their progressively increasing prominence reflecting his rise, and then I read that he was matched to fight the lightweight champion, Jimmy Carter, for the world's title, at one hundred and thirty-five pounds, in Madison Square Garden on the night of June 12, 1953.

The lightweight class has been in a decline in recent years, for reasons as hard to explain as the non-appearance of bluefish in seasons when they are expected. My learned friend Whitey

Bimstein has attributed the extinction of good "bantyweights"—
hundred-and-eighteen-pound professionals—to the increase in
the stature of the human race, but there are still great numbers of
young men visible who stand, say five feet six or seven inches
and can do a hundred and thirty-five, which is the lightweight
limit. Because of the drop in the class's prestige, the Carter–Araujo
bout did not get the publicity buildup that a lightweight-
championship fight would have got in the days of Benny
Leonard, who drew nearly half a million dollars into the Yankee
Stadium when he fought Lew Tendler there in 1923, or even in
the late thirties, when there were lightweights around like Tony
Canzoneri, Barney Ross, Henry Armstrong, and Lou Ambers. Instead of writing about the match for weeks in advance, as they
did when the middleweights Randy Turpin and Ray Robinson
were to fight here in 1951, and when Rocky Marciano was to
fight Jersey Joe Walcott, the sports columnists waited until the
last week, and then gave it one story apiece, unless they happened to be too immersed in baseball to bother about it at all.

Because of this matter-of-fact approach to the fight, I suppose,
Araujo's managers didn't take him to a training camp in the
country before the fateful evening. They must have reasoned that
for a young fighter who has been performing as often as he had—
he was twenty-two and had had fifty-two bouts in the previous
four years or so—a training camp is simply a touch of swank. Besides, it costs money. So a week before the fight they checked him
into the Capitol Hotel, a gaunt hostelry on Eighth Avenue, one
block north of the Garden and three south of Stillman's Gymnasium. He worked out at Stillman's and did his running in Central
Park. Carter, more of a traditionalist, trained in Summit, New
Jersey.

Araujo had been a year short of birth when I left Providence,
so when I climbed the stairs to Stillman's to see him work out
three days before the fight, I had, perhaps, a fuller sense of the
civic responsibility that weighed on his shoulders than he had

himself. As I entered Stillman's the challenger was in the ring sparring with a slightly heavier boy. I could see that he moved gracefully, and with almost too much confidence, in and out under the other fellow's leads, bouncing around as if his legs were so good he enjoyed using them. Naturally, with the fight so near, he wasn't trying to kill his partner. A fight manager watching the workout said that he thought the boy held his hands too low—he was open for a right counter over his left. But I couldn't believe that this was inadvertent; I decided it must be his style, and that he relied on speed of eye and head to slip such punches. It is the style of fools and perfectionists. It is also the kind of thing that only a fellow very sure of himself can do, and to be so sure of himself he must have boxed thousands of rounds. This was in fact the case with Araujo, I learned from his senior manager, Frankie Travis, a sallow, heavyset man with grizzled, wavy hair and a jutting chin, to whom I was introduced at ringside. "I saw George the first day he came up to the Catholic Youth Organization, on South Main Street, and put the gloves on," Travis said. "He was eight years old, and he had so much stuff I said, 'That kid is going to be a champion.' I've been training him ever since." (When Travis said "South Main Street," he brought to my mind a water-front street with flophouses and tattooing shops in eighteenth-century buildings and Portuguese barbershops and ship chandlers' stores whose windows were decorated with prints of Lisbon before the earthquake. It is on the east side of the Providence River, which is the head of navigation on Narragansett Bay, but no great ships have come that far up the bay for a long time. The great ships of Providence's great days as a seaport drew precious little water.) "But he didn't start seriously until he was thirteen," Travis added, as if to discourage the thought that there had been anything unusual about Araujo's childhood. In Providence, Travis is sometimes a Portuguese name—an Anglicization of Tavares. But the manager said his name had originally been Italian—Trevisano. Araujo's other manager was Sammy Richman, a younger, Broadway sort of fellow, who came into the act six months before the Garden fight. He was the outside man, or negotiator, while Travis was the professional instructor and personal counselor. Out-of-town managers, like out-of-town lawyers who have cases in New York, frequently retain metropolitan associates. "He's a good boy," Richman told me, "and I don't think he will get too pent up—you know, freeze."

The boy came down from the ring. He is a mahogany lad, the son of one of those sailors from the Portuguese Cape Verde Islands, off the west coast of Africa, whom New Englanders sometimes call Bravas, although Brava is the name of only one island in the group. Long ago, Cape Verdeans used to make up a good portion of the crews of New England whalers, and hundreds of the islanders still come to New England in sailing schooners every spring to work through the summer on construction jobs and on farms. In the fall the schooners sail back to the islands— thirty-five to fifty days away—occasionally leaving behind a part of their spring complements and carrying home other Cape Verdeans, some of them naturalized American citizens. A lot of Cape Verdeans born in the islands are American citizens because their parents were born or naturalized in New England. They are the last sailing-ship people anywhere, I suppose, who aren't yachtsmen and don't use auxiliary engines; even the Finns have given up their grain fleet. Araujo's father, one of the island-born Americans, sailed to the United States and stayed. He worked on the Providence docks, married, and begot seventeen children, and now there is nothing in his son's voice that isn't New England, and nothing in his manner that isn't Hope High School.

Travis introduced the fighter to me and then sent him along to the locker room for his rub. Araujo, I noticed, had a small head, a compact torso, and big, round arms and calves—not much reach but a good build for endurance and mobility. "He's my baby," Travis said. I asked him if he had had other good boys, and he said, "I once had a fellow named Ernie Mandell that was pretty good, but he got flattened by a Filipino. And I had a boy named Al Mancini that beat Sixto Escobar, but it was over the weight." I figured he had been waiting at least thirty years for a big fighter.

We went into the locker room and sat around the rubbing table in the cubicle rented for Araujo. While the boy sat on the table, we talked about Providence. A fighter I remembered named Eddie Holmes was now a bus driver, I learned, and another named Billy Lynch, who once gave Lou Ambers a lot of trouble until he got a bad cut—the old Providence luck—was a lieutenant in the Fire Department. Young Montreal had a job with a labor union. Knockout Billy Ryan had dropped dead, and old Joe Murphy, the retired bare-knuckle fighter who ran the bottling works on Transit Street, had finally passed on. With the money earned from his fifty-two fights, Araujo had moved his family away from South Main Street and into a neighborhood with less character but more sanitation.

Neither Travis nor George professed any worry about Carter. "He can box, but he's not an expert boxer. And he can fight, but he's not an expert fighter," Travis said. "And he's better than a fair hitter. But he's not getting any younger." This was about what I had heard elsewhere concerning the champion. George had little to say, but he appeared to feel the *Wunderkind*'s contempt for the plodding mediocrity. Travis said he had lost just two decisions in fifty-two fights and had been knocked down only once in his life. That had happened four years before, and he had got up to win easily. I asked George who had taught him most of his stuff, and he said Travis had taught him everything. "I would practice moves with another fighter, and he would coach me," he said. "If a thing didn't work this way, we'd try it that way."

On the night of the fight, I stopped by the out-of-town newsstand in Times Square on my way to Madison Square Garden and bought a copy of the Providence *Evening Bulletin*. It carried a first-page story on the fight by Mike Thomas, the *Bulletin*'s boxing writer, who not unnaturally picked Araujo to win, "home-town view or not." Mike had written, "He should take the decision over the titleholder, Jimmy Carter of the Bronx, in their 15-round go at Madison Square Garden. But there is the distinct possibility he could win on a knockout by the 12th or 13th round. That is, if his plan of speed first and then explosion is not disturbed. He figures to start bombing by the 10th or 11th. By then, the champion ought to be set up for the kill." Thomas said that more than three thousand Rhode Islanders were coming down for the fight. I am not a Rhode Islander, but I had a lot of fun working there, and I had become as partisan as any of them.

I had plenty of time, so I walked on past the Garden to the Capitol Hotel, which I figured would be Providence headquarters because Araujo was staying there. The curb in front of the place was parked solid with cars bearing Rhode Island license plates, and the sidewalk between the cars and the hotel was covered with feet more accustomed to the pavements of Dorrance and West-minster Streets. The air was musical with the flattened "a"s and squeezed "e"s of southern New England speech; a man smoking a pipe to maintain his cam told me that patties had come on by caa and bus as well as by special train. "We've taken over the town," he said modestly, removing his pipe from his mouth and waving it bravely in the direction of the eight million beyond the stock-ade of automobiles. I stood around for a while, half expecting to see somebody I knew, and then left to rejoin my fellow ab-origines.

When I walked into the Garden, a Berber from Morocco was in the ring, whacking away ineffectually at a long, stringy Negro from Cuba; it seemed unbelievable that two men could have come so far to fight so little. The Berber and the Negro banged away awkwardly for a couple more rounds and then disappeared, after one of the least important decisions of the century. Next, a short but barrel-chested Puerto Rican lightweight came on with a thin fellow from Philadelphia; the weights were even, and it was a contest between a vertical line and a cube. This was better—the Philadelphian was resolute, although unduly prolonged, and the Puerto Rican appeared to be a great hitter, in a shot-putting style. "Look at him!" a man behind me cried. "He looks like a monkey—you know, a griller." Having found his *mot juste*, he stuck to it for eight rounds. "A griller!" he would exclaim whenever the Puerto Rican would up to pitch a fist. "A griller! A griller!" The griller did not succeed in converting the Philadelphian into a horizontal, but he made him look like two sides of a triangle in search of a third. "A griller!" the man in back of me said in awe when the boxers left the ring.

The hands of the Garden clock were now so near ten, the mystic hour of television, that the Garden's baritone soloist had to sing the national anthem at the tempo of "The Darktown Strutters' Ball." The heroes of the evening entered the ring without the draggy solemnity that used to enhance the dignity of the beginning of a championship fight. The sponsor was paying fifty thousand dollars for radio and television rights, considerably more than the match was expected to attract at the gate. (It drew thirty-eight thousand dollars.) Carter was longer, leaner, blacker, and older than Araujo—he was twenty-nine—and wore a white robe on the back of which was lettered, with unexpected formality, "James Carter." He had a kind of desiccated look that I mistook for evidence of brittleness. When Johnny Addie, the announcer, introduced Araujo, there was a thunderous cheer from the Rhode Islanders. They greeted Carter with equally thunderous boos. The visitors must have made up half the audience.

At the bell Araujo came out on his toes and started circling Carter, jabbing his left to the champion's face as the taller man advanced. They were flicking, fast jabs, usually double, like a cat striking twice at a butterfly, and, since George was generally going away when they landed, they were not stiff enough to set

Carter back on his heels. If I had not read the *Bulletin*, I would have thought our man had an exaggerated respect for Carter's hitting power, but I knew the battle plan. As the round went on. I thought George looked a good bet. He was on his toes all the way, bouncing wastefully, but his legs were marvels; that kind of underpinning is an asset to be exploited, like reach or hitting power. And he was not using his legs to carry him in one direction; he was moving in and out of range and hitting repeatedly. Carter, bent slightly forward, with his elbows high, moved steadily after him feet flat on the mat, a perfect picture of the deadly hitter I had been assured he wasn't. He had, in fact, knocked out only a small percentage of his opponents up to the previous April twenty-fourth, when he boxed an unfortunate youth named Tommy Collins, in Boston, and bowled him over ten times before the referee stopped the fight. That may have convinced him he could hit. In the first round, though, Carter was missing and George was hitting, and I have never been the kind of fight-goer who gives a fighter credit for chasing an opponent and getting hit.

I was relieved to find that the man and woman in front of me were of my persuasion in this matter, for there is nothing less agreeable to me than having to turn my attention from the ring to explain the rudimentary principles of the sweet science to my fellow customers. At the end of the round I penciled a large "1" on a sheet of yellow paper I had on my knee and marked next to it a large "A." The woman, who had been peeping over her shoulder, smiled and said, "I agree with you exactly." At the end of the next round I marked "2—E," for "even," and the lady said, "Right." In the third Carter caught George in a neutral corner and landed a few solid raps. With an impartiality that aroused my own admiration, I marked "3—C." But in the fourth and fifth, things went so well for Providence that it looked to me "as safe as the Bank," to borrow a phrase from Pierce Egan, the Thucydides of the London prize ring. The mahogany boy opened a cut over Carter's right eye, and in the fifth he began hitting him with left hooks to the stomach. Carter ended the body attack by crouching lower and bringing down his elbows, but he was no nearer nailing Araujo than he had been at the beginning of the fight. They had now covered a third of the course, and it wasn't until the tenth or eleventh round that Araujo was even supposed to open up with his heavy guns. For the moment, I thought Carter might not get that far. But Carter's seconds stopped the blood from the cut and he got going again, while Araujo, gradually coming down from his toes, seemed to take a breather. After both the sixth and seventh rounds I marked a "C," and it occurred to me that just as a man might convince himself he was a hitter by acting like a hitter, so might his opponent fall victim to the same delusion by taking the man at his own valuation. Here were two men of equal weight, equally hard to hurt and, in their records, almost equally damaging punchers—Araujo had actually scored more knockouts in fifty-two bouts than Carter had in eighty-two. Yet the fight was falling into the pattern of a match between a boxer and a puncher, or a light man and a heavy man.

In the eighth the Providence hope did better, beating Carter to the punch, cutting his eye again, and making him look slow, old, and angry. As the hand of the big clock timing the rounds swept past a minute and a half it appeared to me that we were ahead at the halfway mark of the fight, although not far enough to mean anything. The ninth started like every round before it, with Araujo moving and stabbing, landing a succession of those double flicks to the face. Carter hit him with a right to the body that landed below the line. The referee warned the dark, persistent fellow, and then Carter lashed out with a right to the jaw, over that left hand Araujo insisted on carrying low. The boy may have dropped it still lower in involuntary reaction to the body punch. There were a couple more punches, and then Araujo was on the mat. He bounced up almost as soon as he hit the floor. Now, when he was hurt, instead of moving out of danger as he had been doing all evening, he leaped at Carter like a kid in a schoolyard. He went down again, came up again, slugged some more, and then, just before the end of the round, took a wicked right-hander to the jaw that had him wandering aimlessly at the bell.

An older, or a less well-conditioned, boxer would not have lasted out the first thirty seconds of the tenth, but Araujo, moving uncertainly at first, got back on his toes and boxed. He lost the round, of course, but he opened Carter's cut again. The eleventh was even more trying for him, but in the twelfth he seemed completely recovered, jabbing, dancing, and generally fooling the older man, who was beginning to look tired. At the end of the round, I marked my first "A" since the eighth, but the boy was now so far behind on points that he would have to do something sensational to win the decision in three more rounds.

Travis's *Wunderkind* went out to do it in the thirteenth, and for a couple of minutes, changing his style completely, he slugged with Carter, usually beating him in exchanges. The crowd, which always prefers slugging to boxing, roared approval, and this time not only the Rhode Islanders were cheering. But, like Larry's kick the day he was stretched, George's gesture was all pride. Carter caught him with another series of punches, he went down again, and the referee stopped the fight, after two minutes and sixteen seconds of the thirteenth round.

The last thing I remember about the fight is Travis's face as he hauled himself through the ropes to get his boy. It is a big face, and it was wide open, as if he had just seen something he couldn't believe. I don't know what kind of journey home the fellows from Providence had, but I imagine it was quiet.

On the following Sunday morning, I called Travis at his hotel to find out why things had turned out so, and he said to come right over; he would be waiting for me in the lobby. "George is with me," he said. When I got there, the Capitol, which had been buzzing with Rhode Islanders on fight night, was as quiet as a training camp in the Adirondacks. It is a big place, built to be a hotel for the Knights of Columbus, who lost it to the infidels during the Depression, but for some reason the fellow who designed it gave it a lobby no larger than the front room of a police station. Araujo, looking rather subdued, was wearing a sports jacket and slacks. His face was somewhat swollen, and he was even less talkative than he had been before the fight. Travis, like a father who knows his boy has made mistakes but is willing to forgive him, said Araujo had been following instructions by boxing with Carter in the early rounds. "If you're a fighter, and I'm a fighter and boxer, why should I go along with you at your game from the start?" he asked. "Isn't it better if I box you the first nine or ten rounds and cut you? Then I can come on to win. That's what we were planning to do," he added, confirming the battle plan in the *Evening Bulletin*. "It was working, too. George had him cut pretty good. But just when I was going to open George up, we hit the bad luck. He got knocked down, and, never being used to it, he jumped right up. That was stupid!" he said to Araujo. "It was a stupid thing to do."

"I was just angry and excited," the boy said. "I lost my head."

"The bad luck was that he went down with his back toward his corner," said Travis. "If he could have seen us, we would have motioned to him to stay down. If he had taken nine, his head would have been clear, and meanwhile Carter would have had to walk to a neutral corner. George would have gone on the bicycle as soon as he got up, and we would have been all right again before the end of the round."

"Couldn't you have yelled to him?" I asked.

"He couldn't have heard us," the manager said. "In Providence, I might take a chance and run around the ring to where he could see me, but here they might disqualify us for that. And when he got knocked down the second time, he had his back to us again."

"It was my own fault," Araujo said. "I was going good, my wind was fine. In another round, I was going to start to take him."

"It's one of the things we can't ever prove, George," said Travis. "When you bounced up, it was the turning point. I was amazed."

Sammy Richman, Araujo's New York manager, who wandered in just then, had a less tactical, more general explanation. "He didn't make his fight because he was too excited," he said. "You know—too pent up."

Nino and a Nanimal

In the spring of 1954 Whitey Bimstein and Freddie Brown told me about a new talent confided to their care who was *outré* but interesting. "A nanimal," Mr. Bimstein said. "A throwback to the man of the gutter." "A mental case," Mr. Brown agreed, without disapproval in his voice. "By that I mean he's got to be doing something all the time." Managers, like book publishers, make most of the money, but trainers, like editors, participate more directly in the artists' labors. Bimstein and Brown are editors of prizefighters. Mediocrity depresses them; they are excited by talent, even latent. What they dream about is genius, but unfortunately that is harder to identify.

Technically, Whitey and Freddie can do a lot for a fighter— excise redundant gesture and impose a severe logic of punching, as demonstrable as old-fashioned mathematics. When I walked into Stillman's gymnasium one day, for example, Freddie was tutoring a pale, big-boned boy at least as strong as a policeman's horse. ("Strength, most undoubtedly, is what a boxer ought to start out with," wrote Pierce Egan, the Holinshed of the London prize ring, "but without art he will succeed but poorly.") "Throw a left hook," Freddie would say. The boy would pull his left elbow back to a line even with his hip, and Freddie would slap him on the left side of the face and push. "What happened?" Freddie would ask. "I don't know," the boy would say. And Freddie would say, "All right, throw a left hook." The boy would pull his left elbow back again and they would go through the same performance. When Freddie finally saw that the Socratic method was no go, he said wearily, "You dropped your shoulder and I come over it is what happened. Hook with your elbow in." He demonstrated what he meant. After he had sent the boy upstairs to do body exercises, he said to me, "He had a couple of fights in Canada, can you imagine? Up there it is like the amateurs." The next time I visited the gym, the boy wasn't there. He was back in Canada, I imagine.

It is the psyche that makes Freddie and Whitey sweat. Like authors, fighters of exemplary moral quality may be bores. And fighters who do a lot of beautiful things nobody else does may be children emotionally. The good boys get married. The bad ones get in jams. It is hard to tell which may mean more trouble for a trainer. "The worst trouble is assorted maniacs," Whitey says, "because you never know when it is going to break out." A fellow Whitey and Freddie know named Maurie Waxman had a fighter who could move almost as well as Benny Leonard, but he habitually lost his prey. As soon as the other fellow showed signs of damage, Waxman's fighter would back away. One night, in the ring with a tough Puerto Rican, Waxman's fighter hit his opponent in the first round, at which, according to Whitey, "the guy's eye come up like a grape." After that, Waxman's fighter refrained so studiously from hitting the eye that the other fellow made up much of the ground he had lost. Just before the last round, Waxman leaned over his fighter and said, "Julie, I ain't cruel, but just a *touch* on that eye would do it." The fighter looked up at his manager and said, "Maurie, I'm sorry, but I can't. I'm allergic to blood." In relating this to me, Whitey said, "That must of been a nice time to find *that* out." But where you suspect genius, you've got to go along. A harsh insistence on conventional methods may spoil an original style.

I have known Whitey for more than twenty years (he had been a trainer for fifteen years before that), and by now I can tell from looking at him whether he thinks genius is lurking just the other side of the horizon. Four years ago he was desperate for talent. Prosperity had ruined the future, he said; any kid just out of school could get a job for sixty dollars a week, and as a consequence dilettantism was rife in boxing. The faintest frown of fortune would send a boy back to well-paid labor. Boys boxed only to attain social prestige. "Garbage," Whitey said then, when I asked him about the season's vintage. But this spring he was wearing the expression of an editor who has found two new poets and a woman novelist with an acid talent. The mild recession was not solely responsible, he said, although it had made the boys more serious about boxing as a vocation. He and Freddie had three good fighters training at once—two lightweights and one around '30 (130 pounds) who could do '26 to qualify as a featherweight. They also had this animal, Whitey said, who ran fifteen or twenty miles a day on the road and would box fifteen rounds every day if they would let him. Whitey was in the position of the late Max Perkins, with a handful of good established writers and a Thomas Wolfe in training in Brooklyn.

I asked him how big the animal was, and he said it was a colored heavyweight, six feet one and a half and over '90. "His name is Tommy Jackson," he said. "Until you know him, you don't know what you got to put up with." Freddie joined us and said it was a shame they had television. "This kid is still two or three years away," he said, "but how can a learner eat when television's killed off most of the small clubs? The only money is the feature, so they got to fight features or quit. This fellow had fifteen fights and then they made him with Rex Layne and Clarence Henry. Dog eat dog." I asked how the animal had made out against Layne and Henry, and Whitey said he had won big, but the trouble was now he had to keep on meeting name fighters. "How does he fight?" I asked. "He throws a lot of leather," Whitey said. "Like a noctopus!" Whitey is a small man—he used to be what he calls a bantyweight—with a rosy face and white eyelashes. His face and features are small in proportion to his head, and this gives him the look of a medium-old baby, which is disconcerting when he hasn't shaved for a couple of days. "He takes the best punch in the business," Freddie said. "The best thing he has is endurance." Freddie, an ex-featherweight, is bigger than Whitey and has a broken nose. I gathered from the two of them that Jackson won his fights by inducing exhaustion in his opponents, who collapsed like men worn out from slapping at horseflies. He stopped them without knocking them down.

As he talked about Jackson, Whitey looked a trifle self-conscious. "He is a ninstinctive fighter," he said. "He imitates what the other fellow does." "Can't you teach him anything?" I asked, and Freddie said, "Yeah, we are teaching him not to jab with his palms up, which he did so in case he changed his mind he would be ready to uppercut." Shortly after that I read in the paper that Jackson had stopped a fellow named Bucceroni; it was another case of exhaustion.

The first time I saw Jackson, it was on television and he was fighting a small heavyweight named Jimmy Slade, a trickster. Jackson did what I had been told to expect, but Slade didn't collapse. He cuffed Jackson around and made him look silly. I thought this might be good for Jackson, as his managers might now drop him back into his own sort of competition, where he would have a chance to practice. Instead, they got him a match in

Madison Square Garden with a fellow named Norkus, whom he stopped, although he didn't knock him down. Managers have to eat, too. But they didn't take Slade again. Meanwhile the sports writers had adopted Jackson—whom they called Hurricane—as a dull-day subject. They said he couldn't read or write, made up songs, had a punch called the double uppercut, and blamed the Slade defeat on too much fresh air inhaled during roadwork. What attracted them most, I suspect, was the recurrent sports-page myth of the man who can do a complicated thing without learning how. It is an old dream of childhood, and, while it never comes true, people like to read about it.

At Stillman's, after the Norkus fight, I was puzzled to find that Whitey and Freddie themselves were taking Jackson seriously. At least they said they were. The Slade defeat, Freddie said, had been due to an intense but ephemeral romance, followed by a debauch. "Jackson drunk five bottles of Coca-Cola before going into the ring," he said. "Naturally, that slowed him up starting. But in the last round he was getting to Slade." "A nanimal," Whitey said. "You don't know what you got to put up with." But now Whitey and Freddie had persuaded him to swear off soft drinks until after fights, they said, and his mother had broken up the romance. "Mentally, he was below par for Slade," Freddie said, opening new vistas of horror. "He's better now." We stood beside Stillman's No. 1 ring and watched Jackson work, and also the three good boys—Arthur Persley, a colored lightweight, who had an engagement with an Algerian fighter in Atlantic City; Davey Gallardo, a California-Mexican feather, who had a bout coming up in Philadelphia; and Cisco Andrada, another Mexican-American, from Compton, a suburb of Los Angeles. Andrada, like Persley, is a lightweight. He was going to make his New York debut at St. Nick's, Whitey said, and he earnestly advised me to be present. "You will want to say you was there," he said. "He's got everything." All three young men, I noticed, boxed in accordance with the classical verities. They punctuated jabs with hooks, and hooks with crosses, and they uppercut with one hand at a time.

After the workout we all went back to the honeycomb of beaverboard partitions that constitutes the private deluxe dressing rooms at Stillman's. Each one is ornamented by a large sign, reading, "WASH YOUR CLOTHES — BY ORDER OF THE ATHLETIC COMMISSION." It was a hot day, and Whitey stripped to his shorts and rubbed his charges, one by one—a chore that he usually delegates to his assistant, a fat man named Coco. When Whitey takes over, it means he thinks he has something special. Gallardo had been working against extra-tall sparring partners, because the boy he was going to fight in Philadelphia was tall, and also, from the long view, because Sandy Saddler, the world's featherweight champion, is abnormally tall for his weight. Andrada had been working with strong boys, since his opponent at St. Nick's was a crowding type who was expected to have a few pounds on him. Persley, Gallardo, and Andrada are boys who have been to high school, and, as Whitey says, "they talk nice." No maniacs. Whitey kneaded them with esteem.

When Whitey got Jackson on the table, though, the animal began to squeal and laugh. "I'm so ticklish," he said. "Maybe that's why I fight so good." He has a small head, a long, cylindrical torso of no great diameter for a heavyweight, legs like a high jumper's, and long, powerful arms. His skin is a dark-plum color. "I was born under a pine tree," he said. "Maybe that's why I fight so good." I had heard he was raised at Rockaway Beach, where most boys skip school to go swimming, so I asked him if he liked to swim in the surf. "Not me," he said. "I got drowned in an undertow." Subsequent answers were no more illuminating. He looked disturbed, and then the reason for his preoccupation appeared. "Freddie," he said, "get me my wallet. Those nosy rats always lookin' in it." Brown brought him the wallet, and he sat up and spread some money on his knee. "The money is all there

Hurricane," Freddie said. "Twenty-four dollars." Hurricane shuffled the bills cunningly and said, "That's correct. Twenty-four." Whitey slapped him on the back and told him to turn over, and Jackson turned over, putting the wallet under his belly. After Jackson had dressed and gone I asked the partners what they thought he would do to Rocky Marciano if the two should meet. "He could cut him to pieces," Whitey said, and Freddie nodded. Now I know why a lot of the books that get published do. Optimism is the besetting disease of all lovers of the arts.

The I.B.C., however, had already made Jackson with Nino Valdes, a Cuban heavyweight whose personality is more arresting than his workmanship, which is heavy and conventional, like a Spanish dessert. Valdes is very big—he generally fights at about two hundred and eight pounds—and highly experienced, but he has a reputation for laziness. Encountering Charlie Goldman, who edits Marciano, I asked him for an *expertise* on the forthcoming Jackson–Valdes fight, and he said that the Cuban's geniality had led people to underrate him. "He does a few good things, but after he does them, he loafs in between," Charlie said. "Jackson won't let him loaf, so Valdes will kill him."

The next time I saw Jackson was in the offices of the New York State Athletic Commission, at 226 West 47th Street, a few days before the fight. Many of the fights in the Garden in summer are virtually studio shows for television, but the I.B.C. hoped to get some flesh-and-blood customers for this one. Valdes and Jackson had been sent to out-of-town training camps to underline the significance of the match; if Hurricane butchered the Cuban, he would be considered worthy of a fight with Marciano for the world's championship, a press release said. Now the pair had been brought into town for a physical examination, although both fighters were as healthy as mandrills.

When I entered the waiting room outside the office of the Commission's medical examiner I saw Sammy Golden, one of the three men who split Jackson's contract—thirty-three and a third per cent each way. Golden is a diminished, skinny old manager who hasn't had any luck since a fighter named Georgie Ward retired in 1923. Ward was a real good welterweight and is now a cop in New Jersey. I like to talk to Golden, because I know a fellow who used to fight Ward on odd Saturdays in Boston. (On even Thursdays they would fight in Newark.) This time we had barely exchanged greetings when a man named Lippy Breidbart came up behind me and plucked at my sleeve. Breidbart also owned a third of the animal. He is a fattish man who dresses sharp.

I asked Golden whether it was true that Jackson could neither read nor write.

"Ask me," Breidbart said. "I'm the manager. Every time I look at a paper, Sammy is making a quotation. He is strictly Georgie Ward, he lives in the past. The answer is Jackson can read and write, but not good."

"*You're* the manager?" Golden said with spirit. "We should never have took you in."

"Shut your mouth!" Breidbart said. "You're an old man." His tone implied that only Golden's decrepitude protected him.

At this point, Frank Leonetti, the third owner, came up and turned on Breidbart. Golden withdrew to a far corner of the room and made faces. Leonetti is a bulky, bull-necked man, a division superintendent on a bus line, and it was he who discovered Jackson down at Rockaway Beach. "When you make a move, you don't tell us," he said. "You think that's nice?"

"That's a perposterous statement!" Breidbart said.

"Any time I made a perposterous statement, you let me know about it!" Leonetti shouted, shoving Breidbart with his belly.

Breidbart was the manager of record, which means he was the one authorized by the Athletic Commission to make matches and sign contracts for the fighter. He was now advancing the contention that he also had the sole right to make statements. Jackson, who had joined us, put his hands on the shoulders of the two quarreling men. "Why can't you guys get along?" he asked. "I'm the fighter. I'm the one should do the worrying, not you." He turned to Freddie Brown, who had brought him into town on a bus from his training quarters at Greenwood Lake, New York. "I don't like it here," Jackson said. "I want to go back to the mountains, shoot a mouse. No mouses here."

"You can't go back now," Brown said in a soothing voice. Then he turned to me. "Hurricane found a new interest," he said. "He shoots rats with a twenty-two. He calls them mice."

"Mouses," the fighter corrected him. "I shoot them between the eyes." He seemed depressed.

"He finds them on the dump," Freddie said.

When Jackson saw that Freddie wasn't going to take him back to the mountains, he wandered away and sat down, morosely staring at his feet.

"I don't know where he gets the energy," said Freddie, who looked underweight. "The hardest worker I ever seen before him is Marciano, but Marciano works steady and then he rests good. Also he eats good. Jackson don't sleep enough and he don't eat enough. These boys that ain't used to good food, it don't agree with them."

"What kind of food is he used to?" I asked.

"He wants hot dogs," Freddie said. "And also ice cream and pie. We got him to accept hamburgers as a substitute, but you got to watch him all the time. He fell out of a canoe which I had told him not to get into it, and he can't swim good. He wants to ride a horse, he thinks he is Eddie Arcaro. And he could easy shoot himself instead of them rats." Freddie shuddered.

Valdes and his manager, Bobby Gleason, had observed the ruckus between the three owners with polite amusement, like members of Miss Hewitt's Classes visiting a school for delinquent children. "The board of stragedy is having a tough time," Gleason said when I walked over to them. Gleason is a stocky man who runs a gymnasium for prizefighters in the Bronx. Valdes is the color of blond mahogany, and his shoulders look as wide as a door. He was wearing a raspberry steamer cap, a pink silk shirt (18 neck, 37 sleeves), and white pants. Gold teeth provided extra flash. Valdes and Gleason communicate in a lingua franca of English, Neapolitan, and Spanish, and Gleason interprets for others when he thinks it advisable. "Mucho wise guy, Bobby," Valdes says.

When Valdes took the pink shirt off in the medical examiner's office, we could see that he was wearing a gold chain with an amulet around his eighteen-inch neck, which he considers his most impressive feature. He got the neck by carrying three-hundred-and-thirty-pound sacks of sugar on his head when he was a boy. It makes him look slightly pinheaded. Dr. Vincent Nardiello, the examining physician, had the fighters spread their arms, so that he could measure their reach, and it made a good shot for the photographers, who ordered them to go through numerous repeats. Valdes said something in Spanish to Gleason. "He wants to know which one they are measuring for a casket," Gleason told me. The Cuban was six feet three, an inch and a half taller than Jackson, but Jackson had longer arms. Jackson, who had continued to look glum, cheered up for a minute when Dr. Nardiello allowed him to listen to his own heart through the stethoscope. "It sounds good!" he shouted. "Solid!" But soon he was pouting again. In the elevator, going down to the street, he closed his eyes and allowed his chin to droop on his chest, while he leaned his weight on Freddie Brown. "I don't like three men over me," he said. "If you don't take me back to the mountains, I'm going back alone."

Two days later, I heard that Jackson had run away from the mountains, because Freddie wouldn't let him ride a horse, and had reported to Whitey at Stillman's. Whitey had stayed there to handle the three bright boys. Jackson was like a child of divorce running from one parent to the other. When Jackson got to Stillman's, Whitey told me afterward, he said, "This is where I feel at home. No country air in my belly."

On the night of the fight, I was more excited than I had been before any match for years, and for purely subjective reasons. If the animal won, it meant that the Sweet Science was mere guesswork, requiring not even a specialized intelligence. It would be quite a different thing from the victories of immortals like Griffo and Dutch Sam, who were irresponsibles only when they were *outside* the ring. There have been plenty of musicians and painters who didn't have much sense otherwise, and Dostoevski was a political imbecile. I had nothing against Jackson *qua* Jackson, and I wished Whitey and Freddie all kinds of luck with their more conventional clients, but if the animal could beat even a fair fighter, it meant that two hundred and fifty years of painfully acquired experience had been lost to the human race; science was a washout and art a vanity, and Freddie and Whitey had queered their own game.

The preliminaries were unusually good and, from my point of view, reassuring. A tough-looking middleweight from Yorkville, named Schulz, knocked out a boy from Chicago with a short, economical right to the jaw—one out of the book. A dark, knowledgeable featherweight from Harlem prevailed tactically and strategically over a Fighting Newsboy from Columbus, Ohio, who punched in wider arcs. The Fighting Newsboy did not attempt to upset the artistic canon; he simply operated too near its edge. The ancient laws appeared still to be operative when the principals entered the ring for the feature bout. We sang the national anthem, as usual.

Whitey, Freddie, and Breidbart all came into the ring with their primitive. Jackson weighed a hundred and ninety and a half, which indicated that he had overdone his self-induced training sessions. Valdes's weight was announced as two hundred and four, which showed that he had done more work than customary, but not too much. In the first round Valdes, boxing straight up, moved forward methodically and punched at Jackson's body. Jackson, fidgeting about, did not accomplish anything. A Cuban sitting next to me, possibly a political exile, said happily, "Well, Valdes gets cut up tonight, no?" Valdes is for Batista. There was no sign that it would happen.

Jackson stood up in his corner halfway through the one-minute rest period and did what gym teachers call "running in place," at the same time waving his arms. When the bell rang, he rushed out to meet Valdes, dabbing and slapping. Valdes took aim like a bowler and knocked him through the ropes, at which point, since Jackson's body was very nearly horizontal, the referee should have started a count, in my opinion, even though the lower strand prevented the animal's body from touching the canvas. Valdes—"mucho nice boy," as he would have said—turned and went to a neutral corner. The referee disentangled Jackson and upended him, and Valdes knocked him down again a couple of times. Each time Jackson fell—he did even that grotesquely, landing once sitting, once kneeling—he bounced up at the count of two or three. But the referee, because of a fairly new rule of the New York State Athletic Commission, had to stand in front of him and count eight before permitting the opponents to resume action. According to a collateral rule, if one boxer knocks the other down three times in one round, the referee has to stop the fight. (This is well intentioned but silly, because a boxer like Jackson, who doesn't know what to do with his feet, can be knocked down several times without being hurt much, while a fellow who is helpless but remains upright takes a beating without respite, the kind that is most likely to end in permanent injury. It has long been within the referee's discretion to stop a fight at any time, and that's the way the matter should have been left.) By my reckoning—and I was not alone—the second knock-

down was really the third, and the referee, Al Berl, should consequently have stopped the fight there if he was going to be a pre-
cisionist. But Berl let them go to it again. Jackson was fluttering
like a winged bird, making a difficult though harmless target,
and Valdes, conscious of the three-knockdown rule, was following him about, eager to bring him down, even for a half second,
before the round ended. Valdes has had many fights, has always
finished strong, and was in good condition, but he seemed at this
point to be heaving. Perhaps it was merely emotion, for he could
not have anticipated a chance to knock off work so early. Several
times he aimed as deliberately as if he were about to hurl a sack
of sugar at a toad but missed. Finally he missed Jackson's head
with his right fist and, in recovering, hit him on the back of the
neck with his forearm, as big around as a normal collar. He may
simply have been trying to keep himself from falling. Anyway,
Jackson's knees hit the floor, and Berl, perhaps to compensate for
the time he hadn't counted, flung his arms wide in token of
a technical knockout. Jackson promptly jumped up. In Pierce
Egan's time the victor might have offered to knock the loser out
again to satisfy him, but that was before the Athletic Commission. (I know an old boxer who was awarded a fight on a foul because the other fellow was biting him. My friend was enjoying
himself, so he said he would go on with the match if the fellow
would promise to stop biting. The opponent promised, but he
didn't keep his word. "Maybe he hadn't ate lately," my man says.)
Gleason towed Valdes into the corner of the ring farthest from
Jackson and, snuggling against his flank, make him hold up his
right hand for the benefit of the photographers, who got a picture
like one of those circus shots taken under the elephant's trunk.
From the way Valdes was grinning, he had a pretty good program lined up for the rest of the evening.

Meanwhile Jackson was standing in his corner, shaking his
head and refusing to leave the ring. He demanded the privilege
of being hit some more. I could see Whitey and Freddie and a

policeman arguing with him, and then they were joined by Dr. Nardiello, for whom I imagine Jackson has a lot of respect since the incident of the stethoscope. At last they persuaded him to leave.

After an early ending like that most of the customers stay to watch the four-round "emergency" bout that is put on as a postscript. I watched a couple of rounds of it myself. One of the principals had been an early professional opponent of Jackson's a scant twenty months back. On the basis of what I saw, I can't figure how Jackson beat him.

The show had drawn forty-five hundred cash customers—possibly six thousand in all, including deadheads, but even that is only a third of the Garden's capacity, and there was no trouble getting around. The evening seemed so incomplete that I decided to visit Jackson's dressing room, off the corridor on the north side of the arena, to hear the losing faction's story. There were perhaps twenty colored people outside the door, including several attractive girls. As I approached, the door flew open, and Jackson, dressed and carrying a suitcase, dashed through the group and ran up the stairs that lead to an exit on 50th Street, about midway between Eighth and Ninth Avenues. "Tommy, come back!" one of the girls yelled. I followed Jackson out, not knowing quite what he might do, and ran slap into a storm, of which I had been unaware. It was a short, intense squall that had just hit the city, and it seemed to me an exaggerated reaction to the defeat of Tommy Jackson. To him, however, marching off into the rain, it may have seemed a fitting recognition of the occasion. He turned south on Ninth, and my curiosity was not strong enough to draw me more than a short distance into the rain after him. Then I began working my way back toward Eighth, taking advantage of intervening marquees and saloons for cover. At Muller's, on the north side of the street, they have Münchner beer on tap, and I sheltered there longer than at any other place. By the time I got around to the main entrance of the

Garden the storm had died to a drizzle, but there were still a couple of dozen fight people under the big marquee talking about the night's events. I saw a second named Izzy Blanc, who had worked a pair of the minor bouts, and asked him if he knew what had happened to Jackson. "He's walking around the Garden in the rain," he said. "He's been around ten times since I've been standing here." We waited, and within a minute Jackson swung by—silent, head forward, looking like a priest who has found he has no vocation or like an actor hissed from the stage.

I asked Izzy if he had seen the disputed knockdown, but he, a diplomat, offered a good alibi. "After the second knockdown I was on my way to the dressing room," he said. "I had the emergency." He meant he had been engaged to second one of the boxers in the final four-rounder, and he had sensed that it was going to be needed earlier than anybody had expected. "I had my back to the ring," he said.

The rain was easy to ignore now, and Izzy said he was going to walk up Eighth, stopping by a couple of bars where he might meet other fight people. "We'll probably find Whitey at the Neutral Corner," he said. The Neutral is a bar on the southwest corner of 55th and Eighth, and when we got there, Whitey was on a stool smoking a cigar and having a glass of beer. "If they want to rune boxing," he said, "that's the way to do it. He wrastled him to the ground just when the kid was hitting his stride."

"His what?" I said.

"Sure," Bimstein said. "He was just beginning to come on good."

"How about the first three knockdowns?" I asked.

"There was only one knockdown," Whitey said. He rejected my proposition that Berl had let the animal off the time he got knocked through the ropes. "And the second thing he called a knockdown, that was a push, too," Whitey said. He appeared calm, not bitter, and acted as if it were a matter of little moment to him if the Commission wanted to take the bread out of its own mouth. "He was just sizing the fellow up," he said. "And the fellow trips him, and boom, Berl stops the fight." I began to suspect we hadn't seen the same fight that evening.

Soirée Intime

While reading the newspaper *Froissarts'* stories the day after the first Marciano–Charles fight in the summer of 1954, I noticed that there was to be another bout that evening, at Madison Square Garden. This one had been kept so deep a secret during the days leading up to the big match that my discovery made me feel I was getting in on something like a stag show. Even in Tex Rickard's palmy days as a promoter at the Garden, he would never have ventured a show on the night following one of his own ball-park promotions. The theory was that the average fight fan, having spent his money for a big ticket, would have nothing left for a little ticket the same week. This card, however, had a television sponsor, the Gillette Razor Blade Company, and so was economically independent. (The I.B.C. had kept the Marciano–Charles bout off television in the metropolitan district, which had undoubtedly helped the gate.)

The Garden card looked fairly promising, on paper. In the main bout, Orlando Zulueta, the lightweight champion of Cuba, was to meet a fellow named Johnny Gonsalves, out of Oakland, California, who, according to the brief press notices, ranked as one of the best lightweights in the United States. (After what I saw, I hoped he wasn't.) I had never seen Gonsalves, but in 1948 I had seen Zulueta fight in Havana, in the Cuban equivalent of the Garden. That had been for the featherweight championship of Cuba, which has sent out some excellent fighting men in the lighter classes, and his opponent had been an established Havana star named Acevedo, a light-skinned Cuban with a sandy mustache, exceedingly *caballero*. I remembered Zulueta—a tall, thin, dark young Negro with a beautifully educated left hand. He had been on his way up, and Acevedo at the top of the downgrade. The hall was packed with a noisy crowd, jeering and imploring. It was carnival time, very gay. Zulueta had made a fool of Acevedo for a couple of rounds. Then, affected by the carnival spirit, he had stopped stabbing and started slugging with the older man. This had gone well at first, but then Acevedo had nailed him with a few good punches. Most of the crowd was with the old champion, and Zulueta's seconds were yelling frantically. Without understanding technical Spanish, I had known what they were saying: "Stay away from him and box!" He had gone back to boxing, survived the round, and given his man a good pasting. At the end, the judges awarded the decision to Acevedo—as rank a miscarriage of justice as I have seen outside of the Dominican Republic. I remembered that Acevedo's manager carried him around the ring, pickaback, seven times.

Since there was no large sum involved as admission fee, I decided to attend the Garden bout as a customer, a *cochon de payant*. The first preliminary was, as usual scheduled to go on at eight-thirty. I arrived at the Eighth Avenue entrance to the Garden at a quarter to nine and found the place deserted, except for three men at the orange-drink stand in the lobby and four more talking baseball under the marquee. The marquee at least confirmed the report that a fight was supposed to take place that evening. Scouting around among the ticket windows. I found one that was open. The man behind it was reading the next day's entries at Aqueduct, but he looked up when I said "Pardon me." I asked if he had a good ringside seat left, and he looked at me a bit oddly and said. "Second row, right in the center." I asked him how much, and he said "Eight dollars," in a tone that implied he expected me to go away. He may have thought I had mistaken the place for a movie house.

As I entered the door to the Garden proper, I thought I saw the statue of Joe Gans, the old lightweight champion, smile gratefully. The ticket taker, one of the gruff old retired cops who usually look at me as if I were personally responsible for their hurting feet, said, "Nice weather we're having, ain't it?" The program sellers, who ordinarily snarl at you if you can't find the right change, looked so happy to see me that I handed one of them a twenty-dollar bill, just to test his reaction. He counted out the change like a little gentleman, saying, "Nineteen-seventy-five. Right? I'm sorry I have to give you so many singles, Mister." At the beer bar, on other occasions so crowded, I could have been served instantly. Unfortunately, I wasn't thirsty. In the inner lobby, I saw nobody I recognized from the fight mob; no self-respecting character would accept a free ticket that was easy to get. Murray Goodman, the press agent for the I.B.C., entered from the arena, recognized me, and looked as if I had caught him in a humiliating situation. "I gotta be here," he said. "It's my job."

"Is it going to be a hell of a fight?" I asked.

He looked at me suspiciously. "They must think it'll sell razor blades," he said.

A sallow bystander said hello, and Mr. Goodman introduced him to me as Hymie Wallman, Zulueta's manager. Mr. Wallman had been watching the door, and I hoped for his sake that he had not been trying to calculate the gate, because nobody had come in since me. "What percentage are you working on?" I asked, to cheer him up.

"What difference what percentage?" Mr. Wallman inquired bitterly. "You kidding?"

"Hymie isn't doing so bad," Mr. Goodman said cheerily. "He

gets four thousand for his fighter from television. The other fighter gets four thousand, too. The gate receipts are like a tip."

"Yeah? Wonderful," said Mr. Wallman. "You were up at that fight last night?" he asked me. I said I had been, and he said, "If this fight tonight wasn't on television, it would draw fifty thousand dollars." Wiping a tear from the corner of my eye, I said good-by.

No sound was audible from the interior, and I supposed that for some reason the preliminaries hadn't begun on schedule. When I got inside, though, I could see two heavyweights in the ring, belaboring each other in a cathedral hush. It was a private fight. The ushers, who at this point outnumbered the customers, treated me with the courtesy that obtains at the best funeral chapels. One waved me to another, each walking a few steps of the way with me. The usher who accompanied me on the final leg showed me my seat, which was indeed in the center of the second row, on the Fiftieth Street side of the ring. There was one man already seated in the row, and the usher suggested to me politely, "If you went around the other way, you wouldn't disturb him." I went around, and found I had the seat next to my fellow patron. It was like the meeting of Robinson Crusoe and Friday. He had been waiting for an audience.

A round ended, and the referee stopped the bout, because one of the men was outclassed. "I could seeyit," my neighbor said. "It was obvious." In the next bout, a fat, pink boy from Florida, who must have been the pride of the boxing coach at some Y.M.C.A., was in with a Negro welterweight who was not inclined to be severe. I fancied I could hear the Florida boy counting to himself, "One-two, one-two," as he hit out nervously. The colored boy would slap him in the belly and push him away. The white boy was off balance constantly, and my expert got the idea that the colored boy was employing some kind of illegal jujitsu on him. "Seeyit?" he would say. "Seeyit? Why don't they get a referee? It's so obvious." The bout went eight rounds, a tribute to the colored boy's forbearance, and my man was almost tearful with indignation when the judges gave the colored boy the decision.

The next bout brought together two tough young middleweights from Brooklyn. I had heard of one of them, Ray Drake, who once beat Floyd Patterson in the amateurs. After that, Patterson went on to win an Olympic title, and he is a good professional now. Drake has a choirboy face, wavy hair, and big, powerful calves—the kind that, when you see them on a fighter, you know he is going to depend on a lot. Small torso, big legs, you know he will keep moving. Big torso, short legs, he has to be a slugger. Big torso *and* big legs, he's a heavyweight. The other fellow, Rinzy (for Rizzerio) Nocero, had the big torso. When Nocero came up the aisle, he had with him Freddie Brown, who had patched Marciano's eye the night before; Whitey Bimstein, Freddie's partner in the training and seconding business; and Jimmy Coco, their colleague who carries the bucket. It was a corner strong enough for a champion, and it indicated that somebody, somewhere, thought Nocero had a future. It turned out no. They all looked self-conscious, because they are sociable fellows and they felt lonely. A cowbell clanged in the obscurity, and a few brave Brooklyn voices called on Ray and Rinzy. It was the kind of match that in a small neighborhood club would have produced a near riot. But the few hundred fans who had followed the boys from Brooklyn were lost in the empty vastnesses. Fight writers I knew had arrived, and were taking up their posts behind the typewriter ledges around the ring. I felt sheepish alone with the expert in the cash section. It looked as if I were spying on my acquaintances.

At the bell, Nocero rushed in and threw a wicked left hook. Because of Marciano, all the Italian fighters now want to be bulls. When Johnny Dundee, fast and flashy, was the Italian idol, the kids from Italian neighborhoods were all bouncing off the ropes. Drake would jab Nocero silly, cross the right, hit him between the eyes with the top of his angelic head, and then try to tie him up. Seeing Nocero struggling to throw him off, my expert got the idea that it was jujitsu again. Nocero was just trying to get his arms free. The public conscience had found a fellow expert in the row in front of us, which was just beginning to fill up. This second expert had a voice like the Honorable Ray H. Jenkins.

"Seeyit?" my man would scream. "The dirty dog!"

The gentleman in front would say, "Whah, that referee would let him carry a stick of dahnamaht into the ring and hit th'othuh fellow ovuh the haid with it."

All this time, Nocero was catching elbows and heads, and Drake was lying on him. I thought Drake was murdering Nocero, but the two experts thought Drake was being abused. "Seeyit? Seeyit?" the first expert would yell when Nocero swung himself around with Drake leaning on him, as in the start of a dance team's whirl, with the girl hanging on the man's neck. But Rinzy is a strong boy, and he took some of the bounce out of the Drake legs by belting their owner in his narrow waist. The experts outguessed me on the decision, though. They said Nocero would get it, and he did. What we agreed on was that it was a bad decision. The next time I saw Freddie and Whitey, they said Nocero had deserved to win, but I think they had a *parti pris*. "Anyway," Whitey said, "they're bound to fight again." Between rounds, they had used everything on their boy but an iron lung, but Whitey said the kid had been feeling great.

After that, the main bout was mild, but it had its moments of beauty. Señor Zulueta, older, more somber than when I had last seen him, with the weight of maturity on his bones—he went 135—has no more rash moments. Perhaps the gay breath of carnival could again inspire them, but I doubt it. He is like one of those vaudeville jugglers who never changed their routine, or Braque, who paints only little dead fish. He jabs, with exquisite deftness, and blocks the counter by turning his forearm, so his opponent's glove strikes his elbow. If he misses the jab, as the most accomplished juggler sometimes misses a trick, he follows with the elbow, a more effective weapon. So, just as in the case of the juggler, you don't know whether he has missed on purpose. With his right he hits just as accurately, but without putting much behind it. He does not care to advance his greyhound waist to the proximity of a destructive fist. He is reputed to take a good punch to the head, but he seldom has to. When he clinches, it is in the position of a man making a polite bow, with his body in the shape of a question mark. He has weathered many fights with many tough boys since that night in Havana. Nobody hurts him, and he hurts nobody, although he can be humiliating. He gets a lot of points, because he keeps sticking. I can imagine him making a fine fight with a rushing, aggressive fighter—picador and bull. He is no matador, because he never kills. It is a style that makes demands on the bull, too. In the Garden that night, Zulueta had no opportunity to please, because his bull wouldn't fight. Gonsalves is a tall, skinny boy, though not as tall as Zulueta, and he stands with his body straight up, one foot far forward and the other far back. He holds his elbows almost together, and his forearms, too, are straight up. How he would get out of this interesting position if he had to—perhaps in case of an air raid—I will never know, because I will not see him again if I can help it. That night he didn't try. Whenever Zulueta delivered more than the union scale of jabs in any one round, Gonsalves would hit his gloves together in well-controlled fury. If Zulueta had ever knocked anybody out, Gonsalves' caution would be understandable, although no hero should take a match he can't think of a way to try to win. The fact is, though, that Gonsalves will never find a safer opponent to take a chance with.

A fellow who had sneaked into the row behind me began to sing "*Zulueta, gentil Zulueta*," to the tune of "Alouette." My expert yelled, "Whyn't ya go back to the Pacific Coast altogether, Gonsalves!" The bout reached its incomprehensible conclusion, like a play with three first acts, and Zulueta received a unanimous decision. I didn't have to worry about any rush going home. There was no crowding in the aisles, and I hadn't had to endure any commercials. It was like belonging to a small private club for listening to chamber music, and I decided to ask Mr. Goodman to put me on the free list when his series of sponsored recitals began again.

The Neutral Corner Art Group

In the year 1814 the Castle Tavern, a pub in Holborn, came under the management of Tom Belcher, a scientific pugilist whose "mildness of deportment and gentlemanly behavior entitled him to the peculiar consideration and attention of the *fancy* in general." (I quote from *Boxiana*, the *Mille et Une Nuits* of the London prize ring.) The institution from then on became a resort of the cognoscenti, or knowing coves. Of the Castle while Belcher held the license, Egan wrote; "Propriety is the order of the day, and no man appears more scrupulously exact in exerting his rights as a landlord . . . than Tom Belcher. . . . The inquiring stranger, whom curiosity might have tempted to take a *peep* at the scientific pugilists, feels not the least restraint in visiting the Castle Tavern."

I am reminded of Egan's puff whenever I visit a bar at Eighth Avenue and 55th Street known as the Neutral Corner Cocktail Lounge and Restaurant, Steaks and Chops Our Specialty, Meet Your Favorite Fighters and Managers Here. The Neutral, as its familiars call it, is a few doors north of Stillman's gymnasium and is patronized chiefly by fight managers, trainers, and boxers, who are locked out of Stillman's between three and five o'clock every afternoon, and by ex-boxers, who favor a place where somebody is likely to recognize them. There are two training sessions a day at Stillman's—from noon to three and from five-thirty to seven. The second one is a concession to the economic difficulties now afflicting the Sweet Science; an increasing number of boxers have to hold daytime jobs to keep going, and can work out only after hours. The boxers in the Neutral, being in training, do not drink; they eat on credit and occasionally, when their managers endow them with spending money, play Shuffle Alley, a table game in which one slides metal discs in the direction of electrically controlled tenpins. Because they are temperate and of equable disposition, they seldom raise their voices. The trainers feel constrained to offer an example of sobriety; bottled beer and a cigar are about their speed. The managers are afraid to drink, lest some other manager outwit them, and the ex-boxers are usually too broke to tipple. Any unseemly words that may be heard in the place invariably emanate from some socially insecure sightseer without credentials in any record book. Otherwise, a Belcherian propriety reigns.

The scheme of decoration, like the atmosphere, has a Regency flavor. At the Castle Tavern, Egan wrote, "The numerous sporting subjects, elegantly framed and glazed, have rather an imposing effect upon the entrance of the visitor, among whom may be witnessed animated likenesses of the renowned Jem Belcher [Tom's brother] and his daring competitor, that inordinate glutton, Burke . . . the Champion, Cribb, and his tremendous opponent, Molineaux . . . Tom Belcher and his rival, the Jew phenomenon, Dutch Sam . . . with a variety of other subjects, including one of the dog 'Trusty,' the champion of the canine race in fifty battles." The boxers whose likenesses cover the Neutral's walls are of more recent vintages, ranging from John L. Sullivan to one of the bartenders—Tony Janiro, a talented welterweight who retired only a few years ago. The pictures are photographs, instead of hand-tinted engravings, but the faces and torsos are in-

terchangeable with those of 1814. Only Trusty, the champion of
the canine race, has no opposite number on the Neutral's walls.*
Dogfights have gone out of fashion. Janiro has a didactic as well
as a utilitarian function; trainers point him out to young fighters
as a horrible example. He failed to take his profession with suffi-
cient seriousness, and consequently he never became a champion
and is now working union hours. Tony doesn't seem to mind.

I was in the Neutral late one afternoon, enjoying an instructive
conversation with Whitey Bimstein, a Mr. Chips of the boxing
metier, who was showing me a pound of metal slugs he had con-
fiscated from a pair of his charges, upstate boys, who had intended to use them in coin-box telephones. "They never been
away from home before except maybe overnight and they don't
want to get homesick," Mr. Bimstein said. "So they bring the
slugs along to call their girl friends. Crazy kids. They don't know
they can get into trouble that way." He smiled with sympathetic
indulgence for youthful sentiment. "Just when their manager
gets them a match, they could land in the pokey. 'Write your
broad a postcard,' I told them. 'She can wait.' "

Another notable educator present—Charlie Goldman, Rocky
Marciano's trainer—said, "One of the troubles with fighters now
is they don't start before they're interested in dames. When they
used to start at ten, eleven years old, they didn't have the distraction. By the time they did, they knew something." Mr. Goldman, who wears a bowler, bow tie, and chesterfield, in the best
tradition of the Jimmy Walker era, is the Beau Brummell, as well
as one of the Nestors, of the Neutral. He was a barnstorming fly-
weight when he was fourteen, fighting feature bouts in places
like Savannah, Georgia, and he believes that as the twig is bent,

* This is no longer true. A friend outraged at this omission has contributed to the Neutral a photograph of the Dewey Dog, a white bull terrier which won sixty-five fights in
and around 1900.

so will be the nose. It is his greatest regret that he didn't get
Marciano when Marciano was in about the second grade of public
school. "He would have learned to do things right without
thinking," Mr. Goldman says. "Then all he would have to think
about is what he wanted to do."

These pedagogical reflections were interrupted by a fellow
farther along the bar, who was using qualificatives that the
bartender on duty—Chickie Bogad—couldn't go along with. Mr.
Bogad is one of the three proprietors.

"Excuse me, Jack," Mr. Bogad said, "but you got an awful
dirty mouth."

"I don't see no women here," the customer said defiantly.

"There ain't any," Chickie said, "but suppose there was?"

The fellow took this hard. He was a bald, lumpy man with
normal ears, and not even a broken nose to make him look at
home. "I guess I'm just a qualified hoodlum," he said bitterly.
("Qualified" takes the place of a row of asterisks.)

"If you are," the bartender said severely, "this ain't the joint
for you." He moved off toward the beer pumps, under the impression that he had won the argument, but he hadn't. The
lumpy man took off his glasses and put them in his pocket.

"Who are *you* to call me a qualified hoodlum?" he yelled after
Mr. Bogad.

"You said it yourself," Mr. Bogad replied.

The man yelled, "What business is it of yours, you qualified
moralist?"

At that, Mr. Bogad started to come around the end of the bar,
grumbling "I don't have to take that from nobody" as he untied
his apron, but a squad of gentle young prizefighters formed a
wall between him and the customer, while their colleagues
shooed the fellow out onto Fifty-fifth Street, explaining that the
Neutral was no place for that kind of language.

"See that?" Whitey said. "We got a nice class of kids in the
business today. But I sometimes wonder where they going to

wind up." This was an allusion to the technological unemploy-
ment with which television threatens all boxers who are not already headliners. There is hardly a night of the week now that
doesn't offer a nationally televised bout (usually only the main
event is shown), and small flesh-and-blood clubs throughout the
land have gone out of business because they can't meet this free
competition. This condition constantly narrows the opportunity
for development of young fighters and—although Whitey isn't
so sensitive on the subject—young seconds and trainers. The failure of new stars to emerge is hurting the interests of the television programs themselves—a class isn't in a healthy condition
unless it has at least six or eight real contenders—so, as Whitey
says, it all adds up to a vicious circle.

The system is taking money even from the star-bout fighters.
During the late twenties, the last period of comparable prosperity, Friday-night shows at Madison Square Garden regularly drew
from forty to eighty thousand dollars, and each main-bout principal took down from ten to twenty thousand. If the boys
weren't fighting at the Garden, they could get almost as much
out of town. Now principals in the Garden's Friday-night fights
get four thousand dollars each from television, plus a derisory
twenty-five per cent of a gate that would have been subnormal in
Tiverton, Rhode Island, in 1929—less than five thousand dollars
in all. At televised clubs like the St. Nicholas Arena or the Eastern Parkway, they collect about three thousand. In the long view,
the best hope for a revival of the dulcet art is that as the television boxing shows run out of new talent, the big and silly television audience will lose interest in them, and national sponsors
will let them drop. Then the small clubs will start up again, for
the hard core of customers who like boxing well enough to pay
for it but who now get it free. This, the cognoscenti say, will in-
sure not only increased employment but a restoration of artistic
standards.

"The fellow who used to pay a dollar and a half for a seat in the gallery would never stand for feature bouts like the ones now," an old fighter named Al Thoma, who had stopped by at the Neutral on his way to the Plaza's Oak Room, said. "What you don't pay for, you can't complain about." Thoma, when fighting, was always known as a cultivated fellow, like Gene Tunney, but with a faster linguistic change of pace. "The masses are asses," he said with distaste. "There are no more connoisseurs. The way most of these guys fight, you'd think they were two fellows having a fight in a barroom."

Whitey took note of a small, weatherworn taxi-driver, dining modestly off a short beer and a hard-boiled egg. "Benny Tell," Whitey said. "He fought the best. He once fought Pancho Villa." As Villa died after a fight with Jimmy McLarnin in 1925, this placed the hackie chronologically. "How many fights you have, Benny?" Whitey asked.

"About a hundred and fifty," the driver said, pleased at being recognized. All he had to show for them was a moderately thickened left ear. "They don't make them like Villa no more," he said. "You hit me and I'll hit you—that's all they know." He finished his egg and went back to his cab.

"New faces, they want new faces all the time for the television shows," said a trainer named Izzy Blanc, who is younger than most of the sages, but knowledgeable. "But the new faces ain't got the experience, so they get knocked out. And where could they get the experience, with no clubs? Either you got to rush a prospect or let him starve to death."

If television relinquishes its hold on boxing, and open competition matures a new lot of stars, it is, of course, possible that the new stars' names will titillate the curiosity of the rumpus-room audience that sponsors covet. It is also possible that by then television will have gone the way of such other gadgets as radio and the silent movies. In the meanwhile young boxers must live, even though, like modern poets, they have scant means of communication with the general public. Since the Guggenheim Foundation has expressed no concern for their problems, a lot of them run tabs at the Neutral. The tabs are usually guaranteed by their managers, and since the managers can't take the money out of the boys until the boys get a fight, the proprietors of the Neutral show a constructive interest in any move to re-create the pugilistic equivalent of an off-Broadway theater. "If we tried to collect now," Nick Masuras, one of the Neutral's three bosses, said to me, "we would lose our total clientele."

Masuras is an old middleweight—tough, but not classy— who used to box in the armories of the New York National Guard in the twenties, when the state permitted the buildings to be used for professional boxing shows on the condition that all participants were Guardsmen. As the required drills were infrequent and there was no prospect of a war, it was a highly successful form of recruiting. Nick's registration card said that he belonged to the 102nd Medical Regiment. After his unspectacular ring career of thirty-eight bouts, he worked in restaurants and then, in 1949, opened the Neutral. He thought of the name himself. Two years later, he pieced the joint up with Bogad, a former matchmaker at the Garden, and with Frankie Jacobs, a veteran fight manager, who contributed social cachet to the establishment.

My visit to the Neutral that particular afternoon was connected with the first attempt by the Metropolitan Boxing Alliance, which consists mostly of managers who hang out in the Neutral, to run a boxing show of its own, with no television, no promoter, no one-sided matches, and—as it turned out—almost no newspaper coverage. For the most part, the members of the Alliance handled young fighters who appeared in preliminaries and semifinals at New York clubs; many of their boys would be fighting features regularly in small cities if television had not blighted the out-of-town spots. The M.B.A.s were in the midst of a highly personal intra-industry feud with the leaders of the International Boxing Guild, a larger and older association of managers, who handle most of the star-bout fighters. The I.B.G.s, according to the M.B.A.s, tried to use their monopoly of the fighters who appear "on top" (in the features) to control employment "underneath" (in the preliminaries). The trainers, like Charlie Goldman and Whitey, were neutral, since they teach and second boys for members of both groups. But they were in favor of any effort to run more fights.

The M.B.A. show, Whitey had informed me, would be a small gem, because in each of the three feature matches scheduled, both the managers concerned figured that they had a shade the better of it. "For a thousand, they might put their kid over his head," Whitey said, "but not for no three hundred." Each of the principals in the three eight-round feature bouts was to receive three hundred dollars, less a hundred for his manager, the customary fees for his seconds, and, possibly, a payment on account on his tab at the Neutral. The managers, Whitey said, were unwilling to get their boys beaten for small money, so the competition would be extraordinarily keen.

It was a Thursday, one of the two weekday evenings without television competition, and the show was to be held at Sunnyside Garden, a dance hall at 45th Street and Queens Boulevard, in a region that motorists are always so eager to get through on their way to the races that they never remember what it looks like. It was raining like the devil, and nobody at the Neutral seemed to know how to get out there without an automobile. A cross-section of opinion had it that the place was on the B.-M.T., a transportation complex more extensively ramified than the upper Amazon. Mr. Bogad, whom I mistook for the best geographer present, specified that the tributary flowing nearest to Sunnyside Garden was known as the Astoria Line. This was to prove an error of pre-Columbian dimensions, but I didn't know it when I left the Neutral. It was then about six-thirty, and the first bout was to begin at eight-thirty. The last sentence I heard as I stepped out into the rain was "You c'n get there in fifteen minutes."

Since I was not in training to fight anybody, I felt I could sneak out on the Neutral's fare, and I had dinner in a Chinese restaurant near the 49th Street entrance to the main stream of the B.-M.T., which I counted upon to float me under the East River and as far as Queens Plaza. There, I reasoned, I might find a native to guide me to the mouth of the Astoria Line. I was suffering from a severe head cold, a specific for which, I have always believed, is watercress soup and Chinese tea. Over the tangled watercress and, later, on the subway, I read a mammoth, lavish, baby-blue brochure, printed on the best coated paper, which the M.B.A. had put out in honor of the occasion. This publication, entitled "M.B.A., The American Way," assured me that I would see "the cream of the crop" at Sunnyside Garden. The Sunnyside Garden Corporation had taken the inside front cover to convey the best wishes of "The Showcase of Queens," and "Ideal Spot for Club Dances, Social Functions, Banquets, Weddings, Large Meetings, Rallies, Bazaars, Exhibits, Benefit Shows, Special Events, Boxing, Wrestling, Basketball." There was also a panel of portraits of M.B.A. officers, all of whom I knew as conspiratorial faces in the Neutral, and a message from the M.B.A. president, Al Braverman, a former Army boxing instructor who takes a photograph like the late Heywood Broun. "Boxing was never meant for a self-chosen few to force the rank and file members of the boxing fraternity to do as they would have them do," the message said, in not too closely veiled allusion to the I.B.G. "The Gestapo did not work out in Germany, nor will it work out here in our grand and glorious country."

The ads—three dozen pages of them (the revenue was counted on to forestall any deficiency at the gate)—were taken by fight managers (mostly M.B.A. members), fighters' relatives, fight clubs (generously welcoming competition, the International

Boxing Club, which promotes at Madison Square Garden, had taken a full page), fighters' daytime employers (a loyal lot), gyms, pawnshops, sporting-goods dealers, barbershops, luncheonettes, and a gentleman who simply proclaimed himself "Max Greenaut, No. 1 Fight Fan, Always at the Ringside." Among the managers' cards I liked best one that said, "Tony Rojas, Latin-American Manager and Sport." There was a small advertisement of the Claire Bridal Shoppe, of 243 Grand Street, and one of a firm called Time Pleating & Stitching, Inc., which I assumed to be one of Mr. Luce's new tentacles. The journal also included two full pages of "Neutral Corner Boosters," with facsimile signatures (the boys had paid a dollar apiece, I learned later), and a number of greetings from purely social organizations: the Veteran Boxers Association of New York; the Leather-Pushers A.C., of Brooklyn; the Roland La Starza Social Club, of the Bronx; the Cestus A.C., of Newark; and the Village Owls Social Club, of 234 Mulberry Street. By the time I emerged from my Astoria Line train onto a rain-swept mesa that was apparently the head of the navigable stream, I had read every ad in the book, including the holograph signatures. I got back to the Sunnyside by taxi for not much more than it would have cost me to go by a similar vehicle from 49th Street.

When I arrived the first preliminary, an affair of no moment, was already on. The publicity director of the M.B.A., Maurie Waxman, a hyperthyroid fellow who is happiest when strangling with rage, escorted me to the working-press section, which I shared during the evening with a man from the Long Island *Ad - vocate* and a fellow from the *New Yorker Staats-Zeitung*, who arrived just in time for the last bout, in which one of the principals was a German-American. The ideal boxing card, like a music-hall bill, builds from the opening number, and the bout under way when I entered made it evident that the Sunnyside match-maker, an old-timer named Joe McKenna, knew his business. It was the kind of match that is bound to make the next one look like an improvement. The very bad first bout is a pleasant tradition of local clubs. It gives the connoisseurs a chance to find their seats, tune their voices, and warm up their assortment of wisecracks. While doing this, they estimate the size of the gate, upon which, they know, depends the likelihood of more shows at the same address, and try to locate acquaintances in the audience. This time, while the fighters hesitated, a hearty burgher far off in the rear rows landed the first bon mot. "Swing now!" he yelled. "You got the wind wit' ya!" I looked around and was glad to see that the gate was good for a hall the size of Sunnyside. At a neighborhood club, you can count the total attendance early in the evening, because the patrons arrive promptly, to get their money's worth. It isn't like a big fight, where the expense-account hosts and their guests begin to flock in just before the conversation piece, or like off-nights at the Garden, when spectators come late because they are on the cuff. I knew that the boxers and their managers had been out selling tickets, just as in the old days, and the concentrations of sound indicated which areas were tenanted by the delegations brought along by the various boys. At the Neutral earlier in the evening, I had heard the manager of a colored fighter, now going into the ring for the second four-rounder, boast that his boy had sold forty dollars' worth of tickets, and I had no trouble telling where the purchasers were sitting. The boy had against him one of those rigid, determined-looking youngsters who create the impression that they can hit because they obviously can't do anything else. A boxer of this type induces first respect and then incredulity in an inexperienced opponent; by the time the colored boy had decided that the determined fellow was as bad as he looked, he had only a couple of rounds left to slap him around in. The determined fellow, who was white and whose name was Ronnie, had even more friends in the crowd, and they advised him courageously, "Steady up, Ronnie; weave, Ronnie," no matter how hard he got hit. He appeared to be trying to lead the colored boy as a gunner leads a bird, punching a yard or so in front of where the colored boy would have been if he had kept going in the same direction.

By the time the first of the feature eight-rounders came on, the crowd was in fine voice. It was a neighborhood crowd, except for the concentrated groups of fighters' friends, and the neighborhood is not tough but hearty. As it happens, this is the region to which the authentic Manhattan accent has emigrated, according to a learned cove I met at Columbia years ago, who went about making recordings of American regional modes of speech. The more habitable quarters of Manhattan, he told me, have been preempted by successful inlanders who speak Iowese and Dakotahoman; the inhabitants of West Harlem talk like Faulkner characters, and East Harlem speaks Spanish. "Just as the anthropologist who wishes to study pristine African culture must seek it among the Djuka Negroes of Surinam, who were snatched from Africa in the eighteenth century, I must carry my tape recorder to Queens to study the New York speech of Henry James's day," he said.

The contestants in this first feature bout were welterweights with only a pound's difference between them, both Negroes in the dark-umber range, and both with first names that lent themselves admirably to the accent of the Diaspora—Earl Dennis and Ernie Roberts. They were both young and in beautiful condition—"trained up like Kid Lewis," as Captain Hector Macdonald-Buchanan once observed to me when discussing Hitler's Army. (Lewis was a chap who could box twenty rounds without increasing his rate of respiration.) I had once seen Roberts make a savagely correct fight at the Garden, going eight rounds without clinching or stepping back, and I had Whitey's word that Dennis was at least as good. Whitey was in Dennis's corner, along with Mr. Braverman, the author of the presidential message I had just been reading, who is Dennis's manager. With Roberts and his manager, Bennie Allesandro, in the opposite corner, were two seconds, Chickie Ferrara and Jimmy August, both of whom, in the Neutral's idiom, "know what's all about it." Roberts is tall for a welterweight, five feet eight or nine, and has a small, well-shaped head, wide shoulders, and a narrow waist— a classic boxing build. Dennis is a more compact boy—bigger head, longer waist, shorter legs, wide shoulders, and long arms. He has a Sam Langford kind of physique. His face is broader and shorter, too, with wide, white teeth that give him a genially anthropophagous look. It was the sort of contrast in structures that inspires resourceful spectators to devise battle plans for the objects of their interest even before a fight begins.

I knew from talking with their managers that both Dennis and Roberts were married men and fathers, and that they both held down full-time jobs. Roberts, a clerk in a hardware store, got to work at eight each morning and left at seven. His employer let him have three hours off in the middle of the day, during which he trained at Stillman's and had his lunch. After work, he went home to his wife and child, in Harlem, and at five the next morning he was in Central Park, doing his roadwork—five miles in about forty-five minutes every day before breakfast. He was twenty-five. Dennis, who was only twenty-two, although he had been married for five years and had two children, lived in Brooklyn and worked normal hours for a firm on the fringes of the garment center, making women's belt buckles. After work, he went up to the Broadway Gym, a small place near City College, to train, and a couple of hours later headed for Brooklyn. He, too, did his roadwork in the mornings. Roberts had had about forty fights and Dennis about thirty-five. Their daytime bosses were at ringside.

"Hookum, Oil!" a cheerful Queens voice called to Dennis as the men left their corners. Roberts, in purple trunks, received advice just as prompt and resonant—"Up, Poiple! Uppercut!" Roberts came in on a straight line, his waist pulled back, his shoulders and elbows forward. He hit straight or in light arcs— short, jarring punches. Dennis went to meet him scrunched forward, too, presenting the top of his head as the only target of opportunity. ("The head is the hardest part of the human body," Roberts said to me a couple of days later, when I talked to him and Dennis about the fight.) Larry Baker, the fellow I had seen Roberts beat in the Garden, had moved around him and hit from a distance. Roberts may have expected Dennis to do the same thing, but when Dennis didn't, he saw that he would have to make the best of it. ("If you back up, you lose points," he said to me later. "So I knew I had to stay and chalk it up as experience.") Roberts hit fast, but with measured fury, because he realized he had to pace himself. ("When I started out as a fighter," he told me, "I had just a willing heart—threw punches in the wind. I used to punch myself out. When I sampled Dennis's right, I knew I couldn't afford that." Dennis told me that he had formed a slightly optimistic prognosis on the basis of those first short, jarring blows. "Tap, tap," he said. "I told myself, He can't hurt me. Then bam! It really rang bells. I thought, I got a tough boy on my hands. I better play possum and try to let him play hisself out." Dennis, who comes from Wilmington, North Carolina, has a less polished conversational style than Roberts, an old Harlemite.) Dennis and Roberts fought out the round without a second's respite. When two boxers come straight toward each other and don't hit, they wind up in each other's arms, and the same thing is likely to happen if both are swinging wildly; one fellow's arm will go around the other's neck, and he will have to grab to save himself. But Oil and Oinie, as their public hailed them, maintained the minuscule distance between them by hitting each other away. Hitting at such short range, the boxer leaves a correspondingly brief opening; the trick is to take the initiative by anticipating the opening or by moving the other fellow off balance. Having done that, one boy sometimes can land a whole series of blows before the other breaks into the rhythm. And there is never the brief surcease a fighter gets at longer range. A smart old fighter can sometimes slide through ten rounds on the equivalent of one round of such fighting.

I marked that first round for Roberts, though there wasn't much in it, but Dennis won the second. They were fighting the same way, but now Oil's sequences of punches were more sustained, and he was spinning the taller boy when they got near the corners. He had a lower center of gravity and he was using it. Dennis's idea of "playing possum" was to ride out a whole flurry of punches, rolling and bobbing, and then launch a flurry of his own. (He adopted this method of biding his time, he explained to me later, because he had found it safer than retreat. "I used to be a runner," he said, "but more boys get knocked out that way than inside.") Oinie's unpaid second out in left field—"Up, Poiple!"—had noted the diminution of his man's fortunes, and he now showed that his strategy was flexible. "Stickum, Oinie!" he yelled, advising Roberts to stay away and jab. But Roberts would have considered this a species of moral abdication; besides, there is no use in sticking the top of a head. Instead, he came back in the third round with a fine determination to discourage the Brooklyn man. ("I hit him so many times he was visibly out, as far as I could see," he said afterward. "Yet he was still there a second later. Tit for tat, he is the meanest man I ever lived with.") He took the third, and then Dennis carried the fourth. By that time, the man in left field had thought of a refinement. "Stick 'n' hook, Oinie," he was yelling. (Translation: "Punch straight with the left and then hook with it." This is sometimes called hooking off a jab.) The "Hookum, Oil!" man, who was now riding high on a wave of euphoria, howled back mockingly, "Hook 'n' stick, Oil! Givum tha yopposite!" (This, as he knew, was hilarious nonsense; you can't jab off a hook. The laugh he got proved there were other knowing coves present.)

But Roberts carried the fifth—and they hadn't clinched yet, nor had either man taken a backward step except under the impetus of a fist. They moved often, of course, drifting about the ring in a tight circle. ("I thought then I better pace myself so I can finish good," Roberts said afterward. "There is a difference between being too cautious and overcautious, which is to be just cautious enough." At about the same time Dennis, although it still seems incredible, was deciding that he had "played possum" long enough. "At the beginning of that fight," he said, "I was thinking of how tired I was before I went in the ring, even though my boss had given me the day off, yet I couldn't sleep, because of my children in the apartment crying. They been sick with a cold. That was a mistake I made thinking of how tired I must of been, because I wasn't.") In the seventh, Dennis went out and, for the first time, "changed the theme of the fight," to quote his manager, Al Braverman. He began throwing wide, swooping hooks. Possibly because Roberts was "pacing himself," several of these nailed him. If he had been coming in as fast as before, he might have got inside them. ("I should of throwed short hooks," Dennis said. "They would of been even better. But I must have didn't do so bad, because they all applaused me.") In the eighth, Roberts came right back at him, and when the judges and referee agreed to call the fight a draw, everybody was happy—"Hook 'n' stick" as well as "Stick 'n' hook." The general satisfaction was shared by the two managers, each of whom must have thought several times during the battle that he had let his colleague outsmart him. Whitey, who identifies himself with his charges, said with some heat, the next time I met him in the Neutral, "I thought we win it," but Jimmy August, who was there, too, said, "Ain't that funny? I thought *we* win it."

There was a corking club fight after that, in which the chunky young Brooklyn middleweight named Rinzy Nocero beat a redhaired Negro known as Castiron Tommy Dixon, by a decision that might as well have been a draw. But the workmanship was not of the same excellence. The windup fight, between the Yorkville fellow, Irwin Schulz, and a colored middleweight named Bobby Moore, from Newark, was the least exciting of the lot—Moore won it easily—but as the matchmaker, McKenna, said later, it wouldn't have looked so bad if it had been on before the other two. The gate money, McKenna said, had just about covered the purse distributions and the expenses—the show had drawn a net of twenty-six hundred dollars, at two dollars and four dollars a seat—but the advertising in the M.B.A. journal had cleared a profit.

The next morning, I looked at the *Mirror*, the *News*, the *Times*, and the *Herald Tribune*, and all any of them said about the fight was that Earl Dennis, 143½, and Ernie Roberts, 144½, had fought a draw.

Debut of a Seasoned Artist

In a previous sequel to the works of Pierce Egan, the Philippe de Commines of the London prize ring, I felt impelled to chronicle the misadventure of Hurricane Jackson, an unfortunate pugilist with four uncoordinated limbs and three mutually antipathetic managers. I was therefore delighted to hear, after the public demolition of Mr. Jackson, that the next event of importance at air-cooled Madison Square Garden would be the at-long-last debut there of Archie Moore, by popular report the very antithesis of the Hurricane. Moore was an aging academician—thirty-seven, to be precise—of such celebrity that young fighters came from the very Antipodes to study at his feet, which is where they frequently landed. For several years I had been hearing about Moore, a virtuoso of anachronistic perfection in an age when boxers in general are hurried along like artificially ripened tomatoes, and with similarly unsatisfactory results. Moore's art was said to be the product of a fortunate mixture of genius and moderate adversity. (In the growth of any artist, an essential element is a correct dosage of calamity. If the adversity is too adverse, he has to seek work at some useful trade; if it is not adverse enough, he gets a swelled head.) Moore's adversity had taken the form of never getting a big match in New York, which is why I had not seen him. But eighteen years of provincial appearances had kept him in pocket money, and he had even picked up the light-heavyweight championship by defeating Joey Maxim in St. Louis in 1952. St. Louis is Moore's native city, but it has never been suggested that chauvinism affected the decision. Members of the Moore cult thought Maxim hardly worthy of appearing on a Moore program. "It would be like Casadesus playing 'Liebesträume,' " one of them said to me when the match was first suggested. Since then, Moore has given finished interpretations of Maxim in return bouts in Ogden, Utah, and Miami, Florida.

The opponent announced for Moore's Garden debut was Harold Johnson, of Philadelphia, rated by the National Boxing Association as the No. 2 light heavyweight of the country. Like Maxim, he was a slightly hackneyed item in the Moore repertory. The champion had boxed him four times, winning three. Johnson had got one decision, in Milwaukee in 1951, but its authenticity has never been accepted by the cultists. Nobody expected much of Johnson in the Garden match; it is an index of Moore's reputation that the second-best man in his class was not considered to be in his class at all. The advance publicity therefore centered on Moore's alleged difficulty in getting down to the necessary hundred and seventy-five pounds, although he is of just about normal size for a light heavy—five feet eleven inches tall, and not especially massive. If he debilitated himself sufficiently to make the weight, the report implied, he might collapse from malnutrition.

One reason Moore hadn't appeared at the Garden before was, I knew, the character of his manager, Charlie Johnston, who is an independent chap and likes to operate off his own bat, even if it means opening up unfamiliar territory. As recently as 1951, for example, he had Moore working in Flint, Michigan (Herman Harris; K.O. 4), and Cordoba, Argentina (Victor Carabajal; K.O. 3). In 1949 Moore knocked out somebody named Esco Greenwood in two in North Adams, Massachusetts, and in the course of his ten seasons under Johnston's management he has given twenty recitals in Baltimore alone, becoming as much of a local institution as Henry L. Mencken. Since winning the championship, he has shown up in Sacramento, Spokane, San Diego, and Buenos Aires (besides Ogden and Miami), to name a few, and has beaten some of the most unknown prizefighters in the world.

About a week before the fight I telephoned Mr. Johnston, whom I had never met, and arranged to visit Moore's training camp at Summit, New Jersey, to see him work. Mr. Johnston promised to pick me up at the curb on the Broadway side of the Times Tower at precisely noon; he said he would be driving a De Soto sedan. Arriving a minute early, I saw a couple of young colored men standing there who looked as if they might be interested in boxing. Surmising that they were waiting for Johnston, too, I joined them. The De Soto stopped at the curb a few seconds later. Johnston, a ginger-haired middle-aged man with a sharp, merry face, waved me in beside him, the two other fellows climbed into the rear seat, and we were off. I talked to Johnston all the way through the Holland Tunnel without getting an answer. I was beginning to simmer when he turned to me—he had stopped for a light—and announced, with high good humor, that he had a bad right ear. "I'll put up the window at my left, and you can bounce your voice off it," he said, but I shouted that there would be plenty of time for talking after we got to Summit. Meanwhile, the fellows in the back seat were chattering away, so I listened. The larger and darker of the two—he was an inch or two over six feet—was Frankie Daniels, I had learned, and he was on his way to spar with Moore. "I'm going to finish him off—spar with him every day from now until he winds up training," he said, and added that he was looking forward to the opportunity, because he had a fight of his own coming up later in the month and Moore would sharpen him more than he would sharpen Moore. Also, he would get paid for it. "I'm bound to learn something," he said. "Archie so smart he exercise your brain as well as body."

Jimmy Brooks, the other fellow in the back seat, was not a sparring partner but a friend of Sandy Saddler, the world featherweight champion, who is also managed by Johnston and was at the same training camp, preparing for a fight in Venezuela. (The airplane has opened new vistas for a manager with a grasp of geography. Johnston told me later that after Venezuela, where there is a lot of oil money in circulation, he was planning fights for Saddler in Thailand and Japan, two countries that are enjoying featherweight-boxing booms. "They're all little fellows there," he said. "No heavyweights to take the play away." Moore and Saddler both enjoy travel; they are not like a fighter named Terry Young, whom Whitey Bimstein once had to take to Honolulu to substitute for an injured principal in a main bout. They had to fly to make it, and Young was afraid of airplanes. Whitey got him aboard by telling him the trip would take only fifteen minutes. He said Honolulu was in New Jersey.) Brooks wore a black imperial under his lower lip, and was dressed for some improbable Riviera. He said that Saddler had asked him to stay at the camp but that the country was not for him. "I can't stand those crickets," he said. "Keep me awake. I'm a connoisseur. A *boulevardier*." As we got to the top of a rise on a country road among hill pastures Johnston said, "This is the nicest part of the ride." Brooks guffawed. "Old Charlie say that every time he get to this spot," he said. "It's delectably beautiful." Johnston, who didn't hear him, said, "Out here it's quiet. A real training camp. Nothing to do after dark but take a walk or watch television." A hill or two farther on, we stopped under a sign that read, "E H S A N ' S T R A I N I N G   C A M P." There was a farmhouse a hundred feet above the road, and a couple of one-story white frame buildings still higher up, at the end of a path. On the top slope and the crest of the hill was an apple orchard, and under the apple trees were fat sheep. Brooks shuddered.

Johnston drove the car off the road, and we climbed to the farmhouse together. Brooks and Daniels made off up the path. "Moore will be resting until two o'clock," Johnston said to me. "We may as well get something to eat." We entered through the kitchen, where Mr. Ehsan, a parchment-hided man with gray hair, sat snapping the ends off beans. He is a Turk; his mother, known as Mme. Bey, started the training camp about thirty years ago and was so frugal and severe that she attracted the patronage of a conservative class of prizefight managers. Johnston ordered bacon and eggs and coffee, and I did the same. While Mr. Ehsan set about preparing them, Johnston and I went into the bare living room to wait. "This is a serious place," he said, surveying the dismal surroundings with approval. "No bar, no juke boxes. No women from the summer resorts with short pants on." Finding that bilateral conversation was now possible, I asked him how many fighters he had in his stable. "Eight," Johnston said, "but three are in Italy and three are in Argentina. The only ones I've got here are Moore and Saddler."

I knew that Charlie Johnston was a younger brother of the late Jimmy Johnston, an ex-flyweight with a snub nose, indelible black hair, and a derby hat, who had been known in the trade as the Boy Bandit even when he was approaching seventy. Jimmy was a famous manager and promoter, a man of quips, rages, feuds, and funny stories. The current Johnston, like many another younger brother, has jelled in a quieter mold, but he has the Boy Bandit's flair for fighters; I can't remember any other manager with two concurrent world champions. I asked Johnston if it didn't make for jealousy between them, but he said no; Moore is like an older brother to Saddler, who is twenty-seven. Moore is by temperament placid and analytical. Saddler is volatile—a string bean of a man with legs to his chin, and long pipestem arms with which he achieves remarkable feats of leverage. I saw Saddler knock out his predecessor, Willie Pep, so I have great respect for him.

Johnston told me that he had become aware of the financial possibilities of the road while touring with a great, great English fighter named Ted Kid Lewis, who flourished at about the time of the First World War. Jimmy Johnston was Lewis's American manager. "I was fourteen then," Charley Johnston said, "and Jimmy took me into his office. When he was busy with other fighters, he would let me travel with Lewis. Lewis knew everything anyway. He must have fought Jack Britton for the welterweight championship twenty times—every place from New Orleans to Toronto—and they always packed the house. Buffalo, Cincinnati, Dayton, Canton, Atlanta, or Jersey City, it was always a battle. They liked each other all right outside the ring, but when they got inside they would do everything. They were so smart they exasperated each other. Britton was a great, great fighter." By the time Lewis and Britton fought their last match, in New York in 1921 (Britton won the decision in fifteen), Charlie Johnston had learned everything, too. Their performances were encyclopedic.

Mr. Ehsan served up the bacon and eggs, which were excellent. When we had finished, we strolled up the hill toward the gymnasium, one of the frame buildings at the end of the path. As we entered, we were joined by Harry Mendel, an I.B.C. press agent who used to publicize six-day bike races. The day before, the I.B.C. had brought a number of newspaper writers to Summit, and today it was taking the press to the camp of Moore's opponent, near Atlantic City. The wire services and papers were therefore dependent on Mendel for a brief bulletin on Moore's workout and on whether he looked unhappy about his weight. His weight was about the only angle left, Mendel said. Nobody outside Philadelphia expected an exciting fight unless Moore had to cut off an arm. Johnson, although competent and strong, was cautious beyond his years—twenty-six—and the bout was likely to be a bore. This, I reflected, would be one more touch of moderate adversity for Moore, because if he won a dull fight there would be small demand for his reappearance.

The gym at Ehsan's has a standard-size ring and ample room for the boxers, but limited accommodations for spectators. This is the reverse of how things are at the big summer-resort hotels where boxers have latterly taken to training. Moore appeared, a light mulatto with a tinge of red in his bushy hair. He was sporting a black mustache and an imperial, which, Johnston told me, he always wears into battle. They gave him a serene and scholarly aspect, and his long woolen sweat clothes, gathered at wrist and ankle, made him look like an old fellow trying to lose weight in a health club. He wore a cashmere sweater over the sweat suit; the total effect was almost prim. Like Caesar, Moore enjoys having fat men about him. He was attended by two mountainous chaps, Cheerful Norman and Tiny Payne, his habitual handlers, who weigh two hundred and twenty and two hundred and eighty-five pounds, respectively.

Our traveling companion, Daniels, was his first opponent, but it never looked like competition. There was nothing flashy about Moore's style—no superfluous bounce or glide, none of the whacking combinations of socks in the ribs to which some headline fighters treat their sparring partners. He wasn't elusive in the phantom manner, he was a prestidigitator. He picked off punches with his hands, forearms, and elbows, usually as they started, and hit as he willed, moving his man around without shoving him, simply by feinting and keeping him off balance. He himself moved within half-arm length as freely as if he were ten feet off. There was nothing vindictive or even mock-menacing about his expression; as a beginner he may have composed a "fighting face," but if so, he had discarded it years ago. He didn't invite or resent Daniels' sporadic aggressiveness; he simply played an exercise. After two rounds Daniels' stint was over, and Moore worked a round with a blond young Argentine heavyweight who had a Yugoslav face and name. He was a very tall lad, and he attacked as if he were determined to show he cared nothing for reputations. It must have been a curious experience for the boy; he threw a hundred punches and touched Moore's face—just grazed his mustache—twice. Three rounds aren't a severe test of stamina, and at the end Moore wasn't breathing hard. The boy was blown in one. "*Muy astuto,*" he said when he had pulled in enough breath. (I could figure that one out—"A regular cutie.") And then, when he had gulped again, "*Sabe mucho.*" ("He knows a lot.") He sat down on the ring apron, a handler pulled off his gloves, and he began to undo the tapes on his hands. "*Inteligente,*" he said when he had finished. ("Cerebral type.")

Moore's condition didn't astonish me unduly. Unlike old fighters who quit and then try a comeback, he had never been away. Training steadily, never having had to take much punishment, he was sound. Sparring three rounds wasn't fighting fifteen, however, and I couldn't believe he was as good as new.

On the night of the fight, when Moore came to the center of the ring without the cover of the charitable woolens, his age showed. The weight hoax had exploded. In the office of the Athletic Commission, at noon, Moore had weighed a hundred and seventy-three pounds, and admitted he had eaten breakfast. Johnson had weighed a hundred and seventy-two and a half, but as they stood in the ring at fight time, he looked bigger and solider than the virtuoso. Johnson has a heavy, uncertain face, square jowls, and a thick neck, like old Joe Walcott. His body is like Walcott's, too—rounded, heavy-thighed, the diaphragm corded with muscle, the arms good for dock work—and I knew that, like Walcott again, he was a counter-fighter, durable but cautious. He had been knocked out just once in his life, when he was twenty-two, by Walcott himself, who was then about forty. Walcott, though, had been a big heavyweight—a two-hundred-pounder—and a good enough puncher to put Louis, Charles, and Marciano on the floor in their turns. (Of the three, only Charles had stayed there.) Moore didn't look capable of that kind of hitting. His body appeared commonplace. The arms, I reckoned from what I had seen in the gym, were tireless; nobody could know about the legs. Under the circumstances, he would be doing well to outgeneral, bluff, outjab, and cuff Johnson, and that's what I expected him to do, although the way the challenger was made dismayed me. In one sense, I was glad Johnson was a counter-puncher, because it meant Moore could make his own pace, staying away when he wanted to, unless his legs folded irrevocably under him.

The crowd, to my amazement, liked Johnson. I myself have a great prejudice in favor of boxers who are skillful and daring. I wouldn't give the time of day to a professional who won't lead; if he doesn't want to fight, what is he there for? But there are *Lumpen* who come to a fight to see a good boxer beaten. It is an anti-intellectual attitude. There were eight thousand in the audience that night, which is quite a crowd nowadays, although it is not even half capacity. The spectators had all heard of Moore, I suppose, and thought he was a kind of phony, or else why hadn't he been in the Garden before? Also, the *touffe de barbe sous le men - ton* may have struck them as an affectation. Furthermore, he had come into the ring wearing a black silk mandarin robe with gold piping—the sort of touch that probably goes over in Cordoba but is a bit lush for the big time. Moore was old, but the people in the crowd wanted to see him knocked out. When Joe Louis was old, they wanted to see him win. Perhaps it was because Louis was a slugger. He was a pretty good boxer, too, but they forgave him for it. Maybe they hadn't noticed.

For this fight I had cadged a seat in the working-press section, with a shelf in front of it on which I could take notes. I kept track of the fight on a score sheet, marked off in separate boxes for the fifteen rounds, but on looking at it now I find my notes discouragingly fragmentary. My memories, while fuller, are perhaps less accurate; my notation for the first round, "J—2gr," means that I thought Johnson won it, and that he landed two good rights, but it is an unimportant part of what I saw. To make a nice-looking fight against a man who won't lead, and beat him, is a pretty severe test of a fighter's technical resources, and it was what Moore plainly had in mind. Instead of flicking, moving around, and so piling up enough unhurting points to goad Johnson into some possible late activity, he was reconnoitering in close, looking the challenger over as if he had never seen him before. So the true artist takes up a work he has laid aside for years, and attempts a fresh approach. I suspected that Moore was not satisfied with the way he had handled Johnson the first four times they boxed—an aggregate of forty rounds. He had done some nice things, perhaps, but the ensemble had fallen short of perfection. Bent forward, his bearded, Oberammergau head shielded by a mobile elbow, he swayed within Johnson's reach, making sharp tangential prods at the blocky thorax and abdomen, like a sculptor seeking the grain of a rock or a physician asking where it hurts. His jabs to the head, as a discerning colleague has noted, lacked sting; they were tentative, adjusting motions. Experience had evidently convinced Moore that the other procedure was wrong; Johnson was the kind of bird you couldn't suck into a rash gesture. Unlike the novices in the gym, however, Johnson could hit fast and hard; he has knocked out some rough people when they got too temerarious. Examining him so close up is like taking cheese from a set mousetrap. Consequently, even Moore caught a couple at the juncture of the mustache and the imperial, and there was no other way to mark that first round. I thought I caught an expression of slight distaste as he turned away at the bell, but it was more likely self-reproach.

Charlie Johnston, Cheerful Norman, and a grizzled, sailorly-looking man named Bertie Briscoe, Saddler's trainer, were in Moore's corner. (Tiny Payne wasn't in the ring, possibly because he was afraid of weighting it down at one end.) They did not appear discomposed. The Johnson faction in the crowd, though, was howling as if the cerebrator lay weltering in his gore. "Go get him, Harold!" one fellow shouted. "He's an old man!" "Get fierce, Harold!" another bellowed. "He's got nothing left!" Johnson didn't look fierce, though—just meditative. He was trying to figure why Moore was acting as he was. On the margin of my card I find a note, "imp. of H *fierce*," which I take to mean the impossibility of Harold's getting that way, or maybe the impossibility of any Harolds getting that way; if the leaders had switched names, the Saxons might have won the Battle of Hastings.

For the second round, I have just "J," to remind me that the affair continued in the same pattern. For Round 3, I have a very small, doubtful "M—rtb." Moore hit the subject a lot of those light, probing punches, but he also landed one smashing right to the body, as if asking, "Is *that* where it hurts?" And Johnson's eyes said yes. Moore went away as quietly happy as a doctor who has made a promising diagnosis. After that, I have for Round 4 a larger, more decisive "M—1h;" he hit Mr. Johnson at least one left hook in the chops that it is a pleasure to remember not having received. It was just to keep Johnson's mind on higher things, because Moore was still directing his main attack at the body. Then, for Round 5, "M—Take it easy, H," which reflects the fact that while Moore was working calmly at his master scheme, a number of Johnson men in the audience were beginning to yell, "Take it easy, Harold!" as if they feared their man might now do something rash. Apprehension never had less ba-

sis. At the same time, an old, iron-gray cove with a political profile was barking, "Press him, Harold, press him!" The fellows
who were advising caution now began to address their remarks to
this hothead. Johnson himself, between rounds, looked preoccu-
pied, like a habitual loser at roulette who is having a small run of
luck. He had hit Moore some showy, noisy ripostes that sounded
good as they hit shoulders, and it is possible he was ahead on
points then. Certainly he must have thought so. But there was
no place to cash in his chips so he could quit a small winner.

Round 6 is marked with the biggest kind of "M" but no details, and 7 with a big "M—Jn n," which recalls that Moore, jabbing now with dazing snap, had got Johnson's nose bleeding. It
was a wide, flat nose, which bled reluctantly, and the blood appeared to have a sobering effect on its owner. But the more serious blows were still going to the body, and once the challenger's
mouth flew open. He didn't quit, though. He wasn't cowardly—
merely pessimistic. He still never led, but he had so many leads
to counter that he kept busy. Toward the end of the round, Moore
lost him. That alarmed me, because if an executant as skilled as
Moore has a man and then can't finish him, it is a safe bet that
he's tired. Tiny Payne, who will not admit that Moore has ever
been tired in his life, told me afterward that he hadn't been able
to understand this round. " 'Peared Archie had him, and then he
turned away and let him go," he said. I think Moore may have
sensed that Johnson was too strong to take then, and could do
with a bit more softening.

Moore went along well in the eighth and ninth, but Johnson
was getting stronger instead of weaker. I had Moore far ahead,
but my immediate neighbors from the newspapers didn't; they
thought that it was pretty even, and that Moore, at his age, figured to tire faster than Johnson. Moore was also trying to calculate where he stood. He thought that he was ahead on points
right through, he told a reporter after the fight, but he felt that

the crowd was against him and might influence the officials, because "the sentiment was with the underdog." After a couple of hundred recitals, the artist develops a sensitivity to his audience. So in the tenth he was even more aggressive, and had Johnson in real trouble. But near the end of the round Moore was pressing in to get in one more combination of punches before the round ended—and Johnson hit him with a beautiful overhand right to the left side of the head and knocked him flat. It was as if Vladimir de Pachmann had been assaulted by a piano stool. It was an event so unexpected, so unprecedented that even the referee, Ruby Goldstein, lost his head. Goldstein's first impulse must have been to help Moore to his feet and apologize on behalf of the management, but he checked it in time and began to count. He forgot, however, that since this was a championship bout, hostilities were *de règle* as soon as the fallen man got to his feet, which Moore did at "Three." The New York Athletic Commission has a foolish, though well-intentioned, rule governing non-championship matches: Whenever a boxer is knocked down, the referee must stop the fight for eight seconds, even if the man is back on his feet by "One." This is designed to protect boxers from the effects of their own imprudence but has resulted merely in atrophy of their estimative powers. Formerly boxers stayed down as long as they could when they were truly hurt. When they were undamaged, they got up as quickly as possible, in order to minimize the seriousness of their mishap. Now they all bounce to their feet if they are conscious, secure in the knowledge they will get the eight seconds anyway. This substitutes a reflex for an exercise of reason. It is also hard on a fellow who, after staying on the mat until "Eight" or "Nine," might have decided to remain there. In championship matches, this new fangle does not apply. But when Moore got up at "Three," the addled Goldstein stood in front of him, continuing to count, and this precluded further operations, because the ball rang for the end of the round at "Five." In the two lost seconds, Johnson might have hit Moore a couple more licks if Goldstein hadn't been there and the challenger could have prevailed on himself to take the initiative.

The jubilation of the short-end bettors had reached what Colonel Stingo calls a "frenzium." "Go get him, Harold!" they shouted. "You got him!" None were so craven as to counsel caution now. Mr. Johnson's seconds were wagging their jaws like a Gilbert and Sullivan chorus in a patter song. One of them slapped him jovially on the nape of the neck with an ice bag. Johnson alone seemed unamused, reflective. "I got so much different kinds of advice I thought Moore was in my corner," he told a newspaperman later. Johnson could now be sure he was ahead on points; a knockdown counts like the dickens in most judges' minds. He had his choice of two policies: to pursue and try to demolish, or to fence and try to conserve his lead. The first was not in him, and so he built a bridge for his retreating enemy.

Moore used the bridge for about two minutes of the eleventh round, staying away from Johnson as if they had changed roles. Then, having ascertained that Johnson was as meek as ever, he went back to his body-punching. My card says "j" for the eleventh round, but it is a small "j," a diminishing "j," a last "j." Moore opened a cut beside Johnson's right eye—a trifling lesion by Marciano standards, but visible—and he had the pink showing in Johnson's wide nostrils again. He banged the damaged eye with the inside of his left forearm—a palpably illegal maneuver that drew a yell from the Johnson people. Goldstein walked to his corner after the round and spoke to him. Both fighters looked tired, but Moore looked mean-tired behind his whiskers, like Mephistopheles on a hot night.

The twelfth was good Moore, although he did not seem too brisk, and then, in the thirteenth, he began to play that loud part, with the two-handed bangs on the keyboard, that even to the musically uninitiated always portends the windup of a con-

certo. He opened the counter-fighter's mouth with punches between the thorax and the abdomen, and closed it with hooks to
the lower maxillary. He moved him around as if he were trying to
see where he would look best, and he ducked under that weaver's-
beam right arm like a small girl jumping under a skip rope. He
rubbed his bushy hair on all lacerated portions of Johnson's face,
and he buffeted the sore nose with short lateral punches thrown
from a polite bow. When the counter-fighter sat down after the
thirteenth round, he no longer looked like a possible winner. If
Moore finished the last two rounds at the same pace, he was
bound to take the decision and retain his title.

That ending did not accord with Moore's new, mature conception of how to render Johnson, however. He was tired of him.
("Johnson makes you do all the fighting," he told a *Post* reporter
afterward.) Watching the men fight on the side of the ring away
from me, with Johnson retrograding in my direction at a speed
ordinarily observed within town limits, I noted a sudden acceleration of his rearward approach. The synergetic effect of his own
withdrawal and the forward propulsion imparted by Mr. Moore's
right hand sent him into a spin, which failed to impair Mr.
Moore's calm aim. In the gymnasium, Mr. Johnston had informed
me, Moore hits the light bag eight hundred times in three minutes, which figures out to almost five times a second; Johnson
was moving more like a heavy bag, equipped with loose elbows.
The scene reminded me of the immortal Egan's description of
how Dutch Sam finished Tom Belcher: "The ferocity of Sam was
tremendous in the extreme; he followed his opponent to all parts
of the ring, putting in dreadful *facers* and body-blows, dealing
out death-like punishment till his brave opponent fell, quite exhausted." That was about the way it happened, except that Johnson, who had fallen sitting in his own corner, where he could
help himself with the ropes, got to his feet at five, though quite
exhausted, and Goldstein, perhaps feeling he owed him a break,

stepped in front of him and counted to eight. But Johnson was so nearly helpless that the referee stopped the bout a few seconds later.

Getting out of the Garden, I had to walk around Tiny Payne. "They got to match them in the Orange Bowl at Miami," he said. "They got a new public, you understand me? They draw a million-dollar gate."

"Who?" I said, to tease him. "Moore and Patterson?" Patterson is a promising light heavy who turned pro two years before. He was born at about the time Moore was breaking into the record book.

"Moore and Marciano!" Tiny shouted down at me. He must be about six feet four.

But it was certain that Marciano wouldn't fight him during the current tax year. Also, Marciano is the kind of fighter it is sometimes more advantageous to be in the position of challenging than fighting, even for a virtuoso.

Wunderkind

One of the greatest men I ever knew was the celebrated middleweight Philadelphia Jack O'Brien—"Philadelphia Jack O'Brien from Americaw" was the way he liked best to hear it. He would say it that way aloud to cheer himself up when his spirits flagged. "That was how they introduced me at the National Sporting Club in London," he would explain, "and the sonorousness of the effect compensates the redundancy." The "Philadelphia" was to distinguish him from the numerous other O'Briens and pseudo-

O'Briens active in the American ring in his era. (The current edition of Nat Fleischer's record book, *The Ring*, lists only three O'Briens; the Irish are in a professional decline.) The agility of Mr. O'Brien's mind exceeded even that of his footwork, which was the most spectacular of his generation. Once, in his robust, athletic middle years, which coincided with the Depression, he was shy the rent for a gymnasium he conducted atop a Broadway building. He therefore invited the landlord, a dropsical old German gentleman, to a free boxing lesson, in the course of which he pretended that the old fellow had knocked him out. The landlord, fearing a damage suit, avoided O'Brien for months, and never bothered him about the rent.

This, however, is what my (and, during O'Brien's life, his) friend Colonel Stingo would call a labyrinthian digression. What enshrined O'Brien in the memory of millions who never enjoyed the privilege of his personal acquaintance was that in March, 1909, he was knocked into a cerebral hiatus, unique for him, in the last five seconds of a ten-round bout with a less deservedly eminent contemporary called Stanley Ketchel, the Michigan Assassin after he, O'Brien, had won six or seven rounds of the fight. Because the bell interrupted the referee's count, there was no knockout, and under the present rules of the New York State Athletic Commission he would have been entitled to the decision, even though prostrate. The state law then forbade decisions of any kind, and fellows in barrooms have been arguing intermittently ever since over who won the fight. Both O'Brien and Ketchel, according to all qualified observers, were great middleweights, but I sometimes wonder whether their encounter wouldn't be remembered as just a pretty good fight, instead of an epic, if it hadn't ended the way it did.

What made me think of the O'Brien–Ketchel fight was the fact that in the *last* second of the final round of a run-of-the-mill fight at Madison Square Garden in October, 1954, I saw a young colored light heavyweight named Floyd Patterson knock Joe

Gannon through the ropes with a punch that would surely have
been a knockout if the final bell hadn't sounded just as the victim
fell. It's the only time I've seen this happen in what must be several hundred fights I've watched. (I started going to them in
about 1920, and while I've never attended more than about a
dozen cards in a year, they begin to mount up.) Since this was an
eight-round bout, the mathematical odds against the thing's
coming off in the last second were 1,439 to 1. Another odd feature of the bout was that it was limited to eight rounds to protect
Patterson, who is not yet twenty and therefore, in the eyes of the
Athletic Commission, too tender a vessel for a longer course. If
there had been a ninth round, the other fellow wouldn't have
been able to come up for it.

Fight snobs will consider my analogy with O'Brien and
Ketchel sacrilegious, because, as I have said, this Garden bout
wasn't much of a fight. Moreover, it developed later that Gannon
wasn't leading on points in the opinions of the judges, the referee, the newspapermen, or the people watching the show on television. He was walking a tightrope from the first round on. But
for two friends of Gannon's who sat behind me he had run up a
bigger lead than old Philadelphia Jack enjoyed when Ketchel
caught him. I went to the fight because I wanted to see how far
Patterson had progressed since turning professional in 1952, and
I suppose that the same curiosity brought out most of the rest of
the small crowd. Among the exceptions were half a hundred Oc-
cidentals wearing Chinese lampshade hats, whom I took to be
delegates to some convention of Shriners or Red Men of the
World. I learned later they were Philadelphia rooters for a lightweight named Jimmy Soo, whose father runs a Chinese restaurant down there. Soo was fighting in the semifinal.

My interest in Patterson goes back to the summer of 1952, when
he was a member of the United States boxing team at the

Olympic Games in Helsinki, which I attended. There was no boxing ring at Olympic Village, on the outskirts of Helsinki, and the American boxers used to go into town by bus every morning to train in the gymnasium of a workingmen's club in Häkäniemi, the proletarian quarter of town. The club, in a great granite building known as the People's House, stood on a small square, in the center of which was a statue of a completely naked boxer. The daily bus trip gave the American boxers a closer contact with Helsinki and its residents than most of the other athletes got; every morning, a knot of admiring, towheaded small boys and not-so-small girls would wait for the American bus to draw up at the curb outside the People's House, and they would all be there again an hour later to see the boxers leave. The trip made excellent counterpropaganda to the Communist legend of the Land of Lynching, for eleven of the fourteen members of the boxing squad were Negroes. They looked very sharp in their American sports clothes, and the girls quite evidently thought they were beautiful.

There was one working coach with the squad, a jolly, sagacious fellow named Pete Mello, who is head coach of the Catholic Youth Organization boxing team in New York; he had as colleagues a couple of free riders in blue blazers and white buckskin shoes, who stayed far from sweat and Vaseline. On the first morning I met the team, Mello tipped me off to Patterson, who was seventeen and entered in the hundred-and-sixty-five-pound class. Mello picked him as the surest winner for the United States, although the rest of the team included boys who had been amateur stars for years and had won enough watches to stock three hock shops on Sixth Avenue.

Patterson was having no trouble making the weight; he was a tall, straight stick of a boy, slender except for big shoulders. He had a long, straight nose and wore long sideburns; there was something humorously dandified about his appearance. Outside the ring, his favorite position was horizontal. If he saw a bench, he would lie on it rather than sit. Inside the ring he fought with a wild exuberance. He would begin from a crouch, with shoulders and forearms protecting his head, and then would start to wing punches, being as likely to lead with a right as with a left. His style was crude, but his reflexes were so fast he got away with it. His leverage was perfect—his blows hurt, and after throwing one he was almost always in position to hit again. Furthermore, he liked to fight and was as strong as a snake, grabbing his sparring partners and whirling them off balance—an unconventional and technically illegal maneuver that draws only a warning from referees here but is likely to lead to disqualification by the more precise European judges. Mello's one worry about Patterson was that this would happen, and he kept cautioning the boy on the subject. All Patterson's hard fights in Helsinki were in the training ring, against heavier teammates. We had a huge heavyweight there named Ed Sanders, who was a football player from Idaho State College, and an alternate named Norvel Lee, who weighed a bit over a hundred and eighty and had won dozens of amateur titles. Lee, who was twenty-eight, was a law-school man heading for the F.B.I., and he knew as much about boxing as an amateur can know. There was a hundred-and-seventy-eight-pound class in the Olympics, and Lee decided to aim for that. Patterson and Lee liked to fight each other, and Lee, even with his extra twenty pounds and his big edge in experience, couldn't quite hold Patterson even.

There was nothing much to Patterson's Olympic bouts themselves. In the hundred-and-sixty-five-pound final, Patterson met a Rumanian. The fellow was frightened, as well he might have been, and Patterson clowned a bit. He whirled the Rumanian clean around once, and I could imagine Mello blanching. The crowd booed, although he hadn't done anything to harm the fellow—it was a mere *pas de danse*. The judges didn't disqualify him, however, and since the boo had warned him to get down to work, he hit the Rumanian once and knocked him out.

After that, there was "the Olympic ceremony." Three portable platforms were moved into the ring. Patterson stood on the highest, with the resuscitated Rumanian at his right, on a lower level, and a Finn, the winner of third honors, at his left. A girl in Finnish National costume had handed Patterson a big bouquet, and he held it in his left hand. A band played the Olympic fanfare and then "The Star-Spangled Banner," and, tucking his right forearm into his belly, Patterson made a deep, dancing-school bow.

Later, Lee won the hundred-and-seventy-eight-pound final, and got a special cup for being the most skillful boxer in the Olympics. He has a classic stand-up style that goes over big with Europeans. Sanders won the heavyweight title; he was so big that his final opponent, a Swede, simply ran away. The judges disqualified the Swede, who said afterward that it had suddenly occurred to him he might be killed.* The American boxers won five first places out of a possible ten. The mass of unofficial points the Americans picked up in the boxing competition went so far to offset the unofficial points the Russians scored in gymnastics that in the unofficial point score covering all events the United States won a psychologically important unofficial victory. And that was the last time I had seen Patterson in the flesh before I went to the Garden the night he fought Gannon.

In the meanwhile, I knew, Patterson had been doing well, without being rushed unduly. In any art the prodigy presents a

---

* Sanders himself died after a televised bout in Boston on December 11, 1954. He had been knocked out in the eleventh round of a feature scheduled for twelve rounds. It was only his *ninth* professional fight, and he had been a professional for only nine months. In more normal pre-television times a fellow out of the amateurs would spend three years in four-, six-, and eight-round bouts in small clubs before attempting ten. Amateur experience has only a limited relation to serious boxing, since amateurs go only three rounds. Twelve rounds, I should estimate roughly, impose sixteen times as much strain as three, and the transition used to be managed gradually. Patterson, as I have indicated, has had better luck. Two years after turning pro he was being asked to go only eight rounds. But the majority of the fighters who come up under the aegis of the peddling business are not only incompetent, but bad actuarial risks in the bargain.

problem. Given too easy a program, he goes slack, but asked too hard a question early, he becomes discouraged. Finding a middle course is particularly difficult in the prize ring; in comparison, the management of juvenile orchestra conductors, mathematicians, and billiardists is simple. The fighter must be confirmed in the belief that he can lick anybody in the world and at the same time be restrained from testing this belief on a subject too advanced for his attainments. The trick lies in keeping the fellow entertained while enriching his curriculum. In my young manhood, there were two *Wunderkinder* in the light-heavyweight class whose handlers failed to bring it off; one, Young Stribling, was made overcautious by doting parents, and the other, Jimmy Slattery, was made overconfident by adulation. Slattery, like Icarus, made a great splash, though. He was a boy Mozart, a honeydew melon.

In the two years following his return from Finland, Patterson had had seventeen professional fights. Of these, the first thirteen had been with opponents of progressively diminishing unimportance, each picked to contribute something to his education. From the beginning Patterson was a fair television attraction, because of his Olympic fame, and his TV fees served as a kind of scholarship for him. Almost all his fights were on Monday nights—television nights—at a club called the Eastern Parkway Arena, in Brooklyn. His graduation exercises took place in June, 1954, when he went eight televised Eastern Parkway rounds with Joey Maxim, who was still tough and a cutie, or opportunist. Maxim was never a great hitter, though, so he didn't figure to knock Patterson out. I watched the fight from a stool in the Palace Bar & Grill, on West 45th Street, and what impressed me was that Maxim couldn't make Patterson look foolish except at infrequent intervals, and then only for a second or two. He would have handled the Helsinki Patterson the way a rodeo clown handles a bull. In the Olympics, Patterson had wasted much time in aimless body-weaving, and had often launched

himself through the air like a man trying to get through a clos-
ing subway door before the train pulls out. Against Maxim, he
held himself together better and hit more often, with shorter,
quicker blows. Also, he had got pretty cute himself. His greater
vigor more than made up for Maxim's slight margin in acuity, I
thought, and when the ex-champion got the decision, I agreed
with the other patrons of the Palace that Patterson had been
robbed. The newspaper writers the next morning were of the
same opinion. Patterson had proved he could no longer be considered an undergraduate. After these commencement exercises
he knocked out a fellow named Tommy Harrison, who should
have given him a good fight, and then polished off a couple
of light summer snacks while waiting for the rodeo to get out of
Madison Square Garden.

Gannon, the fellow chosen for Patterson's debut on the Garden's Friday-night television program, which paid four thousand
dollars an appearance, figured no better than most of the twenty-
nine-hundred-dollar opponents Patterson had been meeting on
Monday nights, although he was, of course, considerably superior
to a Rumanian amateur. The simplest reason for the match that I
could think of was that the I.B.C. feared Patterson might suffer
from stage fright in his first Eighth Avenue appearance. Gannon
was a fighter calculated to get him over any initial nervousness.
Another reason, I supposed, was that Gannon was managed by Al
Weill, who also manages Rocky Marciano. Weill is a man of
weight and profundity; when he makes a match for one of his
fighters, it often turns out that he has had in view some chink in
the armor of the adversary party. Gannon is an old-looking young
man with a serious, puggy face and a heavy beard, which shows
through his white skin like Senator Joe McCarthy's. According
to the program notes, Gannon was twenty-seven, which indicated
that he must have been something of a prodigy himself in his
time. He was national amateur welterweight champion in 1944,
when, if the program was right, he was seventeen. Subsequently,

however, he renounced his art to become a policeman in Washington, and during his resumed career under Mr. Weill's guidance he had retained a coppish gloom. Sitting in his corner, he frequently looks as though he were counting the number of places he lost on the sergeant's list through his truancy. He is a pretty good conventional boxer, but I couldn't imagine his staying ahead of Patterson. After Maxim, Gannon would be a refresher course in the rudiments.

The purpose of going to a fight isn't always to see a close contest. A great many close fights are hardly worth looking at, while the development of an interesting performer is always an attraction; Native Dancer and Man o' War were drawing cards when they were 1–100 to win. Since I anticipated no strong emotions from the main bout, I went to the Garden early, hoping to see a good preliminary. The small-club atmosphere that has prevailed since television was evident. Perhaps fifteen hundred fans huddled around the ring; the galleries and the mezzanine were empty. By lowering the price of admission to that of a movie theater, the I.B.C. might attract a few more customers, but it is possible that the television sponsor would object. A fight seen on television has the appeal of being something for nothing, and this appeal is increased by the notion that it is something expensive for nothing. It might even help sell beer or razor blades if the I.B.C. made the price for ringside seats fifty dollars instead of eight dollars. Only the elfin Orientals from Philadelphia were animated as a couple of better-than-average colored welterweights, Ernie Roberts and Larry Baker, fought a hard, skillful eight-rounder. "Stop that bloody fight!" one yelled roguishly as the boys slugged away. This insensitivity to what is going on before their eyes is one of the weirdest characteristics of fight crowds. One oaf having suggested that the welterweights were not fighting hard, his companions tried to outdo him in cynicism. They stamped, clapped, and whistled while the welters worked out their tense little problem. Baker, a light-tan boy, worked in from his opponent's flanks, throwing wide hooks and uppercuts, moving around his man. Roberts, bitter-chocolate and grim, worked the inside lines, moving forward, punching shorter and straighter. He took the first round, and then the flashier boy won the next four, anticipating his opponent's blows and hitting him with some notable left hooks to his solidly attached head. In the sixth the dark boy came on, his mathematically superior strategy of the inner lines paying off and his steady hitting taking some of the steam out of the tan fellow. In the last round the enveloper rallied with what I judged to be his last strength, but he was too late, and the straight-mover got the decision. There was nothing theatrical in either performance—just a good professional fight.

Next, Jimmy Soo, whom the Philadelphians had come to root for, went on with a lad named Jimmy Wilde, billed as "a rough, tough lightweight from the Bronx." I learned from my program that Soo, an "undefeated lightweight of Chinese-Irish descent, is colorful, flashy, and talented." He proved to be all that—at least, far too talented for Wilde—but the rough, tough lightweight persisted. The bout was scheduled for eight rounds but was stopped after the sixth, because it was by then ten o'clock and the main bout had to go on for television. Wilde and I were both relieved.

Finally, the main fight went on. Joe Gannon came into the ring—white-skinned, spindly, and determined, knobby of knee and elbow, bristly-jowled, and wearing the expression of a ventriloquist's dummy who knows a secret and won't tell. One of the seconds in his corner was Marciano's friend Al Columbo. Gannon had worked as a Marciano sparring partner. Weill himself wasn't there, though; and neither was Goldman. Patterson came in next, looking about as he had in Helsinki—dark, dandified, and grave.

His handlers wore jerseys with "Floyd Patterson" embroidered on their backs—he had made it; he was an institution. Patterson had not filled out noticeably, and this must be a disappointment to his backers; when you have a seventeen-year-old fighter who is six feet tall, it is only human to hope that he will grow into a real heavyweight. His weight was announced as a hundred and seventy and a half, but he had boxed at the old hundred and sixty-five only a month or two earlier, and he would have had slight trouble making it again. Gannon weighed a hundred and seventy-four and a half, but his arms were thin compared to Patterson's. He walked out bravely at the bell, as if resolved to make an arrest.

At first, I didn't realize what a close fight it was. All I saw was Patterson moving in and Gannon sticking out his left, as if to halt traffic, and then stepping away rapidly—but all too often not rapidly enough. Patterson wasn't exactly killing him, but he was landing three punches for one, throwing them in quick, sharp sequences and driving Gannon in front of him. It was a voice from directly behind my right ear that apprised me of what was actually happening. "Come on, Joe!" the voice howled. "You got him wobbling!"

"I wonder if he can reckernize our voice?" a voice behind my left ear said, and then, before I could roll my head, came, "In da breadbasket, Joe! He don't like dem deah!"

Gannon's mouth was at that moment open, as he stared, glassy-eyed, over Patterson's back while the Negro pounded his belly. "You got him holding now, Joe!" the right-ear voice bellowed.

When the round ended, the left-ear voice said, "He's doing good."

From then on I attended two fights—the one I saw and the one I heard. With my eyes I apprehended poor Gannon—astonishingly brave and astonishingly persistent—sticking and hopping, holding in close for dear life, and taking a beating without ever changing that Boston-terrier expression. Patterson, more patient than in his amateur days, stalked him and outboxed him, nailing him with flurries of blows but never getting him with the one big punch. Sometimes I thought that a spark of his amateur recklessness would help, since Gannon was no hitter. Once Gannon staggered away and Patterson did jump after him. "You got him hopping now, Joe!" my right-ear voice yelled. And as the grim assault continued, the two enthusiasts convinced each other that their friend was far ahead on points.

"He looks good," left-ear voice said after the fifth round. Gannon had lost four, according to all the officials, and five by my count.

"But he gotta knock him out," said right-ear voice. "If he don't knock him out, they'll give it to Patterson. Joe gotta use his right." Joe was already using it, to protect his poor, battered noggin, but left-ear voice and right-ear voice were relentless.

"Hey, Joe, trow your right, huh?" yelled right-ear voice.

"Connect wit' one, Joe, will ya?" concurred left ear.

And they began to chorus, "Trow your right, Joe! Trow your right!"

The sixth round was more of the same. When Patterson, reverting for a moment to his old habit, whirled around in a clinch and, in throwing Gannon out of it, turned his back on him for a split second, right-ear voice yelled disconsolately, "Joe! You didn't take avantage!" But Joe, disregarding their incitements to murder, continued to box correctly—feinting, though Patterson didn't follow; jabbing, though it didn't throw Patterson off balance; taking each smack on the chops unblinking; and holding his right high to pick off punches, which usually arrived from another direction. It was such a one-sided fight that Patterson's problem, patently, was to end it with a flourish. Gannon's mere survival would be a reflection on the *Wunderkind*'s Eastern Parkway education.

Then, in the seventh, Joe reckernized the voices, or else had got bad advice in his corner. He trun rights. Unhappily, one of them connected. Maybe several of them did, but they were of a force incommensurate with their purpose. Patterson reacted with acerbity. He is a vain fellow—a great asset in a fighting man. (Abe Attell, the illustrious featherweight champion turned boulevardier, once said, "I never seen a good fighter who wasn't a conceited son of a bitch.") His temperament is not evil, but he craves admiration. As long as Gannon acted like a man trying to avoid destruction, Patterson had difficulty igniting what Colonel Stingo calls the driving inflatus. Live conspicuously and let live inconspicuously is Patterson's motto. He accepts the fact that others raise their hands against him, but when a fellow like Gannon raises his *right* hand, a fellow like Patterson feels himself belittled. He went straight after Gannon, and Gannon, intoxicated by success or else knocked silly already, disdained to get back on his motorcycle. At the end of the round, right-ear voice was ecstatic. "I tol' him trow da right!" he thundered. "He's *got* um!" howled left-ear.

The eighth was a case of assaulting an officer. Patterson was punching for keeps, raising the tempo to the point at which he used to fight in the gymnasium in the People's House. It is safe to assume that his handlers had been teaching him to pace himself, but with only three minutes left he didn't have to think about that. Poor Gannon moved like a gull on a wave. Now he was in that distressful state when every evasive move brings new disaster, until it seems to the boxer and his public that he is ducking into fists, circling into fists, slipping into fists. His nose was a red circle on his face. But one row behind me he was still winning. "Trow da right, Joe!" the voices were yelling in chorus. "You're in front!" I looked, at shorter and shorter intervals, at the clock dial on which a hand indicates the progress of the round. For the ex-cop's sake, I was glad it was nearly over. Then, as I turned from the clock for one last look at the ring, Patterson hit Gannon with a left hook, and, following him as he staggered across the ring, hit him with five more punches, of which the last, a blow with all the finesse of a pickax, smashed into Gannon's face as he stood straight up with his back to the ropes, where the preceding volley had carried him. Gannon came right on through the ropes, landing flat on his back on the ring apron, out, and the bell rang.

Right-ear voice said, "Well, howdaya like that?"

Left-ear voice said, "It's all over, huh?"

And a minute later, when I turned around, the seats behind me were empty.

Great-and-a-Half Champion

The fighter who dethrones a Pugilant Hero has a hard struggle to win popular acceptance thereafter, as readers of Pierce Egan have reason to know. The microcosm is a worshiper of demigods, like the larger world around it. Gene Tunney is belittled to this day, particularly by fans who never saw him, simply because he whipped Jack Dempsey. The names of the conquerors of Hannibal and Terry McGovern are seldom spoken. The cult of Napoleon envelops the globe, but only Tory biographers have a kind word for Wellington. One thing all these victors have in common is that they went into the ring as long shots; the man who demolishes a concept is never popular.

A protracted terra-cotta-colored prizefighter named Sandy Saddler, whose physique and profile remind me of a praying mantis, has labored under this handicap since the evening of October 29, 1948, four days before the Truman election, when he knocked out a quick-moving Italian named Willie Pep, of Hartford, in Madison Square Garden, and won the featherweight championship of the world. Pep was a 1–3 favorite going in; Dewey, as I remember it, was 1–15. It was to be a week of surprises, and the blushing experts never forgave either winner. Saddler, five feet eight and a half inches tall, was twenty-two and weighed a hundred and twenty-four pounds. Pep, who was twenty-six, is of a height more usual among featherweights—five feet five. Like Saddler he was under a hundred and twenty-six pounds; he had to be, because that is the class limit. Saddler floored the Hartford man twice in the third round and knocked him out with a left hook to the jaw in the fourth. Pep, after the third knockdown, was the theater of a visible psychomachy, or struggle between body and soul. Body won, and he stayed down. Knowing coves—in Egan's phrase—who on the afternoon of the fight had coupled Pep and Sugar Ray Robinson as twin pinnacles on the horizon of the Sweet Science, announced after Pep's defeat that he had been a hollow shell, which is a traditional ex-post-facto metaphor. They even suggested that he had feigned, although his record made this implausible. He had won a hundred and thirty-four fights out of a hundred and thirty-six.

To me Saddler appeared to be what Egan would have called a first-rate bit of fighting stuff, but he never succeeded in making his detractors admit it. He fought Pep three more times—in 1949, 1950, and 1951. In the last two annual renewals he knocked the old champion out, but the critics said that the Pep of 1950 was the mere shell of a shell, while the Pep of 1951 was not even that; he was more like the murmur you hear when you hold a shell to your ear. By that time, Pep admittedly was a bit worn between the shoulder blades, but he was still the second-best featherweight in the world. Part of the public reluctance to accept Saddler is attributable to his height, which spectators feel gives him an undue advantage over his opponents. A moment's cogitation on observed phenomena would tell them the opposite.

There are plenty of tall, skinny kids, but few of them are fighters, because the tubular torso of the asthenic male renders him peculiarly vulnerable to pounding in the middle. His higher center of gravity is a disadvantage in the ring, permitting the other boy to spin him like the lady in a ballroom-dancing act, and his swanlike neck is an overextended line of neural communication, allowing him to be knocked out by a tap that would hardly jog the rudimentary mental processes of a bull-necked lad. Most such physical types, when misplaced ambition brings them to the ring, rely on their reach to peck at opponents and on their legs to keep them out of trouble; in close, they wind their arms about their adversaries' like spaghetti around the tines of a fork. (The United Kingdom has suffered so severely from heavyweight champions of this construction that British growers have now developed a midget heavyweight strain.) Saddler, on the contrary, is relentlessly aggressive. He seldom takes a step backward, and if an opponent occasionally gets a foot under one of his descending ring shoes, he hospitably allows it to remain there. Instead of using his left for jabbing—a gesture of rejection—he prefers to apply a lashing hook to the body, and then bring it up to the jaw. If he misses the second half of the punch, and the other fellow, in straightening up, gets his head wedged under Saddler's crooked elbow, there is little the champion can do about it except uppercut with the other hand to teach him better ring manners. And when a smaller man locks one of Saddler's gloves under his arm, Saddler can hardly be blamed for trying to pull loose, even though he may swing the little fellow completely around in doing so. If at the end of this snap-the-whip he steadies his partner with a chop on the chin, it is, conceivably, to stop him from going through the ropes. Among today's boxers Saddler is almost the last dispenser of the old-fashioned amenities. He himself is built like a bundle of loosely joined fishing poles, but they are apparently pickled bamboo; he takes a good punch, and his thin arms and legs never seem to tire. But the public, instead of appreciating his fresh approach to his role, resents his efficiency.

One boxing man who agrees with me about Saddler is Charlie

Johnston, his manager. Johnston is also the handler of Archie
Moore, the light-heavyweight champion, who has been boxing
since Roosevelt's first administration. One day in the summer of
1954, while I was visiting Ehsan's training camp near Summit,
New Jersey, a pugilistic Yaddo where Moore was doing his thinking for a forthcoming fight, Mr. Johnston made a definitive ap-
praisal. "Saddler is a great champion," he said. "But Moore is a
great, great champion." Saddler was in residence at the time,
training for a couple of bouts Johnston had booked for him in
Venezuela. Since Saddler had spent 1952 and 1953 in the Army,
Johnston was bringing him along on a diet of opponents carefully
graded in significance. Military service is supposed to dull a
fighter's edge, because the Army routine interferes with serious
training. Saddler was training as hard as if he expected a tough
battle; when he went down to Caracas he knocked out his first
opponent in one round and his second in three. Johnston, who
operates from an office on Times Square, drives to Summit every
day when he has one of his champions there, and drives back in
the afternoon. He is a serious man, his champions are serious
fighters, and Ehsan's is a serious place. On weekends, when Johnston thinks the fighters have earned a bit of dissipation, he takes
down a box of jelly doughnuts.

"Doesn't Saddler get bored down here nights?" I asked him.

"Why should he be bored?" Johnston said. "He can talk to
Moore about boxing."

When I read in the newspapers that Saddler was to defend his
title against a fellow called Red Top Davis in Madison Square
Garden on February 25, 1955, I felt as pleased as if I were going
to see a favorite actor in a new vehicle. I knew little about Davis,
but I was confident that Saddler would interpret him in an interesting manner. It would be the champion's first defense of the
featherweight title since his last fight with Pep, in September,
1951.

On the Sunday morning before the fight, I drove down to Summit with Johnston to see Saddler spar. Mrs. Johnston rode in the front seat with her husband; it was such a beautiful day, she said, that he had insisted she go along for the ride. They picked me up in front of my apartment house, and then we drove to the Capitol Hotel, where we collected a radio announcer for the Argentine Ministry of Information; he had a medal to present to Saddler on behalf of Perón. Johnston maintained cordial relations with Perón, and carried on a brisk import-and-export trade in boxers with him. The Argentine, a small plump man with a blue beard, said he hadn't had any breakfast and didn't want any. He told me he traveled to all countries where Argentine athletes competed—especially automobile racers—and broadcast reports to Buenos Aires on how they were doing. The job sounded all right to me. "Three fighters Sandy knock out nineteen-fifty-one in South America," he said. "None them no good never since. Sandy poonch, poonch." Then he fell asleep.

From my seat in back I could converse with Mr. Johnston at the wheel more easily than if I had been sitting beside him, because of his deaf right ear. As we threaded our way between the filling stations and Howard Johnsons of northern New Jersey, I gathered some intelligence about Red Top Davis. Davis, I learned, had gained his position as challenger by beating a fellow named Percy Bassett, who had previously beaten another fellow who couldn't fight at all. On such tenuous foundations are featherweight reputations now reared. Davis, Johnston said, was thirty-one, three years older than Saddler. "As a matter of fact," he went on, "Davis was two of the last six guys Pep licked before the first time we licked Pep. He used to be a sparring partner for Pep, I hear, and that summer Pep decisioned him twice in Hartford in two weeks just to keep busy." Subsequently Davis had campaigned all over the place, losing as often as he won, until the last couple of years, when he started winning more often than he lost. "Some fighters improve late," Johnston said.

In the bare dining room of Ehsan's main building we found Bertie Briscoe, Saddler's trainer. He is a grizzled Brooklyn Irishman who fought as a bantamweight in the Edwardian era. I asked him how Sandy looked, and he said seriously, "How he looks? He's the best fighter ever tied on a glove in the history of the world." Moore, Johnston's other champion, has his own trainers—Cheerful Norman and Tiny Payne. Johnston calls them "Moore trainers," and Briscoe a "Saddler trainer." The Moore trainers were in California, so Briscoe got no argument. "Name me another fighter in the history of the world fought in every country and never brought no soft touch with him to fight," he said fiercely. "We fight the best they got, and we hit them in the old kazazza." He returned, breathing hard with anger, to the perusal of the boxing column in the New York *Enquirer*. "This feller," he said, poking a rectangular index finger into the boxing columnist's photographically reproduced eye, "picks *Davis!*" Johnston equably ventured the suggestion that maybe such talk might bring a few customers into the Garden, but Briscoe, as soon as the manager turned away, glared at his back and grumbled, "Anything for a dollar." He was only half mollified when Mrs. Johnston presented him with a box of jelly doughnuts for himself alone. In the kitchen Mr. Jimmy Brooks, Saddler's *fidus Achates* and junior trainer, was feeding a week-old lamb from a nursing bottle. For Brooks, the dashing Harlemite who admitted he was a boulevardier and connoisseur, this was an unprecedented surrender to the austerity of the environment, and he felt called upon to explain it. "She fell into a pond, and when they fish her out, the mother wouldn't feed her," he said. "She must have smelled different." Looking at the lamb with an affection of callousness, he added, "She wouldn't make but one order of lamb chops." The lamb, having emptied the bottle, made a noise like a baby's rattle, and the boulevardier panicked. "Don't be mad, Baby," he implored. "Daddy going to get you more soon as he can heat it."

When we had had our ham and eggs—the invariable lunch for visitors at Ehsan's—Johnston and the Argentine and I headed for the gymnasium, farther up the hill, where Saddler was working out. Mrs. Johnston stayed in the farmhouse with the Sunday newspapers. The Argentine had managed to eat, and felt better. Johnston had a new Argentine import—a middleweight named Merentino—going at St. Nick's on Monday night, and the announcer said he would broadcast that one. "How is this Merentino?" I asked him, and he said, "Very good poonch, poonch. No much reflection."

Saddler was wearing long sweat clothes like old-fashioned red-flannel underwear, which made him look less like a mantis than usual and more like a Christmas candle. Before he put on his sparring helmet, he pulled a cellophane shower cap over his carefully plastered-down hair. The sweat clothes might have meant that he was having trouble making the weight or merely that he had a sensible aversion to drafts. His sparring partner, Georgie Collins, a chunky, muscular lightweight, operated in the fashion expected of Davis, circling and bobbing much as Pep used to do. (Davis was supposed to have picked up a lot of Pep's stuff sparring with him.) Every now and then he tried to bob up inside the effective arc of Saddler's long arms and work him over in close. Saddler, flat-footed and elastic, practiced assiduously with a long left hook to the region denominated by Mr. Briscoe as the kazazza—the torso between the diaphragm and the waistline. (Mr. Briscoe's slang is as archaic as his lingerie; he wears thick winter drawers that he calls bulletproofs.) The hook to the kazazza of a bouncy fellow is intended to exercise a numbing effect upon his transmission; after a few applications, he ceases to be such a gadabout. When Collins got inside, Saddler would retract his arms to the position of prayer, and uppercut. All was good nature, and I thought I could tell from the way he worked that he wasn't much worried.

I got out to see Davis two days later, on Washington's Birthday. He was training at Long Pond Inn, in Greenwood Lake, New York, and it was to be his final day of sparring before the fight, on Friday night. This trip had more of the air of an official outing than the other; I set forth from the I.B.C., at the Garden, in a hired Cadillac and in the company of Harry Mendel, an I.B.C. press agent, and a free-lance photographer who had been chartered for the day, like the Cadillac. The photographer arrived even sleepier than Sunday's Argentine. "Out of a cold blue sky, they call me on five minutes' notice," he complained.

"You look great—who's your embalmer?" the driver said.

"The same stiff that writes your material," the photographer replied. They must have been listening to the same television comedian. The other members of our company were Al Buck, a sports writer from the *Post*, and Tony Canzoneri, the old featherweight, and then lightweight, champion. (He now weighs a hundred and sixty-five.) Canzoneri was to observe Davis and tell Mendel how he thought he looked; the next day he would go down to Summit and observe Saddler. It would make good publicity for the fight, and also for a restaurant Canzoneri was opening on Broadway. I never see Canzoneri without thinking of the great excitement he used to set up without making a single spurious move. He never took an unnecessary step to call attention to his agility, or threw a silly, slapping punch to catch the crowd's eye; he was an aggressive stylist who kept the pressure on the opposition and then came through with bursts of patterned, synchronized blows that either brought out the best in the other fellow or flattened him.

At Greenwood it was still deep winter. From the windows of

the inn, a long, rambling place on the edge of the lake, we could see men fishing through the ice for pickerel. Inside, the bar was doing a good business. It was a holiday, and up there fighters are a standard attraction, like the Central Park Zoo in Manhattan. The bouts go on in a gymnasium above the long dining room and bar. There is none of the monastic atmosphere of Ehsan's at the inn; it is more cheerful and at the same time more distracting. At the inn the I.B.C. always buys you a steak dinner, and you always meet some trainer you know who is stuck up there with a fighter he can't leave overnight. The trainer's nostalgia for Stillman's is invariably heart-wringing. You would think he was in the middle of the Australian bush.

While I was waiting for my steak I talked with Mush Salow, Davis's manager. He is a large, friendly, youngish man from Hartford, which has long been more of a sporting center than you would think from reading insurance-company brochures. Mr. Salow said his business was installing and servicing cigarette-vending machines, and this, naturally, brought him in contact with a number of people who run saloons where sporting people congregate. Davis, Mr. Salow conceded, had made a lot of bad fights in his early years, but the explanation was simple: he had not had a good manager. Early in 1950, at one of the successive nadirs of his career, Davis had wired from Zanesville, Ohio, his home town, to Pep in Hartford, offering a full contract on his services as boxer, sparring partner, or man of all work for the sum of fifty dollars. Pep had brought the telegram to Salow and recommended the proposition as a good investment. "I took a fifty-dollar bill out of my pocket and handed it to Willie," Mr. Salow said. "I can see it today, when I remember. By then, Willie must have conned himself, too, because he took out two tens and a five and handed them to me. That made us partners. We sent the money, and to our great surprise Davis showed up on the next train. His first fight under our direction, he beat the lightweight champion of Finland." There followed more discouraging days, though, Mr. Salow admitted, and during one of Davis's losing streaks Pep relinquished his twenty-five dollars' worth of the fighter, because, he said, he was disgusted. "That left him all to me," Mr. Salow said, "and look where we are today!" By this time the steaks had arrived, and the bar trade was already beginning to drift away in the direction of the gymnasium. I asked the ritual question—"How does he look?"—and Salow said, "He isn't much of a gymnasium fighter, but he's in great condition. For the first time since I've known him, he's on edge, snapping, and that's a good sign."

Davis turned out to be a dark Negro with a wide face, a strong torso, and stubby, muscular legs, which carried him briskly around the ring on what I should describe as a great-circle course. He was working with Joey Gambino, a six-round fighter who has had about twenty bouts. Gambino played Saddler, and almost every time he threw the imitation Saddler left hook to the kazazza, it landed. It wasn't a natural punch for Gambino, and he threw it awkwardly, but it went in anyway. If Saddler had been throwing those hooks, Davis would have been a tired man at the end of the three rounds he sparred. Coming back to town in the Cadillac, Canzoneri said, "He gets hit too much. But his trainer tells me he's a bad gym fighter."

In consequence of these preliminary investigations, I was not too sanguine of seeing an epic when I took my seat in the Garden on the night of the fight. Uncertainty is not absolutely necessary to my enjoyment of the Sweet Science, however. Davis had what seemed to me an insoluble problem, and I was eager to see how he would apply himself to its solution. He had not knocked out a man of any importance in his entire career, while Saddler hadn't been knocked out once in his hundred and fifty fights. (The record book shows that he was last stopped on March 21, 1944, in his second professional fight, when he was seventeen years old.)

I was pretty sure that Davis wouldn't set a new precedent. His one chance was to outbox Saddler for fifteen rounds, but Saddler was a better boxer. As for Saddler, his procedural details are so entertaining that it is always a pleasure to watch him, even when the opposition is commonplace. It's like seeing Bobby Clark in a musical comedy with an inferior book. Although the fight was on television, there were five or six thousand customers in the Garden—an excellent showing for an era when the Sweet Science has become a free handout to encourage beer sales. I naturally assumed that all these customers were, like me, lovers of art for its own sake; it didn't occur to me that they expected the illusion of close competition. In a wrestling match or a circus chariot race, such an illusion can be prearranged, but not in an honest prize fight.

The semifinal did not long hold my interest, because it was between two young lightweights in such prime condition that they couldn't hurt each other. They exchanged resounding blows with the disregard of consequences that accompanies regular hours, a clean life, and habitual overindulgence in vitamins, and at the end of eight rounds they left a feeling of nothing accomplished. A former member of a college faculty named Eddie Shevlin (he taught boxing) used to say, "You never learn anything until you're tired." He would therefore let his students bat each other about for ten or twelve five-minute rounds before he began trying to teach them, and I sometimes think the trouble with young fighters nowadays is that they are never allowed to become sufficiently exhausted. Even Davis, in all his hundred and ten fights, had never boxed more than twelve rounds in one evening—a circumstance he was destined to recollect before this one was over.

Davis's demeanor when he climbed through the ropes after the departure of the eupeptic lightweights was grave; it is possible that he was even then developing a psychomachy. He was accompanied by Salow, who appeared to be thinking hard about the

fifty-dollar bill, and two trainers—Freddie Fierro and Chickie
Ferrara. He weighed precisely a hundred and twenty-six. Saddler
came into the opposite corner wearing an ensemble that, while it
did not quite outshine the black-and-gold silk mandarin robe
Archie Moore wears into the ring, came within a gleam of it. He
had on a two-piece wool outfit in the Wallace tartan, predomi-
nantly red and black. The Johnston champions find an emotional
outlet in color. With Saddler were Johnston, Briscoe, and Brooks,
all smiling as if they had just split a hamper of jelly doughnuts.
Saddler weighed a hundred and twenty-four and a half pounds, for
a net gain of eight ounces in the six years and four months that
had elapsed since his 1948 bout with Pep. When his handlers removed the plaid coverings, his legs, arms, and torso resembled
cinnamon sticks, but his profile, a sweeping arc from cranium to
chin, rested on his long mandibles as chillingly as it had the first
time Pep saw him. He presented an unfriendly appearance. Harry
Kessler, the referee, a gray-haired, florid official, viewed the two
fighters with the expression of a new Sunday-school teacher who
expects to be hit with a spitball if he turns his head. He had never
refereed Saddler before, but he had heard about his propensity for
bringing out the worst in other fighters' natures.

From the moment Kessler called the two men to the center of
the ring for the conventional admonition—"Now, Sandy and
Teddy, I want a nice clean fight," he said into the microphone—
it became evident that the crowd expected a contest between Saddler and the referee, if not between Saddler and Davis. "Watch
him, Ref!" persons above and behind me shrieked. "Watch dose
tumbs! Watch dose elbows! Watch dat head!" It sounded like the
anatomical-catalogue song about Alouette. The booing of Saddler
began shortly after the first bell. Davis, because he was so much
shorter than Saddler, and because he obviously had very little
chance to beat him, had the public sympathy, and the proximity
of his kazazza to his waistline encouraged partisan outcry every
time Saddler hooked. Encouraged by his supporters, Davis dis-

played brisk but not dangerous activity during the first two minutes of the first round. In one clinch he placed his open left hand
on Saddler's face and felt for an eyeball with a thumb, but the
crowd treated him like Little Lord Fauntleroy; the roles had been
assigned. The Philistines were equally prodigal with advice. Beginning with the first round, a tactician behind me shouted, over
and over, "Trow your right, Davis—he's holdin' his shoulder
low." He forgot that though the shoulder was low, there was a lot
of arm in front of it. Davis didn't forget; Saddler wouldn't let
him. Toward the end of the first round, Saddler hit him with a
left to the head that hurt him sorely, and after that the Davis psychomachy became manifest. This particular battle between body
and soul ended in a draw. Red Top didn't soulfully storm the bar-
ricade of gloves, but he didn't lay the body down, either. He just
kept boxing, moving away, clutching when necessary, jabbing
when it seemed that a jab might make Saddler miss a punch that
counted, and as the rounds went by, the unreceptive public had
nothing to amuse it but Saddler's imaginary conflict with the
rules. Kessler, entering with spirit into his role of public prosecu-
tor, admonished one fighter or the other, and sometimes both, in
almost every round, but after the fight it turned out that he had
not taken a round away from either for foul practice, which
means that in his opinion no serious crime had occurred.

By the end of the third round, the right side of poor Red Top's
head was beginning to swell from the crashing left hooks, and as
the fight continued, it looked like an old, lopsided medicine ball
with features painted on it. Often Saddler, trying to pull loose,
spun Davis about, and the crowd shrieked its outrage; at the end
of one of the middle rounds, Davis spun Saddler, and the crowd
cheered. It wasn't until the eleventh that I heard a kind word for
the long fellow. Then a hero off in the arena seats bravely yelled,
"You're my boy, Sandy!" There was a stunned hush for fully three-
fifths of a second. After the tenth, it was clear to even the most de-
voted rooters for the underdog that nothing was to be expected of

him, and after the eleventh, the vociferation was merely peevish. If I dwell with distaste on this popular reaction to the original artist, it is because it seemed to me to reflect the influence exerted on the fight crowd by television wrestling, which isn't watched as a sporting event at all but as a clash of factitious personalities. Saddler and Johnston had been goaded for a year to risk the title the newspapermen said they had been "keeping in mothballs," and Davis was the best challenger at the weight. In horse racing, when a Native Dancer or Man o' War outclasses the other horses of his age, it does not detract from his popularity. Davis finished the fight on his feet. Saddler's failure to flatten him was thoroughly resented by the same coves who would have hated the champion even more if he had flattened him, and the unanimous decision for Saddler was roundly booed.

I went back to Saddler's dressing room, under the Garden, a few minutes after the champion's faction left the ring. The fighter, reclining on one elbow on a rubbing table, was telling the newspapermen that once Davis had gone completely on the defensive, he had not tried too hard to knock him out—he didn't think he could have, anyway. He said that no punch had hurt him, and that the referee had been O.K. He was not breathing hard, and he was unmarked. Jimmy Brooks, holding a small levee for Harlem friends in a corner of the dressing room, was expansively delighted. "You know how glad I am not to have to go back to the country, my friend," he said to me. "Now for a short-order double helping of gracious living."

Mr. Briscoe, however, was in a mountainous rage, like the mother of a prima donna who hasn't had enough curtain calls. "They booed before he even touched the guy!" he howled.

"He looked pretty good in there, I thought," I said, to cheer him up.

"Pretty good!" he bellowed. "Pretty good! He done the forcing. He done the leading. The feller never come to him, he come to the feller. What other champion ever done that? He ain't rough. Rough fellers, he tames them. He makes altar boys out of them. Right in the kazazza!" Mr. Briscoe appeared to be so near the point of strangulation that I slapped him on the back. It was a mistake. He regained the use of his voice. "He is the greatest fighter that ever tied on a glove in the history of the world," he said.

Johnston was more measured in his praise. "Would you say now that Saddler is a great, great champion, like Moore?" I asked him.

"Well, when he's had as much experience as Moore, he will be," Johnston said. (Saddler had had a hundred and fifty-three fights, but Moore had had more.) "Right now, I'd call him just great and a half."

Next-to-Last Stand, Maybe

In April, 1955, I went up to Syracuse to attend the second last stand of an East Side welterweight named Billy Graham, who was thirty-three years old. The failing practitioners of most arts may be spared pain by critics who pretend not to notice; if such kindness is in default, they can attribute the critics' changed tone to envy. But a fighter knows when he is slowing up, because he cannot reach the openings he sees. (It is a sensation like the dream in which you swing your fist and it floats.) This intimation is confirmed when fellows who have no right—that is, no professional qualifications—to hit him do. In fact, they murder him. The public twigs to the situation in infinitely less time than it takes to catch on to a crumbling Hollywood beauty or a souring statesman. Gamblers no longer bet the odds with the fighter but against him, and friends, solicitous of his health, try to dissuade him from further public appearances before he becomes a mere opponent. (A fighter without significance is described as "just an opponent.")

The fighter is as reluctant as the next artist to accept the evidence of his disintegration, even though it is presented to him so much more forcibly. Between fights he is brisk, active, and lusty, since he is still a young man. He therefore refuses to believe his first couple of bad fights, and blames them on negligence; he has not, he thinks, taken the opposition seriously enough. Then he may lose one or two that he will blame on bad decisions—suspecting, though, that if he had been his old self he would have won easily. Finally, or semifinally, his manager will accept a match for him against a younger fighter on his way up. This is known in the cant of the sports page as the fighter's last stand, although it seldom is, unless it ends in disaster. If the last-standee makes a creditable showing, even in defeat, the fight turns out to have been his next-to-last stand—the first step in a sequence that may repeat itself several times before he finally renounces the active cultivation of his art.

Graham's first last stand, against a twenty-three-year-old fellow—half Chilean and half Italian—named Chico Vejar, in Madison Square Garden on the night of March fourth, was a good fight to watch, even though he lost it. Vejar, a tireless, pressing kind of chap without subtlety, carried the fight to him, and Graham, who would have eluded his rudimentary aggressions with ease a few years ago, had to try to knock him out. For Graham this was a novelty; the chief popular criticism of his best previous efforts had been that they were skillful but unimpassioned. He started boxing professionally in 1941, and until the beginning of 1954 he was as good as a fighter can be without being a hell of a fighter. While all East Side fighters are traditionally tough, most of the really good ones come from the lower East Side—from the streets with names rather than numbers, between Broadway and the East River. While Billy was growing up, the part of the East Side he lived in was a crumbling but still almost genteel neighborhood at the foot of the eastern slope of Murray Hill. It centered on St. Gabriel's Church and St. Gabriel's Park and on Billy's father's saloon, at Thirty-fifth Street and Second Avenue. There was a long line of neat red-brick fronts along the Thirty-seventh Street side of the park, where the East Side Airlines Terminal now stands. The church has since been torn down to make way for an approach to the Manhattan entrance of the Queens-Midtown Tunnel, and the building that housed the saloon fell down of old age. Before these changes came about, the quarter had a provincial air. It had street gangs and street games, but it wasn't enough of a slum to produce a hell of a fighter.

Billy fought plenty of tough fellows who could punch, but he didn't let them punch him often. He was a good boxer inside as well as away, and he made them miss their short punches as well as their long ones. He would hit them enough to win, especially with showy combinations of punches that made him look a bit better than he really was—a knack only his adversaries and their managers begrudged him. Once he came near to winning the world championship from the Cuban Kid Gavilan, in New York, but at the end of fifteen rounds the decision went against him. Gavilan was a hell of a fighter having an off night; he fought Graham again, in Havana, and beat him clearly. In 1953, Graham had a good year, beating three determined, hard-punching fellows who couldn't hit him, and making two appearances in Syracuse against a native hero named Carmen Basilio, who got a decision over Billy in the first bout; in the second, they fought a draw in twelve rounds. But in 1954 Graham began losing to mediocrities, and his first last-stand defeat by Vejar was his third reverse in a row.

Graham's second last stand was also against Vejar. The fight couldn't be held in New York, since the circus had moved into

Madison Square Garden for a six-week run, so the I.B.C. put the match in Syracuse because, by reason of his hard fights in that city, with Basilio, Graham might be expected to draw well there. (The Syracuse promoter, a young man named Norman Rothschild, was to receive a share of the I.B.C.'s television revenue from the fight to protect him against loss in case it *didn't* draw.) Vejar's home town is Stamford, Connecticut, but he has appeared on television so many times that he is well known everywhere. I went to Syracuse, frankly, because I hoped Graham might have learned enough about Vejar to have a plan for taking the youthful bounce out of him; emotionally, I long ago moved over to the middle-aged side of the field, and I root for mature judgment when pitted against the outrageous fortunes of chronology.

I traveled to Syracuse by train the afternoon of the day before the fight, and when I arrived that evening I checked in at the Hotel Onondaga, a big, convivial old pile, which, while not the most modern in town, gets the patronage of visiting members of what Pierce Egan, the Parkman of the London prize ring, liked to call "the fancy." I learned at the desk, while registering, that both the fighters, along with their factions—their trainers, seconds, and managers—were in residence. There was no evidence of their presence, however. The bar of the Onondaga had only a few customers, rather than one of Egan's throngs blowing a cloud over the daffy and heavy wet (gin and beer) while devouring the rich points of a flash chaunt (*chanson à clef*), as there should have been before the combat of two metropolitan heroes in a county town. (Syracuse is the seat of Onondaga County.) I left my bag in my room and went to see how Graham was getting on. The three doors to his faction's suite were locked, but when I knocked at one of them, Irving Cohen, who has been Graham's manager since his first bout, opened it at once.

"Come right in," he said. "Jimmy Wild and I are having a television evening." Mr. Cohen, a short, plump, blond man, and Mr. Wild, Graham's trainer, a short, plump, dark man, were in their undershirts and shorts; they were watching a televised moving picture that had a star who looked exactly like Vice-President Nixon and grinned like him. This chap was trying to find a girl whose picture he had painted from memory. (He had seen her only once, but I came in too late to discover why he hadn't taken that opportunity to ask her name.) Mr. Cohen, who has large, round, blue eyes and a retiring smile, folded his hands contentedly on the front of his undershirt. "A home away from home!" he exclaimed.

Mr. Wild crossed his legs. "Whereya gonna go in Syracuse?" he demanded rhetorically.

I asked about Graham. "He's out catching a double feature," Mr. Cohen said. "We want him to stay up a little late tonight, so he'll sleep late in the morning, not to be restless. We'll wake him just in time to get over to the weigh-in at twelve o'clock."

There are fighters no trainer in his right mind would let get out of his sight on the night before a fight, but Graham isn't one of them. He is an old pro, and a family man. Wild said he had brought Graham up by plane on Monday, three days before; prior to that he had trained for three weeks at Greenwood Lake. In 1926, when Gene Tunney flew from a camp in the Poconos to Philadelphia for his first bout with Jack Dempsey, the flight was intended to be a striking psychological gesture (Tunney got desperately sick), but now it is thought old-fashioned to move fighters by train. "A fighter is condition down fine, he goes crazy, five, six hours on a train," Mr. Wild said. "He wants to get where he's going." Wild, I knew, had been with Graham only a short time; Whitey Bimstein, Graham's usual trainer, had been forbidden by the new state athletic commissioner to work in Graham's corner because Freddie Brown, Whitey's partner, was going to work in Vejar's. It was a sore point with the Graham faction. The explanation of the ruling probably is that the new commissioner, a lawyer, retained in his noodle a legal analogy—that adversaries in a lawsuit should not be represented by the same firm. It is the consensus at the Neutral Corner bar-and-grill that such an analogy is false. The back-room analogy analysts there say that a second is more like a doctor—and can't two doctors in partnership treat two patients in the same room? The commissioner had announced his ruling before the first last-stand fight, and Cohen and Steve Ellis, Vejar's manager, had flipped a coin to see who would have one of the partners in his corner. Ellis won. After the bout Ellis refused to sign for the return match unless he could keep Brown—an arrangement that would automatically bar Whitey again. Since Ellis's man had won, he had the whip hand. "They're crazy about my strategy," Freddie Brown had told me. Vejar, who is not too smart of a fighter, as the cognoscenti say, was thus equipped with a set of self-propelled brains, while Graham, who can do his own thinking in the ring, was deprived of Whitey's ability to read Freddie's mind and find out what Freddie was likely to tell Vejar to do next. Wild is a capable corner man, but he does not know Freddie as well as Whitey does.

Mr. Cohen said that the contretemps over trainers made no difference with a fighter like Billy, who was no dumb kid. But he ventured to observe that in the twenties, when Whitey was partners with Ray Arcel, Whitey and Ray had worked across from each other almost every Friday night in the Garden—"when it really *was* the Garden"—and nobody had ever accused either of them of doing a client less than justice. Mr. Cohen got into the fight business twenty-five years ago, because of his wife's decision to change a small drygoods store that she owned in Bensonhurst into a ladies'-specialty shop. Since that left Cohen with little to do around the place after opening up in the morning, he became a fight manager. He still has the manner of the small shopkeeper, however—eager to please and loath to discuss controversial subjects. Probably because he is that way, he got along beautifully as manager of Rocky Graziano, who was middleweight champion of the world between two fights with Tony Zale. Graziano, a rough rhinestone of the ring, would have blown his top under the needling of a more conventional manager.

Graham came in while Cohen was talking about how things used to be in the Garden. For a doddering old gaffer, he looked paradoxically young in his double-feature clothes—slacks, a sports jacket in a sculptured lattice pattern, and a shirt with the kind of collar that has points so long and so close together that a tie wouldn't show even if you were wearing one. He is of good height for a welterweight—five feet eight or so, in shoes—and has a Roman nose, which his early well-wishers said some friend of the family ought to hit him on with a baseball bat, so he would not devote so much thought to defending his profile. At the end of a hundred and twenty-six battles, the nose still stands as an impressive testimony to Billy's cuteness; it has, in fact, been slightly aggrandized by a bump high on the bridge. Today it is a landmark of Stillman's gymnasium, the graveyard of the Barrymore look.

By this time the guy who resembled Nixon had found the girl whose picture he had painted, but none of us had noticed how, since we were talking of other things. The girl, it turned out, was under the influence of a sinister Russian choreographer. The Russian and the Nixon exchanged high words, and at the prospect of a fight the attention of Mr. Graham, Mr. Wild, and Mr. Cohen became, by professional reaction, fixed upon the screen. But instead of squaring off with the Russian, the hero employed a mysterious, invisible judo hold and led him tamely from our view, after which we heard the sound of a blow offstage, as if someone had crushed an inflated paper bag. Mr. Wild got up and switched the set to another show. "I guess they didn't want to spoil the crease in their pants," he said.

"We lose nothing," Graham said. "I never see a good fight in the movies yet, except a newsreel. They always corny it up."

"I saw one picture where a guy was training in a gym the day of the fight!" Mr. Cohen said, his eyes extra wide with astonishment. "What kind of a manager did he have?" Even children—or at least, fight people's children—know that a fighter *rests* on the day of a fight.

"I see one," Graham said, "where the two guys are having their hands taped before they put on the gloves, and who does it? The *Boxing Commission physician!*"

"And how many times they always have to be knocked down in the beginning, the heroes!" exclaimed Mr. Cohen. "They got to get murdered or they can't win. The best tip who to bet on in a movie fight is the guy who loses the first fourteen rounds."

"He makes a miraculous recovery," Graham said. "His strength is renewed. But the tops I saw on television last winter—the guy is going to defend the world championship the next night and he says to his wife he is sick of the whole business."

"He's with his *wife* the night before the championship?" interjected Mr. Cohen.

"He says he won't fight no more," Graham said. "But his little kid, about five years old, comes in in pajamas and says, 'Daddy, box with me.' So he has to put on the gloves with the kid, and the kid says, 'Daddy, I heard what you said. I'll take your place against that bum'—well, the kid didn't say 'bum' exactly in the television—and the old man begins to cry. So he goes through with the fight and knocks the guy out. How do you like that? What I really go for is Westerns; then I can't tell when they're cornying it up."

As I got ready to leave, Graham and the others were watching a show called "Public Defender," in which a man who had a .45, a gray Ford, and a record as long as his arm had been charged with killing a fellow who had been shot with a .45 by a man in a gray Ford. All the Public Defender had to do was to get him off.

"Good night," Mr. Cohen said to me. "We'll be sitting here some time yet."

Before going to bed I took a turn through the lobby to look

for the members of the opposing faction, but they must have
been upstairs, too, and it was now too late to go calling. Although the bar had livened up a bit, the customers, I learned
from the barman, were not followers of the milling art but basketball fans. The Syracuse professional team, the Nationals, he
said, had just defeated the Fort Wayne, Indiana, Pistons, in the
first game of the World Series of basketball. Syracuse had won
the Eastern and Fort Wayne the Western championship for the
regular season. The Nationals' home court was the War Memorial Auditorium, where the milling coves would perform next
evening, and the basketball teams would play there again on Saturday, in the second game of the World Series. Billy had been
crowded out of the Garden by the elephants, and now he was being sandwiched in between two performances of a troupe of
human giraffes. In a city the size of Syracuse—population, two
hundred and fifty thousand—it was reasonable to assume that the
publics for all kinds of sports would heavily overlap, and that
basketball followers, under the necessity of shelling out the bus-
tle twice in three days for the World Series, would skip the fight.
The bout was due to be overshadowed in the metropolitan press,
too, because there was a more important battle in Boston, where
the welterweight champion, Johnny Saxton, was defending his
title against a Bostonian named Tony De Marco.

I slept late myself next morning, and then made my way over
to the weighing in, at the auditorium. Syracuse is not one of
those cities that win your heart at first glance—which this was
for me—but it was a fine day. In the Onondaga Coffee Room, I
had observed the members of the Fort Wayne Pistons having
breakfast. They twined their long legs around the table legs or
doubled them back under the chairs. It occurred to me that life
must be very difficult for a traveling collection of men who are
from six feet six to nearly seven feet tall. They might have special
long beds at home, but they could scarcely carry them with
them, and they must either bend or step back several paces to

look in a shaving mirror. An awareness of their altitude seemed to oppress them—I could imagine how many times they had been asked how the weather was up there—and their heads, at the ends of such long necks, looked small, like guinea hens'. I was rapidly becoming depressed myself, until I thought of what a liberation it must be for a man of that height to get into the company of others who could see eye to eye with him. Instead of feeling himself set apart, he probably begins to think of anyone under six feet five as subnormal. He goes back to his home town a giant refreshed.

Arriving at the auditorium, the outside of which is carved all over with the names of battles, from Belleau Wood to Iwo Jima, I was further gladdened by the sight of a number of familiar Eighth Avenue faces. Freddie Brown and Chickie Ferrara were there with Vejar, who is a shorter but more compact welterweight than Graham. So was Ellis, a swarthy, hand-pumping kind of man who, aside from being a manager, narrates sports events on television. Brown was in an expansive mood; another fellow he trains, named Giovanelli, had scored a knockout earlier in the week against a four-to-one favorite, and he must have felt that this was a good omen. Cohen and Wild were on hand with Graham, whose beard showed dark through his pale skin. Vejar's tawny cheeks seemed beardless. A moonfaced, jolly trainer named Jimmy August had driven up from New York with a middleweight named Ray Drake, who was fighting in the semifinal. Drake, like Graham, is a student of the niceties of tactics, specializing in leverage. An expeditionary force from the I.B.C. office in New York had also appeared, under the command of Billy Brown, the Garden matchmaker, who is no kin to Freddie. All the briefly expatriate faces shone with a special polish for their out-of-town adventure, reflecting, first, a *souci* for the Big Town reputation for elegance, and, second, a realization that, as Whitey Bimstein long ago observed to me, "Out of town, anything is liable to happen. You gotta keep your eyes open every minute." On the scales, before an Athletic Commission inspector, Graham weighed 149 1/2 pounds and Vejar 154 1/2, or two and a half pounds more than he had for their first fight. When, after being weighed, the two men posed together for the Syracuse newspaper photographers, the difference in their ages was more apparent than when they wore clothes. Graham was in excellent trim, but his pale skin appeared stretched over his lean body, while Vejar's darker skin seemed molded to his flesh to form a single substance. The Graham legs, which had served him well so often, looked spindly compared to the younger man's. Some joker called to Billy, "Howya feeling, Pop?" and he didn't look too pleased.

When Graham had his clothes on again, I asked him what he thought of Vejar's weight, and he said, "I think it's good. He'll be slow. Won't be able to run away so fast." Before the group broke up, there was quite a bit of talk—more of it about the fight in Boston than about the one in Syracuse, which was natural, since it was an easier fight to talk about without picking against parties present. The universal opinion of the knowing coves was that Saxton, the champion, would win.

I spent the afternoon walking around Syracuse and appreciating the weather, and then had dinner with a fellow I had known during the war, who is now a clubman and engaged in the paper business up there. He said that by then the odds were two to one on Vejar. My friend and I arrived at the auditorium just before the beginning of Drake's bout. My forebodings about the gate had been borne out. The basketball patrons had stayed away, and the hall was only about a third full. The New York newspapermen had gone to the Boston fight, and Billy's second last stand would be chronicled exclusively by the press associations and the locals. With the house lights out, though, there was a feeling of a crowd and of partisan excitement. A fight crowd in a secondary city like Syracuse is different from one in New York or Chicago, or even Philadelphia—when there is a local man fighting, it is intensely partisan; when both are outsiders, it is objective and skeptical. In this case, Drake was boxing a boy from Poughkeepsie, and although that city is much nearer to New York than to Syracuse, it shares with Syracuse the mystic quality of being upstate, which means in permanent, suspicious opposition to the metropolis. The Poughkeepsie entry, a redhead named Eddie Prince, consequently got a lot of encouragement and benevolent advice, while Drake, who prides himself on a worldly, self-possessed air, impressed the crowd immediately as a fellow one couldn't trust.

Prince, who had an honest face and a willing heart, fought from a semi-crouch, hitting hard but seldom anything. "Short moves, Eddie, short moves!" the fans who had adopted him called when he missed his long punches. When Drake took him by the right elbow, as if helping him to alight from a taxicab, and then shoved him gently away and hit him with a left hook, a Syracusan shouted, "None of that Bowery rough stuff!" Drake boxed rings around Prince, who kept trying, however. Drake's good will was evident; on one of the two occasions when he pushed the upstater all the way through the ropes, he helped pull him back; on the other hand, when Prince kicked Drake in the instep, the chaw-bacon did not even stop to shake hands. In the fourth round, or perhaps the fifth, Prince scored a clean and unexpected knockdown. (Drake later said that he had seen the right starting but, instead of forestalling it with a conventional left, had tried to beat it with his own right. "It was incorrect," he said. "He hit me right on the chin.") Rising, disdainful, although forced to accept a count of eight, Drake resumed his demonstration of how to keep your feet even when the ring seems greased for your opponent. "Floor him again, Eddie!" the upstate Republicans chorused, and after every round they yelled to the referee, "Take that one away from Drake!" Annoyed by his own incorrect reaction to the right hand, Drake showed no elation when he got the decision. He is a perfectionist and, I fear, doomed never to be satisfied.

It was a nice fight, providing an excellent emotional warmup for what was ahead. A pair of powerful Negro heavyweights then went at each other for four rounds, going the distance rather to their own astonishment. The bout ran over onto television time, so Graham and Vejar were allowed to go about their business without further delay.

Graham had found in his first last-stand bout that he was no longer fast enough to outbox a man like Vejar all the way; the Stamford fighter has a good jab and quick reflexes, as well as plenty of bottom, which is the London prize-ring word for stamina, and sounds better. He had also found that he couldn't make his own pace—resting and then spurting, and so winning a series of short fights instead of one long one. This was because Vejar wouldn't let him rest, or at least because Vejar's corner wouldn't let Vejar let him rest. The younger man could go the whole ten rounds at a fast rate. And Vejar wouldn't spurt when Graham wanted him to, which, of course, was when Graham had already hit him and was in position to hit him again. For a young fellow, and a Latin, Vejar is a cool customer. He is not, however, an exceptionally dangerous hitter. Billy didn't have to worry much about Vejar's taking him out with one punch. In none of Graham's hundred and twenty-five fights had anybody ever done that. In their first fight, though, Graham had nailed Vejar with several beautiful rights to the head—some almost straight punches and some that were more conventionally angled in. I had never before seen him stand so flat or punch so hard. So I suspected now that the older boxer's best chance to win might be by knocking the rough young slugger out, but I didn't know how Billy was going to go about it.

In the first round Billy didn't enlighten me. He boxed with the habitual Graham elegance. Going under Vejar's elbows and around him, flicking him with long lefts, like an old-fashioned lightning portrait painter in a variety show, and occasionally getting in a stylish left and right to the body, he made him look crude, but Vejar's jab, when he landed it, appeared to have more power; in fact, it looked faster. Vejar punched away, too, and although he missed any target worth aiming at, his blows landed on Graham's arms, his shoulders, his back as he ducked under punches, and his ribs now and then in clinches—all attentions calculated to take some of the steam out of a fellow of Billy's seniority and to impress the judges, at least, with Vejar's aggressiveness. The referee, Ray Miller, who was once a good fighter himself—maybe even a hell of a fighter—could be relied on not to be overimpressed, but judges are usually less discerning. I wouldn't have given Graham that round myself, for all my admiration of him. After the bell, he looked virtually middle-aged. His hair, which he wears rather long, and flattened to his head, hung lank, the gloves had left welts on his white skin, and his nose had been reddened, although not bloodied, as if by a prolonged course of the daffy.

It was clear that salvation did not lie that way; there was even a danger that Vejar would wear Graham down and have him hanging on before the end. The second round was better; Billy caught Junior with one hard right, but Chico got away and took the curse off it with more flurries of elbow busters. In the third, Graham seemed to be tiring, and after that it was all Vejar for a while. Graham's defensive boxing was brilliant, but he didn't even look like trying to score points with his left. He was in, under, and out a lot, leaving Vejar looking silly and baffled, but the boy was doing most of the punching, such as it was. I had Vejar winning five of the first seven rounds, and one even.

Then, halfway through the eighth round, Graham nailed Vejar with a right as the boy came off the ropes on the opposite side of the ring from where I sat. Vejar tried to counter and Billy hit him again; Vejar tried to slip away and the right went in a third time. Graham landed at least five hard rights to the side of the

head within five seconds, but none hit the jackpot, and the
strong young legs carried Vejar away. Blood was streaming from
a cut behind and above his left eye, and the theretofore neutral, half-contemptuous crowd—"That'll be all, Willie!" they had
been yelling a minute earlier—roared for Billy to finish him. He
tried with the prescribed calm to set the boy up, but he couldn't.
His legs wouldn't keep him close enough. The clock over the
ring showed thirty seconds of the round left, then twenty, and
the classic boxer discarded finesse. With his lank locks flying
around his head, he stood flatfooted and threw the right after Vejar's circling form like an old woman throwing a pie, but then
the round ended, and he walked very slowly to his corner, while
the fighter with a future stumbled toward the ministering arms
of Drs. Brown and Ferrara. Brown, who stops the flow from the
mountainous crevasses in the craggy countenance of Rocky Marciano, did one of his customary jobs on Vejar. The boy came
out looking like the "after" picture in a "remove unsightly
blemishes" ad.

Graham's grim task was to open the cut again, but this objective was so obvious that it put him at a tactical disadvantage. Vejar knew what Graham had to try to do, but Graham didn't know
what Vejar was going to try to do. All he *had* to do was keep the
left side of his face intact and he would win the decision, even if
he lost the last two rounds. Actually, Vejar did better. He caught
Graham with a left hook that turned him halfway round, which
would have been unthinkable if the cute boxer hadn't been
so intent on getting that right over. Later, Graham hit the patch
once—blood showed again—and then the round was over. The
last stand would have no movie ending.

Both men came out strong for the final round—"very gay,"
Egan would have said. It was a fine, hard round, and Billy won it,
I thought, but there was no doubt where the decision would go.
It was unanimous for Vejar.

After the fight, I went back to Graham's dressing room. All

the veteran artist's wounds were on his back and shoulders—probably scrapes from glove laces—although the nose showed an extra bump, and stood taller than ever. Also, Graham had somehow developed a painful blister on the big toe of his left foot. Everybody said he had made a great fight—better than the one in New York—and I asked him if he had been trying from the first to set Vejar up for the right. He said, "Yeah, but he knew I was looking for him." He talked to Cohen and Wild about the blister on his toe and they decided not to cut it. He was talking easily, as if he hadn't been fighting. His wind was good. After a while he said wistfully, "Gee, did you see that cut bleed in the ninth when I hit it just once?"

Wild said to me, "We were going for his gut in those middle rounds, to bring his guard down. But he wouldn't go for it. Anyway, this guy couldn't get in there like he could have once."

A reporter for a press association asked Cohen whether Graham would retire now, and Cohen replied, "We are withholding any announcement at present."

Half an hour later, I was at the Onondaga bar again, waiting for train time, which was a couple of hours away. I was with my Syracuse friend who is in the paper business, and I was lamenting my failure to have bet on a horse named Bobby Brocato, which had won the feature race at the Jamaica opening and paid 19 to 1. I was sure that if I had been there, I would have played him. We were also discussing the news from Boston. The Boston fellow, De Marco, had knocked out Saxton in the fourteenth round and won the welterweight championship. The paper man said, "You could have had three to one against him."

We were standing at one end of the bar, near the telephone. Graham came in, wearing a dark suit with even a tie, and put in a call to his mother. He drank beer with us while he waited for the call to go through; he was pretty thoroughly dehydrated. Af-

ter a while he got the connection, and said, "It's me. . . . I'm all
right. . . . Sure." For such an old, ring-wise fellow, he sounded
strangely like a small boy minimizing a bad school report. His
mother must have known by then how he'd made out, if she had
a television set or neighbors. After listening to her for a bit, Graham said, "Oh, sure. They're all satisfied. They all said I made a
good try, but I guess it wasn't good enough."

Donnybrook Farr

The Sweet Science, like an old rap or the memory of love, follows
its victim everywhere. When Phil Drake, a horse, not a prizefighter, won the Epsom Derby of 1955 at odds of 12 to 1, I had
five nickers (Mayfair for pounds) on his nose. After deducting another five I had bet on one of the losers I had a net profit of fifty-
five quid, better than one hundred and fifty dollars, which I took
with me to the Champagne Bar under the grandstand. After a
race won by a 12-1 shot, it is the most accessible section of the
buffet. While there, I caught sight of some English boxing writers I know and wanted to see; they were struggling to reach a
more animated and less expensive sector of the bar. It was a
shame I had to down my champagne so quickly, but there wasn't
enough to go around, so I finished it off and then sneaked up behind them, saying something about the smallness of the world.

It was at the bar, with my profits in my pocket and my champagne in me, that I learned there was soon to be a fifteen-round
fight in Dublin for the featherweight championship of Europe.
The defending champion, a Frenchman named Ray Famechon,
had been induced to go there to fight the challenger, a boy from
the North of Ireland, but not a Protestant, known as Billy Spider

II Kelly. This Kelly, my friends said, was the British and British Empire champion, and a man of promise. One could fly to Dublin in a little more than an hour, and return just as expeditiously the morning after the battle. But what decided me to go was the news that the fight was going to be held in Donnybrook, an outlying part of Dublin that is universally synonymous with an unofficial, free-for-all fight. Professional fights have been less numerous in Dublin, but some of them have been illustrious. Pierce Egan, the Blind Raftery of the London prize ring, was a part-time Dublin man himself, and has recounted the triumphs of Dan Donnelly, the first great Irish heavyweight, against two Englishmen, whose names escape my memory. They fought on the turf of the Curragh, a racecourse where, I am reliably informed by Tim Costello, a restaurateur of my acquaintance, small boys are still led out to view Donnelly's heelprints. Dan was no tippytoes fighter, and although he fought the Englishmen separately, he could have beaten them both together, make no doubt of it. Within my own lifetime, Battling Siki, the ingenuous Senegalese known to legend as the Ignoble Savage, was lured to Dublin to defend the world's light-heavyweight title, which he had acquired from Georges Carpentier, against Mike McTigue, an Irishman polished by travel. The bout was on March 17, 1923, and McTigue got the decision. McTigue's home-grounds success appeared to be the precedent most plausibly applicable to the proposed match at Donnybrook, for I knew that Famechon, who has boxed in the United States, was hardly likely to fell Kelly like an ox; the biggest piece of an ox Famechon has ever felled, I imagine, is a *tournedos*. The boxing writers told me that the referee was to be a neutral, appointed by the European Boxing Union, but even a neutral might prove suggestible at Donnybrook.

When I got my Aer Lingus ticket and reservation (Aer Lingus is the Irish airline), I found that the line had put on extra flights, rolling out old DC-3s, which take two and a half hours for the trip, to supplement their new English-built Viscounts, which take only an hour and twenty-five minutes. Because I applied late, I was put on a DC-3. When I came aboard, the only vacant seat was next to a large, fair-haired man of resolute and familiar appearance. The seats were narrow, the leg room was limited, and it was easy to see why the place next to the big fellow had been left to the last. To establish relations, I asked him how much he weighed, and he said, as if used to being asked the question, "Fourteen stone eleven and a half," which works out to two hundred and seven and a half pounds. I said, "I weigh sixteen stone, very nearly"—very nearly seventeen, I meant. We scrunched together like bulls in a horse trailer, and he grunted, "I'm only three pound more than when I fought Joe Louey."

"*Did* you?" I asked politely.

"If I didn't, I don't know 'oo put the rooddy loomps on my 'ead," he said pleasantly, and the hand-stitched face, with the high cheekbones, narrow eyes, and Rock of Gibraltar chin, came back to me out of the late thirties. He was Tommy Farr, the old Welsh heavyweight who went fifteen rounds with Joe Louis in 1937. There is a half-established legend in Britain that he was twisted out of the decision, which he wasn't. Farr does nothing actively to favor the myth, but he doesn't discourage it, either. He also fought a series of savage bouts, with varied fortunes, against fellows like Max Baer, and against them, he thinks, he got all the worst of it when he lost. "But I love the States," he said. "I made a lot of money there. That's what I fought for, eh? Money." He rubbed a thumb like a hammer against a rectangular index finger. "Two hundred and ninety-six fights I had. Do you think it was for a rooddy lark?"

I said no, and he said, "It was my profession. I well and truly served my apprenticeship, and then I wanted money. That's why they didn't like me over there at first—the press didn't like me. Because I didn't let them mess me about, that's why. I wanted my rest. Didn't want them banging about downstairs after eleven.

My manager had a fridgeful of liquor for them, and 'e'd bring
them in all hours. All right for '*im* wasn't it? '*E* didn't 'ave to
fight. They liked '*im* fine. Robbed me of fifty or sixty thousand
quid, they did."

I asked him how the American press had robbed him of fifty
or sixty thousand pounds, and he explained that it was by saying
he would have no chance against Louis. "Spoiled the gate, they
did," he said.

I tried to console him by recalling how extravagantly they
had praised him after the fight, but he grumbled, "That didn't
'elp the gate."

Somehow the money had slipped between the hard knuckles.
So now, he said, he was launched on a second career. I asked him
what it was. He was looking fit and prosperous, in a smashing
dark-gray pin-striped suit, and wearing a good thin watch. In the
light of this exterior, I was scarcely prepared for his answer.

"I'm a write-ter," he said. "I love write-ting. I give it to them
straight. No split affinitives, you know, or other Oxfer stooff. Oh,
of coorse I split an affinitive now and then, to show I know how,
but I don't believe in it." He was writing boxing, he told me, for
the *Sunday Pictorial*, a once-a-week tabloid, with a circulation of
five and a half million, that was creeping up on the eight million
circulation of the older-established phenomenon, the *News of the
World*. "I thank God I 'ave found a way to make a living for
my dear wife and kids," Farr said. "It seems I'm a natural-born
write-ter. I've hod five revisions of contract since I came with the
Pictorial."

He was going to report the fight, and I asked him for a bit of
professional inside on Kelly. "He's a very good methodical boxer,"
he said, "with a fine sense of anticipation." It was to prove a practically perfect synopsis of Kelly; he might have added only that
Kelly too often anticipates the worst. Farr's experience in the
United States was much in his mind. "I couldn't be a good-time
Charlie," he said. "When I was a kid, I was taught not to talk or

joke or laugh at the table. 'You come 'ere to eat,' my old man used to say to me. 'When you eat, go.' A man can't change from what 'e's brought up to be, can he? He wasn't a bad old man. He taught me the importance of a good left. He was very aggressive. When he was fighting, they used to say 'e was a throwback to the cave man. 'When you go into the ring, you're a hoonter,' he'd say. 'Don't hop about like you were fighting in a rooddy balloon on the end of a stick.' "

Farr told me he had written in the *Pictorial* that Don Cockell, the Englishman who recently tried to take Marciano's heavyweight crown in San Francisco, had no sympathy coming. "He had sixteen pound on Marciano," Farr said. " 'E should of set about *'im*. I got 'oondred and eight letters, all approving. My boss got nineteen letters, all disapproving. He phoned me up. 'That's grand,' he said. 'Keep up the good work. They'll be something extra in the post for you tomorrow.' "

Farr said he was going to spend the night at the Royal Hibernian Hotel, where his paper had reserved a room for him, and it was there that I, too, eventually found a room. I met him again at dinner; he was eating with three businessmen from Derry, young Kelly's home town, whom he had taken into the aura of his greatness. Between courses he autographed cards for the young busboys and the waiters. "Is it true that you fought Joe Louey, Mr. Farr?" they would ask him, and he would reply, with a rugged laugh, "If I didn't, I don't know 'oo put the rooddy loomps on my 'ead." It had happened before the little busboys were born, and they thought of it as something historic.

After dinner—a modest collation of honey dew melon and *darne de saumon au Chablis*, the Irish salmon being exceptional—the five of us drove to Donnybrook in the Derrymen's car. The streets were full of automobiles from the North of Ireland and the three free counties of Ulster; my associates could pick them out by the license plates. One car we came up behind had a hand-lettered sign on its rear window reading "Won't you come into my parlor? said the Spider to the Ray." Farr, who, like most Welshmen, can sing, paid his passage with "The London-derry Air." "It used to be my speciality," he said, and broke forth:

> *"Oh, Danny Boy—ta loora loo loo loora loo,*
> *Oh, Danny Boy—ta loora loora loo!*
> *Oh, come ye* BACK—*"*

We were the success of the cavalcade.

The fight, as I knew by that time, having had a chance to read an evening newspaper, was to be held in a monster garage, just built by the municipality to house all the omnibuses of Dublin. Six thousand seven hundred and fifty chairs had been borrowed from caterers and undertakers; the one I got was tagged "O'Connell's," but I don't know which line of work O'Connell is in. The bout was being staged by Jack Solomons, the London promoter, with the cooperation of the officials in charge of An Tóstal, a kind of Gaelic old home week, which included an ecclesiological exhibition at Maynooth, a children's art competition, and an event listed in the papers as "Dun Laoghaire—Blackrock Ceili—an Tóstal, Aras an Baile (8 P.M.)," and evidently reserved for Gaelic speakers. Famechon was to get three thousand pounds, which makes a tidy sum in francs (three million), or even in dollars (eight thousand four hundred). Kelly was to get two thousand pounds and, in the unanimous opinion of the Derrymen, the European featherweight championship as well, after which Solomons had promised him a match with Sandy Saddler for the world's title. Saddler fought Famechon in Paris last year, and knocked him out in six rounds. Now Famechon was thirty years old and Kelly twenty-three, and both had made the featherweight limit of a hundred and twenty-six pounds at two o'clock that afternoon. Famechon had been around a long time—a very good fighter by European standards but not top-class by ours. I had heard at the Neutral Corner Restaurant, in New York, which is an international exchange for trade information, that he was definitely on the downgrade.

I had expected a delay at the gate, but Mr. Farr swept me in with him—in the double capacity of journalist and celebrity, he had the run of the house—and an usher conducted me to the O'Connell chair, in the second row ringside, where my neighbors regarded me with the respect due my illustrious sponsorship. The low ceiling of the bus garage kept the cigarette smoke down, and, although the soirée had not progressed past the first preliminary, the ring was enveloped in a blue haze, giving the scene the look of a painting of a club fight by Bellows. The strained, awkward boxers in the ring carried out the motif; the salient feature of "Stag at Sharkey's," I have always thought, is that both the central figures are simply pushers. The principals in this bout were a Dublin man and a Belfast man, of whom the former was the more inept. After the fifth round the master of ceremonies announced that the Dublin man had "retired," and a buzz of sympathy ran through the hall. The restraint was studious, as if each member of the audience had come to the hall determined to keep his temper.

The ushers, who wore badges denominating them "stewards," were fanatical about making customers crouch in the aisles while any boxing was going on, and conducted them to their chairs only during the one-minute intervals between rounds. It was like Town Hall during a séance of the New Friends of Music. Since horizontal distances were great in the garage, it took some arrivals from two to four rounds to reach their seats. The round before the Dublin man retired, a small, merry-looking man with a pointy nose and an even more finely pointed waxed mustache passed along the aisle in front of the first ringside row, bent over like a crab. The man next to me pulled my arm. "It's Alfie Byrne, the Lord Mayor," he said. His Lordship was taking no chances of alienating a voter. There was a large Irish harp in electric bulbs on one wall and another, in green paint, on the wall opposite. I saw no tricolors.

The *ambiance* warmed a bit with the next bout—a lightweight match between a heavy-muscled, pyknic Galwayman, not much more than five feet tall, named McCoy, and a more conventionally constructed fellow from Belfast, named Sharpe. (Belfast, like most industrial cities, produces a large crop of boxers.) Galwaymen, in popular myth, are hot-tempered and unpredictable, and transplanted Galwaymen, of whom there were many in the audience, are vociferously loyal. The little fellow started out at a terrific pace, moving his arms as if in a pillow fight. A cry of "Up, Galway! Come on, McEye!" spontaneously dispelled the decorum of the evening. It seemed impossible that McEye could keep on moving his arms at that rate for more than a minute, but he did, and the astonished Belfast man, after waiting for him to run down, joined in the fun. But each time Sharpe administered to the animated half keg a conventional uppercut to the chin—he knew the antidotes academically prescribed for a violent attack by a short opponent—McEye would loose a flurry of blows that reminded me of a passage in "The Song of Roland": "I will strike seven hundred or a thousand good blows." Six hundred and ninety-nine or nine hundred and ninety-eight would miss, but for the Belfast man it was like trying to hit through an electric fan. The fellow sitting next to me jiggled with the effort of maintaining his composure; he seemed to be in the grip of an electric vibrator. After every round, he would grab me and ask, "Would you say the little fellow is ahead now?" I would nod, and he would turn and grab the fellow on the other side, a sporty type who was escorting a platinum blonde. This Blazes Boylan—it is impossible to be in Dublin without Joyce—was a purist. "Sharpe is landing the cleaner punches," he would say. The man between us would wait until Blazes turned back to the blonde, and then pluck my arm again. "Do you know," he would say in a conspirational way, "I don't agree with that man at all." Neither did the referee, who gave the decision to McEye and perpetual motion. There are no judges at European professional bouts, and the referee decides. My neighbor and I exchanged friendly glances, secure in our connoisseurship.

The announcer now had his great moment. "My Lord Mayor, ladies and gentlemen!" he called, and began introducing visiting celebrities—Freddie Mills, the Englishman who briefly held the light-heavyweight championship of the world before Joey Maxim won it; my sponsor Farr, who got a great hand; and, climactically, "the original" Spider Kelly, the father of the hero of the evening. (I had heard of at least one earlier Spider Kelly, the man who said to his seconds, "What I need ain't advice—it's strength." But that had been in California, and it would have been a quibble to bring it up at Donnybrook.) The original Irish Spider Kelly was a puckish little man with a red face and heavy black eyebrows. He had held the British and British Empire featherweight championships himself twenty years before, I knew from my newspaper fill-in, and had guided Spider II's instruction from his first tottering essays at footwork. The audience included many fathers, more sons, and quite a number of mothers and sisters. (There was also a good speckling of Roman collars.) A cheer for old Spider was an endorsement of the principle of the family, and he got it.

A fanfare of hunting horns was sounded at the remote end of the garage, and another cheer began, distant at first, louder as its object approached the ring. It was Spider II, surrounded by his faction. He was a baby-faced boy with a crew cut, who looked more like eighteen than twenty-three. The calves of his legs resembled those of a school quarter-miler—large and rounded—but his torso and arms, white and boyish, were less impressively developed. The Frenchman, whose entry was heralded by another but less enthusiastic fanfare, was sleek, wide-shouldered, long-armed, and spindle-shanked. He looked not much younger than

Spider I, but his antiquity inspired no comparable demonstration of respectful affection by the crowd. The master of ceremonies implored the audience to stop smoking during the coming contest, and all the men within my sight extinguished their cigarettes. He next introduced the boxers, giving their weights to the ounce—Kelly had a ten-ounce weight advantage—and, finally, the referee, who received a polite, unsuspicious cheer. I did not hear his name, but the man next to me said, "Some kind of a Dutchman." It appeared likely, for the referee had the buttery tint so common among Hollanders, and walked about the ring with the exaggerated spryness of a Teuton being dashing. He had a snipe nose that pointed at the ceiling, and held himself so straight that his Adam's apple created a noticeable deviation from the vertical, pushing a neat bow tie in front of it.

The gong rang, and the men came timidly from their corners amid thunderous cheers. "Don't let us pretend to be impartial," a fellow wrote in the *Irish Press* the next morning. "We all wanted the best man to win, and Billy Kelly was the best man for us." Confirming Farr's description, Kelly went to work methodically; he landed a light tap on the Frenchman's nose, parried a return with his right, and then tapped twice more. Famechon floundered at him a bit, like a fellow reaching over a man's shoulder to shake hands with someone behind him, and the round ended with no damage to either. The man next to me turned his face from the carnage and said, "Is he doing all right?" I showed him my program, on which I had marked the round even, and he said, "That other fellow has a very dangerous look."

After the second round, Kelly settled down to work, and a very promising workman he looked, drawing leads, popping the slower Frenchman with fast, precise jabs, and once, in the fourth, even landing a really good right uppercut to the diaphragm in close. When Famechon started a punch, Kelly would be going in another direction. Usually when the Frenchman got close to him, Kelly would cease trying to do harm and concentrate on escape, as if he were fighting a middleweight instead of a gaffer his own size. He was good at ducking and slipping away, but nobody was ever hurt by being ducked away from. Still, he outboxed his man round after round—I gave him four in a row—and the bus garage swelled with the sound of shouting. The jabs had little sting, but since Kelly was younger than Famechon, it appeared reasonable that he would keep on piling up points as the fight went on, and at the end would take the decision. By the seventh, Famechon, having apparently decided that the boy couldn't hurt him at all, was rushing after him, slapping and pushing but unable to accomplish much. And so they went, round after round—Kelly almost never using his right except to block and never following an advantage beyond a second or third light pop when he had his man set up for a real one. At the beginning of every round he crossed himself, and whenever Famechon's slaps strayed low he would look appealingly at the referee. As they came up for the fifteenth, I had them all square on my card—six rounds for each and two even—but I had a feeling that Kelly's margins had been a trifle clearer. I gave him the final round, which was as tantalizingly ineffectual as all the others, and as hard to pick a winner in. Just the same, I was sure that Spider II deserved the decision—and meanly suspected that he would be sure to receive it even if he hadn't done quite so well. It was then that the Dutchman, to quote one Irish writer, "rose" Famechon's hand. I thought I could write a fair account of what followed, but when I saw the story on the first page of the *Irish Press* next morning, I realized that the writer, a Mr. John Healy, had probably had more experience in that kind of going:

> There was a long pause as a stunned audience, who had watched the young Spider swap punches at a terrific pace in the last two rounds, slowly gathered what it meant—Billy Kelly had lost the fight.
>
> And then, slowly at first, until it gathered momentum

and burst like a rumbling volcano, they got to their feet and cut loose with a solid barrage of catcalls, boos, whistles and shouts. Angry spectators swarmed up to and tried clambering over the Press table. A bottle whizzed over my head into the ring. [I missed this, or at any rate it missed me.] A coat, flung in rage, flapped on the ropes. [It did.] Chairs were bumbled. A squad of Gardai and plainclothes detectives surrounded the ring. ["Gardai" is Gaelic for uniformed police, and monstrous big ones these were.]

They were still booing and cheering Billy when he was escorted from the ring minutes later. All down that long avenue of jam-packed people, they screamed their admiration. "You're the winner, Billy!" or "You're the champ!" Grown men cried their rage in the sea of faces. . . .

That's just about the way it was. Taking a more moderate line, a Mr. Ben Kiely, on the sports page, wrote, "There's no doubt in the world about it—the raising of Ray Famechon's hand was one of the greatest shocks in Franco-Irish history. Because for the crowd in the Donnybrook Garage Billy Kelly was the man for their money."

Famechon, whose hundred-and-third professional fight it was, looked relieved but not astonished. He probably thought he had won, as any fighter does who has made it at all close. Kelly sat in his corner with head almost between his knees, the picture of dejection, like a bright boy who has failed to get 100 in an arithmetic test because the teacher came up with the wrong answer. He had played it safe for fifteen rounds and failed to obtain the reward of thrift and diligence. The most interesting figure in the ring, for many reasons, was the referee; the man about to get lynched is undeniably the center of attention at a lynching. It is unlikely that it had occurred to him when he rose Famechon's hand that he would be immoderately happy to see the Amsterdam airport again. The Kelly rooters were standing in the aisles and on the undertakers' chairs, which assumed a new significance. Devil an usher could make devil a customer sit down. The referee, encouraged by a number of big men in mufti, probably detectives, who had entered the ring, got as far as the ropes, climbed through them to the ring apron, and stood there like a fellow who has never gone off a diving board and wishes he hadn't walked out to the end. He was as pale as the inside of a Gouda cheese. The Gardai marched to the edge of the ring below him and formed a phalanx, into which they lowered him down. They then marched forward, with the Dutchman in the center. A small man in a raincoat tried to cut in from the rear, swinging a punch under a cop's armpit. The Garda turned around, laughing, and slung him about twenty feet, using the man's raincoat as a hammer thrower uses the wire on the hammer. The Lord Mayor slunk out as self-effacingly as he had entered. The wild shouting continued, the ushers were ignored for another five minutes, and then everybody began to laugh and chat and light up cigarettes again, in preparation for the bouts that would wind up the program. (It was apparently permissible to suffocate all boxers except those in the main event.) Since the tag end of the program was of small interest, I soon made my way out into the night and a pouring rain.

By the time I got back to the Royal Hibernian, Mr. Farr was established before a late snack of cold chicken and cold ham, with a few bottles of Guinness. He said he had already filed his story for the *Sunday Pictorial*, and readily recited what he thought the best bits of it for me. Like me, he thought Kelly had deserved to win. "Kelly hos nothing for the seeker of blood and thunder, but those who enjoy the grace of movement and textbook poonching will be fully satisfied by the Derry craftsman," he said, which is the way it appeared in the *Pictorial*, except for the Welsh stresses. He writes a very pretty style. He thought, though, that Kelly had been overcautious—that he had had little to beat. We adjourned to the lounge, in which bona-fide residents are allowed to drink as late as the night porter, a crabbed old humorist, will serve them, and there were joined by a number of gentlemen from Northern Ireland, including the trio who had transported us to the fight. Before bringing us a new round of drinks, the porter would make each of us give his room number, and we would count off, beginning with a Mr. Cassidy from Derry—I think he had No. 58—and going all the way round to a man from Donegal whose name I forget but who weighed eighteen stone seven and collected first editions. It was not so much that the porter expected our bona-fide status to change between rounds, I think, as that he wished to determine our degree of responsibility. A fellow who forgot the number of his room might have been refused the next drink. But nobody did forget.

Mr. Farr, who had switched from Guinness to Cointreau, was naturally the oracle of the occasion, and won the golden opinion of all until he burst out ingenuously, "The truth is that the lod fights like he was in a rooddy balloon at the end of a rooddy stick. Every time t'other lod 'it 'im in the goot, 'e looked ot the referee. Is the referee 'is rooddy grondmother? Was he too prroud to reciprrocate?" He rose, granitic and dignified. "I must take an early plane in the morning," he said. "Bock to my sweet wife and wonderful children. Each Saturday afternoon I take the kids to the cinema and tea. High tea." He made his way to the lift, the pattern of a literary man who leads a sane family life.

I stayed on until the porter himself decided to go to bed, at dawn. He has insomnia in the dark, he said.

Ahab and Nemesis

Ahab and Nemesis

Back in 1922, the late Heywood Broun, who is not remembered primarily as a boxing writer, wrote a durable account of a combat between the late Benny Leonard and the late Rocky Kansas for the lightweight championship of the world. Leonard was the greatest practitioner of the era, Kansas just a rough, optimistic fellow. In the early rounds Kansas messed Leonard about, and Broun was profoundly disturbed. A radical in politics, he was a conservative in the arts, and Kansas made him think of Gertrude Stein, *les Six*, and nonrepresentational painting, all novelties that irritated him.

"With the opening gong, Rocky Kansas tore into Leonard," he wrote. "He was gauche and inaccurate, but terribly persistent." The classic verities prevailed, however. After a few rounds, during which Broun continued to yearn for a return to a culture with fixed values, he was enabled to record: "The young child of nature who was challenging for the championship dropped his guard, and Leonard hooked a powerful and entirely orthodox blow to the conventional point of the jaw. Down went Rocky Kansas. His past life flashed before him during the nine seconds in which he remained on the floor, and he wished that he had been more faithful as a child in heeding the advice of his boxing teacher. After all, the old masters did know something. There is still a kick in style, and tradition carries a nasty wallop."

I have often thought of Broun's words in the years since Rocky Marciano, the reigning heavyweight champion, scaled the fistic summits, as they say in *Journal-Americanese*, by beating Jersey Joe Walcott. The current Rocky is gauche and inaccurate, but besides being persistent he is a dreadfully severe hitter with either hand. The predominative nature of this asset has been well stated by Pierce Egan, the Edward Gibbon and Sir Thomas Malory of the old London prize ring, who was less preoccupied than Broun with ultimate implications. Writing in 1821 of a milling cove named Bill Neat, the Bristol Butcher, Egan said, "He possesses a requisite above all the art that *teaching* can achieve for any boxer; namely, *one hit* from his right hand, given in proper distance, can gain a victory; but three of them are positively enough to dispose of a giant." This is true not only of Marciano's right hand but of his left hand, too—provided he doesn't miss the giant entirely. Egan doubted the advisability of changing Neat's style, and he would have approved of Marciano's. The champion has an apparently unlimited absorptive capacity for percussion (Egan would have called him an "insatiable glutton") and inexhaustible energy ("a prime bottom fighter"). "Shifting," or moving to the side, and "milling in retreat," or moving back, are innovations of the late eighteenth century that Rocky's advisers have carefully kept from his knowledge, lest they spoil his natural prehistoric style. Egan excused these tactics only in boxers of feeble constitution.

Archie Moore, the light-heavyweight champion of the world, who hibernates in San Diego, California, and estivates in Toledo, Ohio, is a Brounian rather than an Eganite in his thinking about style, but he naturally has to do more than think about it. Since the rise of Marciano, Moore, a cerebral and hyper-experienced light-colored pugilist who has been active since 1936, has suffered the pangs of a supreme exponent of *bel canto* who sees himself crowded out of the opera house by a guy who can only shout. As a sequel to a favorable review I wrote of one of his infrequent

New York appearances, when his fee was restricted to a measly five figures, I received a sad little note signed "The most unappreciated fighter in the world, Archie Moore." A fellow who has as much style as Moore tends to overestimate the intellect—he develops the kind of Faustian mind that will throw itself against the problem of perpetual motion, or of how to pick horses first, second, third, *and* fourth in every race. Archie's note made it plain to me that he was honing his harpoon for the White Whale.

When I read newspaper items about Moore's decisioning a large, playful porpoise of a Cuban heavyweight named Nino Valdes and scoop-netting a minnow like Bobo Olson, the middleweight champion, for practice, I thought of him as a lonely Ahab, rehearsing to buck Herman Melville, Pierce Egan, and the betting odds. I did not think that he could bring it off, but I wanted to be there when he tried. What would *Moby Dick* be if Ahab had succeeded? Just another fish story. The thing that is eternally diverting is the struggle of man against history—or what Albert Camus, who used to be an amateur middleweight, has called the Myth of Sisyphus. (Camus would have been a great man to cover the fight, but none of the syndicates thought of it.) When I heard that the boys had been made for September 20, 1955, at the Yankee Stadium, I shortened my stay abroad in order not to miss the Encounter of the Two Heroes, as Egan would have styled the rendezvous.

In London on the night of September thirteenth, a week before the date set for the Encounter, I tried to get my eye in for fight-watching by attending a bout at the White City greyhound track between Valdes, who had been imported for the occasion, and the British Empire heavyweight champion, Don Cockell, a fat man whose gift for public suffering has enlisted the sympathy of a sentimental people. Since Valdes had gone fifteen rounds with Moore in Las Vegas the previous May, and Cockell had excruciated for nine rounds before being knocked out by Marciano in San Francisco in the same month, the bout offered a dim opportunity for establishing what racing people call a "line" between Moore and Marciano. I didn't get much of an optical workout, because Valdes disposed of Cockell in three rounds. It was evident that Moore and Marciano had not been fighting the same class of people this season.

This was the only fight I ever attended in a steady rainstorm. It had begun in the middle of the afternoon, and, while there was a canopy over the ring, the spectators were as wet as speckled trout. "The weather, it is well known, has no terrors to the admirers of Pugilism of Life," Egan once wrote, and on his old stamping ground this still holds true. As I took my seat in a rock pool that had collected in the hollow of my chair, a South African giant named Ewart Potgieter, whose weight had been announced as twenty-two stone ten, was ignoring the doctrine of Apartheid by leaning on a Jamaican colored man who weighed a mere sixteen stone, and by the time I had transposed these statistics to three hundred and eighteen pounds and two hundred and twenty-four pounds, respectively, the exhausted Jamaican had acquiesced in resegregation and retired. The giant had not struck a blow, properly speaking, but had shoved downward a number of times, like a man trying to close an overfilled trunk.

The main bout proved an even less grueling contest. Valdes, eager to get out of the chill, struck Cockell more vindictively than is his wont, and after a few gestures invocative of commiseration the fat man settled in one corner of the ring as heavily as suet pudding upon the unaccustomed gastric system. He had received what Egan would have called a "ribber" and a "nobber," and when he arose it was seen that the latter had raised a cut on his forehead. At the end of the third round, his manager withdrew him from competition. It was not an inspiring occasion, but after the armistice eight or nine shivering Cubans appeared in the runway behind the press section and jumped up and down to register emotion and restore circulation. "*Ahora Marciano!*" they yelled. "Now for Marciano!" Instead of being grateful for the distraction, the other spectators took a poor view of it. "Sit down, you chaps!" one of them cried. "We want to see the next do!" They were still parked out there in the rain when I tottered into the Shepherd's Bush underground station and collapsed, sneezing, on a train that eventually disgorged me at Oxford Circus, with just enough time left to buy a revivifying draught before eleven o'clock, when the pubs closed. How the mugs I left behind cured themselves I never knew. They had to do it on Bovril.

Because I had engagements that kept me in England until a few days before the Encounter, I had no opportunity to visit the training camps of the rival American Heroes. I knew all the members of both factions, however, and I could imagine what they were thinking. In the plane on the way home, I tried to envision the rival patterns of ratiocination. I could be sure that Marciano, a kind, quiet, imperturbable fellow, would plan to go after Moore and make him fight continuously until he tired enough to become an accessible target. After that he would expect concussion to accentuate exhaustion and exhaustion to facilitate concussion, until Moore came away from his consciousness, like everybody else Rocky had ever fought. He would try to remember to minimize damage to himself in the beginning, while there was still snap in Moore's arms, because Moore is a sharp puncher. (Like Bill Neat of old, Marciano hits at his opponent's arms when he cannot hit past them. "In one instance, the arm of Oliver [a Neat adversary] received so paralyzing a shock in stopping the blow that it appeared almost useless," Egan once wrote.) Charlie Goldman would have instructed Marciano in some rudimentary maneuver to throw Moore's first shots off, I felt sure, but after a few minutes Rocky would forget it, or Archie would figure it out. But there would always be Freddie Brown, the "cut man," in the champion's corner to repair superficial damage. One

reason Goldman is a great teacher is that he doesn't try to teach a
boxer more than he can learn. What he had taught Rocky in the
four years since I had first seen him fight was to shorten the arc of
most of his blows without losing power thereby, and always to
follow one hard blow with another—"for insurance"—delivered
with the other hand, instead of recoiling to watch the victim fall.
The champion had also gained confidence and presence of mind;
he has a good fighting head, which is not the same thing as being
a good mechanical practitioner. "A *boxer* requires a *nob* as well as
a *statesman* does a H E A D, coolness and calculation being essential
to *second* his efforts," Egan wrote, and the old historiographer was
never more correct. Rocky was thirty-one, not in the first flush of
youth for a boxer, but Moore was only a few days short of thirty-
nine, so age promised to be in the champion's favor if he kept
pressing.

Moore's strategic problem, I reflected on the plane, offered
more choices and, as a corollary, infinitely more chances for error.
It was possible, but not probable, that jabbing and defensive skill
would carry him through fifteen rounds, even on those old legs,
but I knew that the mere notion of such a *gambade* would revolt
Moore. He is not what Egan would have called a shy fighter. Besides, would Ahab have been content merely to go the distance
with the White Whale? I felt sure that Archie planned to knock
the champion out, so that he could sign his next batch of letters
"The most appreciated and deeply opulent fighter in the world."
I surmised that this project would prove a mistake, like Mr.
Churchill's attempt to take Gallipoli in 1915, but it would be
the kind of mistake that would look good in his memoirs. The
basis of what I rightly anticipated would prove a miscalculation
went back to Archie's academic background. As a young fighter
of conventional tutelage, he must have heard his preceptors say
hundreds of times, "They will all go if you hit them right." If a
fighter did not believe that, he would be in the position of a Eu-
clidian without faith in the hundred-and-eighty-degree triangle.

Moore's strategy, therefore, would be based on working Marciano into a position where he could hit him right. He would not go in and slug with him, because that would be wasteful, distasteful, and injudicious, but he might try to cut him up, in an effort to slow him down so he could hit him right, or else try to hit him right and then cut him up. The puzzle he reserved for me—and Marciano—was the tactic by which he would attempt to attain his strategic objective. In the formation of his views, I believed, Moore would be handicapped, rather than aided, by his active, skeptical mind. One of the odd things about Marciano is that he isn't terribly big. It is hard for a man like Moore, just under six feet tall and weighing about a hundred and eighty pounds, to imagine that a man approximately the same size can be immeasurably stronger than he is. This is particularly true when, like the light-heavyweight champion, he has spent his whole professional life contending with boxers—some of them considerably bigger—whose strength has proved so near his own that he could move their arms and bodies by cunning pressures. The old classicist would consequently refuse to believe what he was up against.

The light-heavyweight limit is a hundred and seventy-five pounds, and Moore can get down to that when he must, in order to defend his title, but in a heavyweight match each Hero is allowed to weigh whatever he pleases. I was back in time to attend the weighing-in ceremonies, held in the lobby of Madison Square Garden at noon on the day set for the Encounter, and learned that Moore weighed 188 and Marciano 188¼—a lack of disparity that figured to encourage the rationalist's illusions. I also learned that, in contrast to Jack Solomons, the London promoter who held the Valdes–Cockell match in the rain, the I.B.C., which was promoting the Encounter, had decided to postpone it for twenty-four hours, although the weather was clear. The decision was based on apprehension of Hurricane Ione, which, although apparently veering away from New York, might come around again like a lazy left hook and drop in on the point of the Stadium's jaw late in the evening. Nothing like that happened, but the postponement brought the town's theaters and bars another evening of good business from the out-of-town fight trade, such as they always get on the eve of a memorable Encounter. ("Not a bed could be had at any of the villages at an early hour on the preceding evening; and Uxbridge was crowded beyond all former precedent," Egan wrote of the night before Neat beat Oliver.) There was no doubt that the fight had caught the public imagination, ever sensitive to a meeting between Hubris and Nemesis, as the boys on the quarterlies would say, and the bookies were laying 18–5 on Nemesis, according to the boys on the dailies, who always seem to hear. (A friend of mine up from Maryland with a whim and a five-dollar bill couldn't get ten against it in ordinary barroom money anywhere, although he wanted Ahab.)

The enormous—by recent precedent—advance sale of tickets had so elated the I.B.C. that it had decided to replace the usual card of bad preliminary fights with some not worth watching at all, so there was less distraction than usual as we awaited the appearance of the Heroes on the fateful evening. The press seats had been so closely juxtaposed that I could fit in only sidewise between two colleagues—the extra compression having been caused by the injection of a prewar number of movie stars and politicos. The tight quarters were an advantage, in a way, since they facilitated my conversation with Peter Wilson, an English prize-ring correspondent, who happened to be in the row behind me. I had last seen Mr. Wilson at White City the week before, at a time when the water level had already reached his shredded-Latakia mustache. I had feared that he had drowned at ringside, but when I saw him at the Stadium, he assured me that by buttoning the collar of his mackintosh tightly over his nostrils he had been able to make the garment serve as a diving lung, and so survive. Like all British fight writers when they are relieved of the duty of watching British fighters, he was in a holiday mood, and we chatted happily. There is something about the approach of a good fight that renders the spirit insensitive to annoyance; it is only when the amateur of the Sweet Science has some doubts as to how good the main bout will turn out to be that he is avid for the satisfaction to be had from the preliminaries. This is because after the evening is over, he may have only a good supporting fight to remember. There were no such doubts—even in the minds of the mugs who had paid for their seats—on the evening of September twenty-first.

At about ten-thirty the champion and his faction entered the ring. It is not customary for the champion to come in first, but Marciano has never been a stickler for protocol. He is a humble, kindly fellow, who even now will approach an acquaintance on the street and say bashfully, "Remember me? I'm Rocky Marciano." The champion doesn't mind waiting five or ten minutes to give anybody a punch in the nose. In any case, once launched from his dressing room under the grandstand, he could not have arrested his progress to the ring, because he had about forty policemen pushing behind him, and three more clearing a path in front of him. Marciano, tucked in behind the third cop like a football ball-carrier behind his interference, had to run or be trampled to death. Wrapped in a heavy blue bathrobe and with a blue monk's cowl pulled over his head, he climbed the steps to the ring with the cumbrous agility of a medieval executioner ascending the scaffold. Under the hood he seemed to be trying to look serious. He has an intellectual appreciation of the anxieties of a champion, but he has a hard time forgetting how strong he is; while he remembers that, he can't worry as much as he knows a champion should. His attendants—quick, battered little Goldman; Al Weill, the stout, excitable manager, always stricken just before the bell with the suspicion that he may have made a bad match; Al Columbo—are all as familiar to the crowd as he is.

Ahab's party arrived in the ring a minute or so later, and

Charlie Johnston, his manager—a calm sparrow hawk of a man, as old and wise in the game as Weill—went over to watch Goldman put on the champion's gloves. Freddie Brown went to Moore's corner to watch *his* gloves being put on. Moore wore a splendid black silk robe with a gold lamé collar and belt. He sports a full mustache above an imperial, and his hair, sleeked down under pomade when he opens operations, invariably rises during the contest, as it gets water sloshed on it between rounds and the lacquer washes off, until it is standing up like the top of a shaving brush. Seated in his corner in the shadow of his personal trainer, a brown man called Cheerful Norman, who weighs two hundred and thirty-five pounds, Moore looked like an old Japanese print I have of a "Shogun Engaged in Strategic Contemplation in the Midst of War." The third member of his group was Bertie Briscoe, a rough, chipper little trainer, whose more usual charge is Sandy Saddler, the featherweight champion—also a Johnston fighter. Mr. Moore's features in repose rather resemble those of Orson Welles, and he was reposing with intensity.

The procession of other fighters and former fighters to be introduced was longer than usual. The full galaxy was on hand, including Jack Dempsey, Gene Tunney, and Joe Louis, the *têtes de cuvée* of former-champion society; ordinary former heavyweight champions, like Max Baer and Jim Braddock, slipped through the ropes practically unnoticed. After all the celebrities had been in and out of the ring, an odd dwarf, advertising something or other—possibly himself—was lifted into the ring by an accomplice and ran across it before he could be shooed out. The referee, a large, craggy, oldish man named Harry Kessler, who, unlike some of his better-known colleagues, is not an ex-fighter, called the men to the center of the ring. This was his moment; he had the microphone. "Now Archie and Rocky, I want a nice, clean fight," he said, and I heard a peal of silvery laughter behind me from Mr. Wilson, who had seen both of them fight before. "Protect yourself at all times," Mr. Kessler cautioned them unnecessarily. When the principals shook hands, I could see Mr. Moore's eyebrows rising like storm clouds over the Sea of Azov. His whiskers bristled and his eyes glowed like dark coals as he scrunched his eyebrows down again and enveloped the Whale with the Look, which was intended to dominate his will power. Mr. Wilson and I were sitting behind Marciano's corner, and as the champion came back to it I observed his expression, to determine what effect the Look had had upon him. More than ever, he resembled a Great Dane who has heard the word "bone."

A moment later the bell rang and the Heroes came out for the first round. Marciano, training in the sun for weeks, had tanned to a slightly deeper tint than Moore's old ivory, and Moore, at 188, looked, if anything, bigger and more muscular than Marciano; much of the champion's weight is in his legs, and his shoulders slope. Marciano advanced, but Moore didn't go far away. As usual, he stood up nicely, his arms close to his body and his feet not too far apart, ready to go anywhere but not without a reason—the picture of a powerful, decisive intellect unfettered by preconceptions. Marciano, pulling his left arm back from the shoulder, flung a left hook. He missed, but not by enough to discourage him, and then walked in and hooked again. All through the round he threw those hooks, and some of them grazed Moore's whiskers; one even hit him on the side of the head. Moore didn't try much offensively; he held a couple of times when Marciano worked in close.

Marciano came back to his corner as he always does, unimpassioned. He hadn't expected to catch Moore with those left hooks anyway, I imagine; all he had wanted was to move him around. Moore went to his corner inscrutable. They came out for the second, and Marciano went after him in brisker fashion. In the first round he had been throwing the left hook, missing with it, and then throwing a right and missing with that, too. In the second he tried a variation—throwing a right and then pulling a shoulder back to throw the left. It appeared for a moment to have

Moore confused, as a matador might be confused by a bull who walked in on his hind legs. Marciano landed a couple of those awkward hooks, but not squarely. He backed Moore over toward the side of the ring farthest from me, and then Moore knocked him down.

Some of the reporters, describing the blow in the morning papers, called it a "sneak punch," which is journalese for one the reporter didn't see but technically means a lead thrown before the other man has warmed up or while he is musing about the gate receipts. This had been no lead, and although I certainly hadn't seen Moore throw the punch, I knew that it had landed inside the arc of Marciano's left hook. ("Marciano missed with the right, trun the left, and Moore stepped inside it," my private eye, Whitey Bimstein, said next day, confirming my diagnosis, and the film of the fight bore both of us out.) So Ahab had his harpoon in the Whale. He had hit him right if ever I saw a boxer hit right, with a classic brevity and conciseness. Marciano stayed down for two seconds. I do not know what took place in Mr. Moore's breast when he saw him get up. He may have felt, for the moment, like Don Giovanni when the Commendatore's statue grabbed at him—startled because he thought he had killed the guy already—or like Ahab when he saw the Whale take down Fedallah, harpoons and all. Anyway, he hesitated a couple of seconds, and that was reasonable. A man who took nine to come up after a punch like that would be doing well, and the correct tactic would be to go straight in and finish him. But a fellow who came up on two was so strong he would bear investigation.

After that, Moore did go in, but not in a crazy way. He hit Marciano some good, hard, classic shots, and inevitably Marciano, a trader, hit him a few devastating swipes, which slowed him. When the round ended, the edge of Moore's speed was gone, and he knew that he would have to set a new and completely different trap, with diminished resources. After being knocked down, Marciano had stopped throwing that patterned right-and-left combination; he has a good nob. "He never trun it again in the fight," Whitey said next day, but I differ. He threw it in the fifth, and again Moore hit him a peach of a right inside it, but the steam was gone; this time Ahab couldn't even stagger him. Anyway, there was Moore at the end of the second, dragging his shattered faith in the unities and humanities back to his corner. He had hit a guy right, and the guy hadn't gone. But there is no geezer in Moore, any more than there was in the master of the Pequod.

Both came out for the third very gay, as Egan would have said. Marciano had been hit and cut, so he felt acclimated, and Moore was so mad at himself for not having knocked Marciano out that he almost displayed animosity toward him. He may have thought that perhaps he had not hit Marciano *just* right; the true artist is always prone to self-reproach. He would try again. A minute's attention from his squires had raised his spirits and slicked down his hair. At this point, Marciano set about him. He waddled in, hurling his fists with a sublime disregard of probabilities, content to hit an elbow, a biceps, a shoulder, the top of a head—the last supposed to be the least profitable target in the business, since, as every beginner learns, "the head is the hardest part of the human body," and a boxer will only break his hands on it. Many boxers make the systematic presentation of the cranium part of their defensive scheme. The crowd, basically anti-intellectual, screamed encouragement. There was Moore, riding punches, picking them off, slipping them, rolling with them, ducking them, coming gracefully out of his defensive efforts with sharp, patterned blows—and just about holding this parody even on points. His face, emerging at instants from under the storm of arms—his own and Rocky's—looked like that of a swimming walrus. When the round ended, I could see that he was thinking deeply. Marciano came back to his corner at a kind of suppressed dogtrot. He didn't have a worry in the world.

It was in the fourth, though, that I think Sisyphus began to get the idea he couldn't roll back the Rock. Marciano pushed him against the ropes and swung at him for what seemed a full minute without ever landing a punch that a boxer with Moore's background would consider a credit to his workmanship. He kept them coming so fast, though, that Moore tired just getting out of their way. One newspaper account I saw said that at this point Moore "swayed uncertainly," but his motions were about as uncertain as Margot Fonteyn's, or Arthur Rubinstein's. He is the most premeditated and best-synchronized swayer in his profession. After the bell rang for the end of the round, the champion hit him a right for good measure—he usually manages to have something on the way all the time—and then pulled back to disclaim any uncouth intention. Moore, no man to be conned, hit him a corker of a punch in return, when he wasn't expecting it. It was a gesture of moral reprobation and also a punch that would give any normal man something to think about between rounds. It was a good thing Moore couldn't see Marciano's face as he came back to his corner, though, because the champion was laughing.

The fifth was a successful round for Moore, and I had him ahead on points that far in the fight. But it took no expert to know where the strength lay. There was even a moment in the round when Moore set himself against the ropes and encouraged Marciano to swing at him, in the hope the champion would swing himself tired. It was a confession that he himself was too tired to do much hitting.

In the sixth Marciano knocked Moore down twice—once, early in the round, for four seconds, and once, late in the round, for eight seconds, with Moore getting up just before the bell rang. In the seventh, after that near approach to obliteration, the embattled intellect put up its finest stand. Marciano piled out of his corner to finish Moore, and the stylist made him miss so often that it looked, for a fleeting moment, as if the champion were indeed punching himself arm-weary. In fact, Moore began to beat him to the punch. It was Moore's round, certainly, but an old-timer I talked to later averred that one of the body blows Marciano landed in that round was the hardest of the fight.

It was the eighth that ended the competitive phase of the fight. They fought all the way, and in the last third of the round the champion simply overflowed Archie. He knocked him down with a right six seconds before the bell, and I don't think Moore could have got up by ten if the round had lasted that long. The fight by then reminded me of something that Sam Langford, one of the most profound thinkers—and, according to all accounts, one of the greatest doers—of the prize ring, once said to me: "Whatever that other man wants to do, don't let him do it." Merely by moving in all the time and punching continually, Marciano achieves the same strategic effect that Langford gained by finesse. It is impossible to think, or to impose your thought, if you have to keep on avoiding punches.

Moore's "game," as old Egan would have called his courage, was beyond reproach. He came out proudly for the ninth, and stood and fought back with all he had, but Marciano slugged him down, and he was counted out with his left arm hooked over the middle rope as he tried to rise. It was a crushing defeat for the higher faculties and a lesson in intellectual humility, but he had made a hell of a fight.

The fight was no sooner over than hundreds of unsavory young yokels with New England accents began a kind of mountain-goat immigration from the bleachers to ringside. They leaped from chair to chair and, after they reached the press section, from typewriter shelf to typewriter shelf and, I hope, from movie star to movie star. "Rocky!" they yelled. "Brockton!" Two of them, as dismal a pair of civic ambassadors as I have seen since I worked on the Providence *Journal & Evening Bulletin*, stood on Wilson's typewriter and yelled "Providence!" After the fighters and the hick delinquents had gone away, I made my way out to Jerome

Avenue, where the crowd milled, impenetrable, under the "El" structure.

If you are not in a great hurry to get home (and why should you be at eleven-thirty or twelve on a fight night?), the best plan is to walk up to the station north of the stadium and have a beer in a saloon, or a cup of tea in the 167th Street Cafeteria, and wait until the whole mess clears away. By that time you may even get a taxi. After this particular fight I chose the cafeteria, being in a contemplative rather than a convivial mood. The place is of a genre you would expect to find nearer Carnegie Hall, with blond woodwork and modern functional furniture imported from Italy—an appropriate background for the evaluation of an aesthetic experience. I got my tea and a smoked-salmon sandwich on a soft onion roll at the counter and made my way to a table, where I found myself between two young policemen who were talking about why Walt Disney has never attempted a screen version of Kafka's "Metamorphosis." As I did not feel qualified to join in that one, I got out my copy of the official program of the fights and began to read the high-class feature articles as I munched my sandwich.

One reminded me that I had seen the first boxing show ever held in the Yankee Stadium—on May 12, 1923. I had forgotten that it *was* the first show, and even that 1923 was the year the Stadium opened. In my true youth the Yankees used to share the Polo Grounds with the Giants, and I had forgotten that, too, because I never cared much about baseball, although, come to think of it, I used to see the Yankees play occasionally in the nineteen-'teens, and should have remembered. I remembered the boxing show itself very well, though. It happened during the spring of my second suspension from college, and I paid five dollars for a high-grandstand seat. The program merely said that it had been "an all-star heavyweight bill promoted by Tex Rickard for the Hearst Milk Fund," but I found that I could still remember every man and every bout on the card. One of the main events was between old Jess Willard, the former heavyweight champion of the world, who had lost the title to Jack Dempsey in 1919, and a young heavyweight named Floyd Johnson. Willard had been coaxed from retirement to make a comeback because there was such a dearth of heavyweight material that Rickard thought he could still get by, but as I remember the old fellow, he couldn't fight a lick. He had a fair left jab and a right uppercut that a fellow had to walk into to get hurt by, and he was big and soft. Johnson was a mauler worse than Rex Layne, and the old man knocked him out. The other main event, *ex aequo*, had Luis Angel Firpo opposing a fellow named Jack McAuliffe II, from Detroit, who had had only fifteen fights and had never beaten anybody, and had a glass jaw. The two winners, of whose identity there was infinitesimal preliminary doubt, were to fight each other for the right to meet the great Jack Dempsey. Firpo was so crude that Marciano would be a Fancy Dan in comparison. He could hit with only one hand—his right—he hadn't the faintest idea of what to do in close, and he never cared much for the business anyway. He knocked McAuliffe out, of course, and then, in a later "elimination" bout, stopped poor old Willard. He subsequently became a legend by going one and a half sensational rounds with Dempsey, in a time that is now represented to us as the golden age of American pugilism.

I reflected with satisfaction that old Ahab Moore could have whipped all four principals on that card within fifteen rounds, and that while Dempsey may have been a great champion, he had less to beat than Marciano. I felt the satisfaction because it proved that the world isn't going backward, if you can just stay young enough to remember what it was really like when you were really young.